AFRICAN THEOLOGY
TODAY

AFRICAN THEOLOGY TODAY SERIES

VOLUME I

The African Theology Today series is intended to bring to the attention of the African continent itself and especially to the wider world, the often hidden riches of African theology. These are to be found in the frequent Inter-African theological meetings and conferences and in the stream of articles published in a variety of theological journals. Unfortunately, since neither of these initiative and sources is well known outside of Africa, the University of Scranton Press has launched this modest series of books to make them better known. It will consist of three major categories: first, carefully selected and edited selections from various African theological journals. Second, original works by African theologians. And third, reprints of valuable classic works of this type drawn from the past.

It is hoped that these contributions of ideas and culture will, to the benefit of all, add to the history, growth, and culture of Christianity itself and deepen the healthy dialogue already begun within Africa itself and with other Christian theologians, churches, and general readers around the world.

Questions concerning the African Theology Today series should be directed to the series editor:

Dr. Emmanuel Katongole
The Divinity School
Duke University
Box 90068
Durham, NC 27708
Tel: 919-660-3465
Fax: 919-660-3473
Email: ekatongole@div.duke.edu

AFRICAN THEOLOGY TODAY

Edited by

Emmanuel Katongole

Scranton: The University of Scranton Press

© 2002 by The University of Scranton Press

Library of Congress Cataloging-in-Publication Data

African theology today / edited by Emmanuel Katongole.
   p. cm.
Includes bibliographical references and index.
ISBN 1-58966-012-9 (pbk.)
1. Theology, Doctrinal–Africa–Congresses. I. Katongole, Emmanuel, 1960-

BT30.A4 A37 2002
230'.96–dc21
                                           2002024348

Distribution:

The University of Scranton Press
Linden & Monroe
Scranton, PA 18510
Phone: 1–800–941–3081
Fax: 1–800–941–8804

PRINTED IN THE UNITED STATES OF AMERICA

CONTENTS

PERMISSIONS

I am grateful to the publishers of the following books and journals for permission to reproduce these articles:

Mercy Amba Oduyoye, "Acting as Women," from *Daughters of Anowa*, (Orbis, Maryknoll, NY, 2000).

Mika Vähäkangas, "African Approaches to the Trinity,"from *African Theological Journal*, 3/2 (2000): 33–50.

Aidan G. Msafiri, "The Church as Family Model: Its Strengths and Weaknesses," from *AFER* Vol. 40, No. 5 & 6, 1998.

Clement Majawa, "The Church's Role in Defining Genuine Democracy in Africa," from *AFER* Vol. 42, No. 1 & 2, 2000.

Emmanuel Katongole, "African Renaissance and Narrative Theology in Africa. Which Story? Whose Renaissance?" from *The Journal of Theology for Southern Africa* 102 (1998): 29–40

INTRODUCTION

The idea of a series in *African Theology Today* was born sometime in the Spring of 2000 while at dinner with Prof. Richard Rousseau. At that time, I was completing my one-year stay as visiting professor of African Theology at the University of Scranton, and Dick Rousseau was contemplating retiring from his faculty position and becoming full-time director of the University of Scranton Press. During our conversation, Dick kept lamenting how little was known in the United States about the developments and discussions within African theology. Part of the problem was the lack of readily accessible publications which carried work or essays by African theologians, apart from African theological journals, whose circulation tends to be limited to academic institutions. It was in the course of this dinner conversation that the need was felt to periodically publish a collection of essays by African theologians. Such a collection would be a step in making the work and discussions within African theology more readily accessible to a wider audience. It was also hoped that such a collection would allow its audience, particularly in the West, some familiarity with the range and breadth of concerns that characterize African theological discussion, which would allow and encourage dialogue between African theology and other theologies in this era of Christianity as a global religion.

It is against this background that I present with pleasure the first collection of essays in the series of *African Theology Today*. The book brings together twelve essays representing a wide range of topics, discussions, and methodologies in African theology. Even though we might try to organize future volumes around one theme, it was felt that the first volume should give our readers a chance to experience the breadth of concerns as well as wide-ranging methodological orientations that characterize African theology. While the diversity in concerns and methodologies bears witness to the richness and vitality of African

ix

theological reflection, it may be the source of a certain amount of frustration on the part of the reader. For what the variety of thematic and methodological persuasions also points to is the absence of comprehensive and sustained discussions on any one topic as well as the lack of sufficient dialog among various theologians who might be working on different themes or employing different methodologies. A number of reasons account for this frustration. First, there are the usual economic and institutional limitations that make systematic and sustained research in African theology way beyond the means of many theologians in Africa. Second, the occasional and contextual nature of the reflections in African theology somehow also reflects the changing events/situations in Africa, and the attempts by African theologians to stay abreast with these changes and to respond to them theologically. The reader will get a feeling of this attempt to respond theologically to new trends or ideologies such as the New World Order (Mugambi's "From Liberation to Reconstruction") and the African Renaissance (Katongole's "African Renaissance and the Challenge of Narrative Theology in Africa" and Louw's "The Merging of Globalization with the Notion of an African Renaissance").

For easy reading the essays have been arranged loosely around five clusters. The first three essays deal broadly with issues of *biblical hermeneutics*. Chris Manus' essay is exploratory and gives the reader a chance to see what has been going on in the area of biblical scholarship in the West African subregion. The essay by Gerald West represents a more recent direction of engaging biblical hermeneutics from a postcolonial perspective—a trend, however, that is becoming increasingly popular, especially in South Africa. Musa Dube is one of the leading African feminist theologians who engages biblical hermeneutics from a feminist postcolonial approach. Accordingly, her "Rereading the Bible" provides this particular approach, which she combines with a concern for social justice.

The fourth and fifth essays are set within what might be loosely characterized as *inculturation hermeneutics*. Mika Vähäkangas' "African Approaches to the Trinity" provides a good introductory survey to the various models that have been used to understand the Trinity—all drawn from African culture. Aidan Msafiri's essay, on the other hand, assesses the merits and demerits of the recently proposed (as typically African) ecclesiological model of the Church as God's family. Then there are two essays (the sixth and seventh) which deal with *social/political concerns* mostly arising from the dysfunctional nature of the nation–state in Africa. The two essays, however, adopt radically different assumptions and recommendations on how theology should engage the social order. Clement Majawa's essay represents the more standard approach and seeks to explore how the churches can contribute to genuine democracy in Africa. Katongole's essay is suspicious of this standard approach and instead seeks to position the Church's own life and practice as an alternative to the story of the nation–state in Africa, what he depicts as "King Leopold's Ghost." The two essays by Maluleke and Oduyoye respectively also deal with similar issues relating to *African agency* and the role of Christian theology in advancing or inhibiting that agency. Tinyiko Maluleke's essay, "The Rediscovery of the Agency of Africans," provides a helpful survey of the old and new paradigms within African theology, and suggests a direction in which African agency can be meaningfully recovered. Oduyoye's "Acting as Women," on the other hand, is a challenge by the leading African female theologian for the Church and theology to take African Christian women agency seriously by taking a conscious effort to rise against patriarchy and chauvinism. And, finally, there are the three essays by Jesse Mugambi, Emmanuel Katongole and D.J. Louw, which as I already pointed out are either occasioned by or seek to provide a response to *emerging or new ideologies* on the African scene. In the face of the New World Order, Mugambi proposes a new paradigm (Reconstruction) for African theology. Against the background of a projected African renaissance, Katongole calls for alternative readings (narratives) from African theology, while Louw attempts to provide a practical, theological, and pastoral assessment of the notion and its collusion with the forces of globalization.

By bringing together essays drawn from these five clusters of concerns, we hope the reader will find the volume a helpful resource in beginning to appreciate the wide-ranging discussions within African theology. Moreover, we have tried to bring together not only essays that survey what has been (or is) going on, but also essays that reflect the creative restlessness as well as new directions within the various areas of African theological scholarship. As the reader will notice, some essays have been previously published, while others are appearing in publication for the first time. I would like to thank various authors who submitted their essays for consideration. I would have loved to publish all the submitted essays, but for obvious reasons that was not possible. I am in special debt to those whose essays I have included in the collection, as well as to the publishers who have given permission for reproducing previously published articles. A great thank you to Richard Rousseau, Patty Mecadon, and the whole staff of the University of Scranton Press for making this publication possible.

Emmanuel Katongole
May 30, 2001

CHAPTER 1

Methodological Approaches in Contemporary African Biblical Scholarship: The Case of West Africa

Chris Ukachukwu Manus

Introduction

The integration of religiocultural insight into the academic interpretation of the Bible in West Africa has, since the departure of the European missionaries, been steadily rising, revealing, in fact, a growth rate quite unparalleled in other regions of black Africa except perhaps the now Democratic Republic of the Congo, where inculturational theology has best been championed and accepted by the church. Biblical research in the West African sub–region shows, among other things, the strengths and viability of pluralist approaches in biblical exegesis and interpretation. Such pluriform methodological approaches include those reflected in the works of comparativists like J.J. Williams and K.A. Dickson; the thematic interpreters and authors like J. Ngally and N. Onwu; the conceptualists such as S.O. Abogunrin and D.N. Wambutda, in whose list could be included the inculturationists mainly represented by Teresa Okure and J.S. Ukpong, the Catholic Institute of West Africa School of thought; the culturalists—Christologists like K.A. Bediako, Ukachukwu Chris Manus, and A.O. Nkwoka. Certainly, there are others, but these names make the lead, at least for now.

The works of these scholars demonstrate that West African Bible scholars have, in spite of their training in methodologies developed in European and American colleges, seminaries, and universities, continued to steer the course of biblical research toward safety on the African shore. The orientations of these authors attest to the fact that they have been grappling with the problem of how to make the teaching, the understanding, and the message of the Bible relevant in the West African subregion and in Africa as a whole. It must be agreed that culture contact between the "West and the rest of us," as the Nigerian

1

author, Chinweizu, has auspiciously coined the encounter, has not been a balanced interactive phenomenon. Each methodology, though valuable in its own right and in the time it was devised, is derived from the Judeo–Christian traditions with its biblical heroes. Africans can contextualize God's word in the light of their own cultural thought–forms and idioms. Taken together, the approaches reveal an emerging range of methodological options in West African biblical scholarship, a fact which points to the likely progressive direction toward which African biblical research is moving in the 21st century.

The Comparativists

Discussion on the comparativists' approach was started off with J.J Williams' 1930 sensational work, *Hebrewism of West Africa*. I regard this work as sensational in the sense that Williams is the earliest author to address a comparative analysis of the most bizarre type with a West African cultural lifestyle—namely the cultural similarities between the Ashanti of Ghana and the Hebrew race of ancient Palestine. In his own words, "somewhere in the remote past there was an infiltration of the ancient Hebrews in the parent stock from which the present Ashanti were evolved" (Williams 1930:35). Williams picks out some Ashanti words and finds their equivalents in the Hebrew language. He considers an Ashanti word *Obayi*, witch, as the equivalent of *ásah óbh*, the art of necromancy in Hebrew magic. In his structural analysis of both Hebrew and Ashanti languages and phonemes, he argues that varieties of vowels in their consonantal structures, verbal conjugations, and other linguistic traits have a lot in common. For Williams, many Hebrew terms and constructions had been superimposed on the Ashanti lexical forms. To further justify his claims, Williams asserts that since scholarship uncovered many parallels between the Sumerians of late Babylonia and the Hebrew languages, why could there not be similarities between Hebrew and Ashanti languages? From such assertions, Williams reaches the conclusion that the Ashanti could not be but scions of a Hebraic racial group, perhaps the lost tribe of Israel.

All Africa Council of Churches (AACC) in January 1965 held a Consultation at the Immanuel College, Ibadan, Nigeria, whose main purpose was to provide the churches of Africa the "opportunity of thinking together of the Christian faith which had come to them from the older churches of the west through missionaries of a different cultural background who . . . could not fully appreciate the reactions of their converts to their practices" (Dickson & Ellingworth 1969:vii). The theme of the symposium was biblical revelation and African beliefs. The task pursued in the symposium was to provide an answer to the question: "whether there is any correlation between biblical concept of God and the African concept of God, between what God has done and is doing in the light of biblical record and teaching and what God has done and is doing in Africa according to African traditional beliefs" (Dickson & Ellingworth:16). Of the work that was published thereafter, eight chapters were written on topics such as God, priesthood, sacrifice, man, eschatology, and so on. The volume contains no serious biblical exposition or exegetical enquiry on the subject matter. At a critical reading of most of the papers, what appears is that our "path finders," made up of eleven contributors out of whom seven were working in West Africa at that time, sued for the search for comparative elements and identical biblical patterns which they dressed up in the garb of systematic theological argumentations. The work is one of the best of the West Africans' study on "correlation of African and Christian ideas" (Dickson & Ellingworth:159).

In 1972, Kwesi Dickson advanced this comparative/correlation method a synthetic step further in a study, "African Traditional Religions and the Bible," done for the Jerusalem Congress on Black Africa and the Bible. In this essay, he nuances the idea of "comparisons between African religions and the Bible" by accepting that common grounds do exist (Dickson 1972:158–160). For him, "similarities of thought between the Hebrews and Africans have pedagogical values in so far as their common findings can clarify certain elements of human interest in the Old Testament" and thereby enable African students "to gain some measure of insight into those Old Testament customs which have near counterparts in African life and thought, customs and ideas" (Dickson:161). Dickson finds out those elements such as magical arts, divination, faith in nature deities, sacrifice, transference of sin (scapegoatism), purification, contrasts in OT and African conception of time, death, and the hereafter. The keen interest Dickson had shown on comparative approach can be read from his lament on the dearth of (comparative) biblical scholars in the region. In his own words, "Regretably West Africa has not produced enough researchers in Biblical ideas and customs" (Dickson 1975:93).

In a 1979 article in the *Bulletin de Theologie Africaine*, Vol. 1, No. 2, Dickson presses further his comparative method in the OT and its identity with African thoughtforms. He explores the Marcionist position, its European and Asian followers, and their distaste for the OT in the Church Scriptures. He discovers that for neo-Marcionists like Schleiermacher and Harnack and some Indian theologians the OT is unsatisfactory in its story of God in human history. But according to Dickson, in Africa, the opposite is the case. The OT is much more appreciated and its value is found more relevant to the needs of the African students. The OT, he observes, is almost the spiritual book of the African independent churches who use it to the extent that OT norms have become preferred by the adherents of many of the African indigenous Christian churches. Unveiling the rationale for this over-whelming attachment to the OT in Africa, Dickson, as in his earlier works, affirms that similarities abound in the OT, African religious ideas, and the African traditional life and thought. For Dickson, there are three levels of continuity between the OT and African custom: namely, theological, religiocultural, and the interpretative/hermeneutical approaches. Of particular interest to us is Dickson's advice that in the hermeneutical angle, "the text and the African, or the Black American or the Latin American, or the Asian or the European are bound together" (Dickson 1979:192). Moreover, it is Dickson's opinion that the hermeneutical continuity has not received the urgency it deserves from "African theological educators and students" (Dickson:192). In sum, he advises that approaching the OT with questions and problems relating to one's own time brings the African interpreter face to face with Christian theology as he/she is forced to measure the answers he finds against the teaching of Christ. In this respect, I wish to remark that before its popularization in Europe and America, this West African OT scholar had pointed the way toward the reader-response criticism by which many people read the Bible texts today.

The Thematic Approach

With the inception of university colleges in preindependence West Africa, such institutions as the University College of Ibadan, Nigeria, then of London, the Fourah Bay College of the University of Durham, the University of Ghana, Legon, as well as those in the Francophone countries of West Africa, the Europeans who lectured in the Departments for the Study of Religions and Theology in West Africa had taught courses in both the OT and NT studies with European and American methodologies. Interpretative models such as the Graf–Wellhausen's Documentary and Fragment hypotheses, the Historical Criticism, Formgeschichte, and lately the Redakionsgeschichte develped and popularized by German scholars like H. Gunkel, O. Eisfeldt, R.

Bultmann, and W. Marxsen were drummed into the ears of West African college students. These methodologies, though scientific to the core, were not easily actualizable in the African situation. The overriding question is: Did such approaches help bring the message of the Bible down-to-earth in any way for the Africans to comprehend? Or did they help promote evangelization and the establishment of a virile church growth in the African soil? How about the Christian religion? Did such methodologies make Africans in any way better in their understanding of the good news preached by Jesus Christ? What are the relevancy and the fruits of such models that can be found today in the works of West African students who were so schooled in those days?

In recent times, and since their Western training, many African theologians fully embrace the thematic approach. But what exactly is the thematic approach? And how has it been used in biblical studies in West Africa? According to a dictionary definition, a theme is a unifying idea, image, or motif repeated or developed throughout a work (Hanks 1979:1506). The thematist biblical interpreter is therefore engaged in the search for an idea or motif in the Bible which can vivify his/her African cultural concepts and symbols. According to Charles Nyamiti, "with the thematic approach, the theologian elaborates his theology from some particular subject(s), theme(s) or categorie(s) usually taken from the African cultural context," (Nyamiti 1993:135). Amplifying further, he states, "It is in this way that the African categories such as "ancestor," "chief" and "healer" have been applied by some writers to Christ in view of an African Christology" (Nyamiti: 135).

In the *Bulletin of the All Africa Conference of Churches* (AACC), January–February 1975, composed of papers assembled by the Churches' Theology Unit as a kind of its *Instrumentum Laboris* for the WCC Fifth Assembly in Nairobi, Kenya (1975), Jacques Ngally, the Camerounian OT scholar's "Bible Studies from an African Perspective" took its starting point from the thematic approach. His Christology is founded on themes like "the revelation of the Son of God," "Christ crucified," "Liberator" and "Unifier" of all mankind. The Liberation motif had continued to hold great fascination for Ngally. In another article which appeared in the *Ecumenical Review* in the same year, Ngally beckons his readership to see Jesus as the Liberator from all diseases, hunger, poverty, tyranny, legalism, tribalism, and militarism— all evils quite endemic to the West African subregion. In his study on Genesis 1–4, he develops a sound theology of labor based on the theme of the dignity of labor and mankind's duty in the creative work of God

(Ngally 1978:222–232). Six years later, N. Onwu, a Nigerian NT scholar, pursued the theme of liberation further afield. He pertinently observes that liberation has become a popular subject of analysis by African exegetes since the concept is biblically rooted and "inherent in their concept of salvation" (Onwu 1984/85:37). "In the African context, and in the Bible," Onwu admits, the theme of "salvation as a theological concept cannot be complete without liberation as a sociopolitical concept."[1]

In 1980, Monrovia, the capital of Liberia, hosted scholars of the All Africa Lutheran Consultation. Their Proceedings, *Christian Theology and Strategy for Mission*, contained many chapters on mission in Africa studied in the light of mission themes in the Bible. From biblical themes, the authors map out a mission strategy which could deliver West Africa of the eighties to the Lutheran Confession. In the same year, Christiansme et Identité Africaine: Point de vue exégétique, was published as the *Acts of the First Congress of African Biblists* (now PACE). Even though the title of the entire volume was written in the French language, three Anglophone West African Roman Catholic exegetes (Bishop J. Onayeikan, P.D. Akpunonu, and Th. Onoyima—all Nigerians) made their contributions to the volume. They invented luxuriant themes to address the topical issues which concerned the church in its task of evangelization at that time in black Africa. The exegetes who collaborated with some of their European colleagues and former teachers sought with exegetical rigour themes to establish the continuity and discontinuity between the OT and NT as Kwesi Dickson had initiated in the seventies and that between both Testaments and African religions as was done by the AACC in 1965 at the Immanuel Theological College, Ibadan, Nigeria. Such themes as the identity of the African Christian person and Christology were discussed. Jesus was seen, inter alia, as the bridge between God and all peoples in their concrete historical and cultural settings. Since the appearance of this premier volume, the Pan-African Catholic Exegetes' Association (Karen, Nairobi) has successfully published three other thematically arranged proceedings in which a number of West African biblical scholars have consistently contributed their own quota in the scientific exegesis of the Congress themes.[2]

In 1983, the Sixth Assembly of the World Conference of Churches (WCC) deliberated on the theme: Jesus Christ—the Life of the World. African theologians who attended the assembly prepared a study titled "An African Call for Life." A quick overview of the subjects shows that top on the agenda of the African contingent was the theme of a "Christology developed by a dynamic didactic method with its focus on the study of a number of biblical images of Christ and its relationship to life" (ma Mpolo 1983:165). Themes such as human rights, freedom, poverty, and hunger—factors which make life worthless in the black continent were addressed. The Bible stood as the reference point of the authors. For them, biblical titles of Jesus as Living Water (John 7, 37), Bread of Life (John 6, 35–51), the Narrow Door and Path leading to eternal life (John 10, 7ff; 14, 6) establish the salvific work of Jesus Christ. Their real point of departure is the anchorage of the socioeconomic and political realities of contemporary Africa since independence in the sixties on the theme of Jesus' role as Liberator. According to them, for the Africans, the saviour of all mankind "is incarnate in the daily life of those who are hungry and thirsty, those from whom the bare minimum of justice is withheld" (ma Mpolo: 165).

So, one can see that West African–born biblical scholars who had worked with the thematic approach have one common denominator. They represent, in fact, the earliest attempts to relate biblical themes to Africa's harrowing experiences in changing political and socioeconomic hard times. Therefore, it can be argued that African biblical exponents joined hands with the elderstatesmen to address the problems of liberation which in the biblical sense included salvation, mission, self-determination, and sociopolitical freedom. For this crop of scholars, the Bible speaks the word of salvation, liberation, and well-being to the oppressed and famished African peoples. Thus scholarly interpretation of the Bible which adopted this method in the sub-region in the sixties and up to the early eighties had focused on the search for biblical-theological solutions to problems associated with Africa's temporal and - spiritual experiences.

The Contextualists

The preoccupation of the exegetes using the contextualist method is to express the Christian message and mode of worship in forms that are conducive to their native and cultural patterns of life. As far back as 1947, Christopher Dawson had recognized the nexus between religion and culture. He asserts that both realities are often inseparable, for religion cannot escape the necessity of being incarnated in a culture. Due to his work, contextualization has become a concept which African scholars have discovered to be relevant in virtually all disciplines. As a working methodology, contextualization is being employed by many

West African biblical scholars whose interest, among others, is to make
the gospel take deep root in the full life of their communities and
thereafter to grow into its full stature in the people's cultural contexts.
Elsewhere, I have noted that contextualization demands entering a given
cultural context, discerning what God is doing and saying in that
context, and speaking out and working for needed change (Manus
1985:25)

Further amplifying the concept, Joseph Osei-Bonsu, A Ghanian
theologian, states:

> Contextualization (not only) involves introducing elements from the
> indigenous culture into Christianity, making use of thought-forms and
> concepts pertaining to the given culture; it also involves Christian-
> izing the indigenous culture, injecting it with Christian values, thereby
> transforming and reshaping it to produce a new creation. (Osei-Bonsu
> 1990:148)

On the same methodology, J.S. Ukpong, a Nigerian, notes:

> We define the context as an existing society (with its many patterns
> of social relations) into which Christianity is introduced. Thus the
> context is something dynamic with its values, needs and aspirations.
> Religious beliefs, habits and customs, societal problems and issues—
> all make up the context to which the Christian message is to be made
> relevant. Hence, . . ."Contextualization" is seen as an umbrella term
> for all endeavours aimed at making the different forms of Christian
> expression of Christian thought and practice in terms of the thought-
> forms and the idiom of particular cultures as well as relating the
> Christian message to the concrete life experiences of people. (Ukpong
> 1987a:152).

In the light of the foregoing definitions, scholars whose approach
resembles that of the contextualists among West Africans are legion.
A.O. Igenoza, a Nigerian, in an article, "African Weltanschauung and
Exorcism," addresses himself to "the ministry of exorcism in the
contextualization of Christianity in Africa" (Igenoza 1985:179). In
recognizing the importance of the ministry of exorcism for a more
dynamic contextualization of Christianity in Africa, Igenoza asserts that:

> biblical Weltanschauung and that of traditional Africa have many
> striking similarities in their perception of spiritual realities . . . and as
> such the ministry has a unique role to play in the effective procla-
> mation of the reign of God in Africa. (Igenoza:190)

In a 1986 article, "Biblical Research in Africa," S.O. Abogunrin raises pertinent questions on the relevance in Africa of the methodologies developed in the West. He asks, among others, "Can we completely remove the Bible from its cultural milieu and impose the Western cultural understanding upon the text as if the Bible originated from the West a few centuries ago?" and "What is the role of culture in the contextualization of the Biblical message?" (Abogunrin 1986:13). For him, Western approach to biblical interpretation is nothing more than a "colonizing religion." Abogunrin instructively proposes some guidelines for biblical interpretation in Africa. Realizing that the Bible "is like a box of treasure" for many African Christians, he suggests that "Africans should possess the key to open the box of treasure; namely to acquire the principles of interpretation" (Abogunrin:16). For him, it is biblical scholars who, through their fresh impulses, should provide the "tools for the contextualization of the biblical message and for the laying of a strong theological foundation for Christian theology in Africa" (Abogunrin:16). While he correctly argues that "Scripture must be interpreted by comparing one Scripture with another," Abogunrin submits to the comparativists' position as he states:

> Our duty as African scholars is not to impose an African meaning on any passage but to appeal to parallels where they exist and draw illustrations from the rich cultural heritage of Africa. (Abogunrin:19)

In his essay, "The Synoptic Gospel Debate: A Reexamination in the African Context," Abogunrin reexamines the current synoptic problem debate, castigates the Western proponents of numerous hypothetical sources and theories of dependence, and challenges African biblical interpreters to have recourse to African values embedded in both written and unwritten historical traditions as main sources of African history. He admonishes them to examine such ancient traditions in order to see their implications on the sequential order of the Gospels.[3]

In an article devoted essentially to the general import of con-textualization in contemporary missiology, J.S. Ukpong draws our attention to contextualization as a method which has its origin and place in biblical studies. He reminds us of its earlier origin in the work of Herman Gunkel, the doyen of Sitz-im-Lebensforschung. According to Ukpong, Gunkel employed the term to describe "the real situation in people's life or the socio-cultural setting from which a literary genre (Gattung) of the Bible originated" (Ukpong 1987a:150). As Ukpong asserts, Gunkel's original perception has, today, blossomed into the generally accepted sociocultural as well as the sociopsychological angle in the reading process of biblical texts. Since the time of Gunkel, modern biblical interpretation has laid much stress on "the contextual study of texts," "what a text meant to its original writer and audience,"and "the context of present–day audience," observes Ukpong (Ukpong 1987a:151). In another article, "Contextualizing Theological Education in Western Africa: Focus on Subjects," Ukpong restates much of his earlier views on the significance of the contextual method. He however goes beyond his former position to prospect for the subjects which ought to be included in theological education syllabi "within the framework of . . . emerging new paradigm" in the West African theological institutions (Ukpong 1987b:59).

The Inculturationists

At the present stage of theological education in West Africa, it is no longer necessary to present a detailed definition of inculturation. Much as P. Schineller has done justice to a holistic understanding of the concept (Schineller:1990), let me briefly rehearse the methodological perspectives offered by some West African theologians. As I have elsewhere noted, "Inculturation presupposes the tabernacling of the gospel message as it encounters other cultures, especially as it moves from one cultural soil to another" (Manus 1992:541). For me, inculturation is a process which the African church is passing through quite tardily. The process is admittedly tied to the problem of gospel and culture and the amenability of the mainline church leadership to innovations. As E.E. Uzukwu would want us to take it, inculturation methodology is that approach which enables theologians to "work towards the encounter of . . . structural history and the heart of the proclamation of the gospel" (Uzukwu 1985:26). Justin Ukpong offers a rather perceptive analysis of the process. According to him:

> It involves enquiry at four levels. First is enquiry into the sources of the Christian faith—the Bible and the Church's theological tradition —from the local cultural background; the third level involves a meeting of faith and culture, and at each level is involved posing appropriate questions. Thus inculturation takes place at the point where biblical exegesis, the Church's theological tradition and the local cultural perception meet. In the process any dead–wood in the transmitting or receiving culture falls apart and there emerges a new inculturated form of Christian expression (Ukpong 1987a: 155).

Bishop K. Sarpong of Kumasi, Ghana, pastorally defines the concept. According to him, "Inculturation represents the efforts of Christians in particular places to understand and to celebrate their Christian faith in a way peculiar to those contexts" (Sarpong 1990:2). Vatican II allows that

> the Church is not tied exclusively and indissolubly to any way of life, customs and practices but can enter into communion with different forms of culture, thereby enriching both itself and the cultures themselves. (GS. 58; Ad Gentes. 22)

Bishop Sarpong wonderfully and succinctly outlines the agenda of inculturation. For him,

> Inculturation is not imposition which is belittling, it is not translation which is superficial, it is not adaptation which, in the last analysis, is a subtle form of imposition. It is a kind of indigenization, making things native, taking into account what is peculiar to a context or a culture. It is hence contextualization which implies weaving the gospel into every particular situation and making it part of the situation. Contextualization affects situations in which the gospel must be incarnated. (Sarpong 1990:3)

Foremost among Bible interpreters who seek scriptural basis for the promotion of the inculturational method in the West African Christianity is Teresa Okure, SHCJ. Teresa's cardinal interest and objective is, inter alia, to establish "the scriptural and theological foundations for inculturation" (Okure 1989:39). According to her, the New Testament church struggling to pass on the good news was confronted with problems: the messianic and the Gentile questions. In Teresa's opinion, to respond to these questions and to live by their implications, the early Christians engaged in inculturation. The task before them was how to transform the mind and cultural attitude of their listeners so that they could recognize that Jesus of Nazareth was "God's unique and final agent of salvation for all peoples" (John 4, 42; Acts 4,12) (Okure: 39). Given this background, Teresa insists that NT inculturation implies that "the mystery of Christ and his definitive role in God's plan of salvation holds the key to the true understanding and correct implementation of inculturation in the Nigerian context (Okure: 44–45). In sum, it is Teresa's opinion that the similarities between the New Testament setting and the Nigerian situation call for comparison and application.

If these ideas are supposed to be what inculturation implies in the mind of West African theologians and church leaders, reflections on God's original revelation are therefore constantly called for. Even though as Robert J. Schreiter admits, "Human cultures, while good, are skewed by sin" (Schreiter 1981:547); inculturation ought to provide a mutual symbiosis of the gospel message and the West African ways of life in order to promote the emergence of a new Christian culture in the subregion.

The Culturalist Method

The term *culturalist* sounds enthusiastic, but it is just a cliché I am using to identify a group of West African biblical interpreters, including my humble self, who are currently engaged in seeking a culturalist approach toward the understanding of the Christ image in the West African church and society. Like Bishop Peter K. Sarpong advises, their prime objective is "to look to Africa for a Christ yet to be discovered, a Christ who, to use the words of Pope John Paul II, in the members of his body, is himself African" (Sarpong 1990:2). Let me offer some West African regional efforts and the methodologies adopted to create viable West African biblical Christologies to respond to the Lord's original question: "Who do you say I am?" (Mark 8, 29 par.).

In the article "Biblical Christologies in the Context of African Religions," K. Bediako, a Ghanaian evangelical missiologist, addresses the "Christological problem as it confronts us now" (Bediako 1983: 139). He devises a method with which he groped for the solution of this problem in the worldview and religious traditions of his own people, the Akan of Ghana. Bediako reads the scriptures in the light of Akan traditional religiosity and aims at proposing a Christology "which deals with the perceived reality of the ancestors" (Bediako:143). He relates his Christological findings to the realm of the ancestors as the encounterpoint for Africans with the Christ event. In the tradition of Kwesi A. Dickson, Bediako relates Christian faith with African (Akan) culture and tradition as the basis at which "we can be authentic Africans and true Christians" (Bediako:142–143).

In a much earlier article of mine, "The Centurion's Confession of Faith" (Mark 15, 39), I employ the hermeneutical method to expose the significance of the Christology implied in the confession of the Roman military officer who supervised the execution squad that nailed Jesus on the cross at cavalry vis à vis some emergent rustic cultures that some modern Africans consider valuable today. Among other things, it is discovered that in the mouth of the Centurion, Mark's notion of divine sonship muted at the commencement of his Gospel in the enigmatic expression "the gospel of Jesus, son of Mary, son of God" (Mark 1, 1) is amplified. The Synoptists narrate the story of the Centurion's confession with variations in the titles. For Matthew and Mark, Jesus is *huioj tou Qeou Theou*, son of God, while for Luke, he is *dikaioj*, innocent. The methodology helped me reach the conclusion that the title *dikaios* was much more primitive and was probably adopted as the pious equivalent to the title son, which "stood for the quality of a man justified to claim God as his father in the Palestinian–Syrian region where the Q–Community thrived during the later part of the first Christian century" (Manus 1993:58).

But in the mouth of the Centurion, the concept seems to carry with it pagan connotations associated with the idea of the *divus filius* usually ascribed to men who were held as saviours, benefactors, emperors, rulers, and great philosophers in the Hellenistic world. For me, the relevance of the text is not so much the meaning of the title as "what message Mark intends to convey via the Centurion to a believer in contemporary times" (Manus:58). In Mark, son of God is a high Christology which involves suffering, rejection, and death. It is proof of Jesus' divine Sonship and Messiahship (Manus 1985:271). But what is the importance of this Christology for African Christians?

My method helps reveal that the evangelist conveys a message of hope and faith to all who are underprivileged and subjected to all forms of structural oppression and man's indignity to humanity. Through rejection and death, Jesus becomes the innocent Messiah, seated in glory as the Judge of all. Mark's insight into the divinity of Christ invites all Christians in rural and peasant Africa to bear a living witness to Christ. The barrenness of the sociopolitical culture, the destabilizing economic as well as the spiritual bankruptcies prevalent in the West African contemporary societies, are not without drastic consequences to the people's ethos. Official corruption, dictatorship of the national leaders, bad governing by local rulers and overlords, and their unprioritized policies aggravate and impoverish the living conditions of man in the West African world. That spirit of heroism and fortitude which Jesus exhibited on the Cross that baffled the Centurion and made him confess faith in the divinity of Jesus should embolden West African Christian leaders to have, in times if crisis, confidence in the Eternal Ruler of the universe, the Lord of history to whom, with his son Jesus, every ruler should obey in order to become a "winner."

In his article, "Jesus As Elder Brother (Okpara)," A.O. Nkwoka attempts to deepen our understanding of the Igbo concept of Okpara Chineke. The concept, according to him, had been adopted as a translation equivalent to Son of God in the *Archdeacon Dennis Igbo Union Bible*. He explores the significance of Okpara in Igbo tradition and culture in order to underscore its Christological import to Igbo Christians (Nkwoka 1991:87). Among the Igbo who have a semblance of monarchical culture, the Okpara Eze (King) is the King's arm of government through whom the King coordinates both priestly and social leadership functions in his community. In such acephalous communities as the Igbo peoples, the Okpara is the father's confidant who alone knows his secrets and the extent of his estate. It is to the Okpara that the father confers all essential prerogatives of inheritance and possessions, and he alone has the right to distribute property to all the juniors as he wills. Thus, for Nkwoka, and the Igbo subculture he belongs to, administratively, the Okpara acts as the second father, and religiously, he is the family priest, the link between the family members and the ancestral spirits. On the sociopolitical sector, the Opkara, Nkwoka admits, executes his role as both the family's socialite and the "traditional prime minister" (Nkwoka:93). Thus *Okparaship* in Igbo sociology points up the beneficial significance of Jesus as Elder Brother in Igbo Christian families. Okpara Christology implies that Jesus, Okpara Chineke (Son of God), is to the various Igbo family groups the only exemplary Okpara (son) they know. In sum, Nkwoka states:

> The place of Okpara in Igbo cosmology has proved to be a very fertile ground for the contextualization of Jesus as both the Son of God and a very living "big brother" to man irrespective of his lot in life. This, we believe, might have contributed in no small way to the massive embrace of Christianity by the Igbo. (Nkwoka:99)

There is no doubt that the cultural approach toward the portrayal of the image of Christ in West Africa can still be done by exegesis of NT texts. Both Chris. U. Manus and Justin. S. Ukpong (our mentor), both now professors, had in separate publications written in different places and time, addressed themselves to the exegesis of Matthew 25, 31–46 using the cultural approach and hermeneutics (Manus 1991:19–41; Ukpong 1992:55–83). Aware of the emerging consensus among Euro-American Matthean scholars that there is hardly any Christological category adequate to express the Matthean view of Jesus' identity, Ukpong in agreement with David Hill affirms that Jesus' identity must not be reduced to a single title. Thus he, like Manus, reads the story of Matthew's eschatological discourse with African spectacles. Both adopt the synchroni-diachronic approach to interpret the passage in the African context. Both attempt to uncover "who is Jesus and where he is to be found in Africa today" (Ukpong:63). Both interpret the text differently, yet their findings complement each other's.

While Manus sees an Endzeit judgment scenario in the text where "Matthew depicts a situation where all peoples shall be gathered and judged for their refusal to promote the cause and the realization of the humanum" (Manus:31), Ukpong recognizes the text as "a scene of the judgement of all humanity for whom Jesus is Lord and King" (Ukpong: 60). For Ukpong, Matthew's Jesus is "God be with us" and which, according to him, is "an adequate presentation of Matthew's christo-logical framework" for the African audience (Ukpong:58), while for Manus, Matthew depicts a "King-Judge" at home in Africa. While for Ukpong, the passage projects Jesus as one who "has identified himself with the less fortunate in society—the hungry, the thirsty, the stranger, the naked, the sick, the prisoner, etc." (Ukpong:62), for Manus, Matthew has skillfully employed traditional motifs . . . to portray Jesus "as the Christ-King, the Judge of all nations . . . who reigns in his exclusive status as God's representative" (Manus:36). Diachronically both address the implications of their Christologies to the sociopolitical problems in today's Africa: Manus on the evils still associated with the South African apartheid policies and Ukpong on "all the needy and afflicted," "the different categories of the less fortunate Africans" (Ukpong:62).

Quite recently a paradigm shift may be said to have begun in the field of contextual theology in West Africa. Here, I have in mind a vast number of authors whose works are not immediately available to us due mainly to communication problems and poor circulation of theological literature in Africa. In this regard, the appearance of a number of my publications written from the religiocultural tradition approach and the New Testament—that is, using African cultural texts to interpret the New Testament—are noteworthy.[4]

Conclusion

The West African sociopolitical landscape has been witnessing dramatic upheavals and unrest. These crises had had no small con-sequences in the lives of her peoples. Hunger, disease, and death daily stare the populace in the face. Many a head of state in our sub–region rule with an avalanche of draconian decrees, repress the opposition, and resist populist calls for progressive governance and the democratic rule of law. Can a census of the woes of some of the states help us appreciate what is meant? By the time this essay was being composed, Liberia was ravaged by civil war, after which it was choosing its leaders and lawmakers for the first time since seven years with reports and allegations of election malpractices. Today, that nation has not known peace even under the elected leader Charles Taylor.

Nigeria and the Ivory Coast lead a teeming angry mob whose anger was feared to explode any time if the immiseration of the people continues unabetted. Has it now not dawned on us that the keg of fuel in the Ivory Coast has dangerously exploded? The once peaceful and economically stable nation in the subregion is now a curfew-guided nation. The socioeconomic consequences of the cancellation of the federal polls of June 12, 1993, in Nigeria by General Ibrahim Gbadamosi Babangida created flagrant political crises that have demoralized many a Nigerian family. Today, Justice Oputa's Human Rights Violations Commission is unearthing the horrendous events of those regimes to the amazement of Nigerians and the outside world. Cameroon was virtually economically unviable and politically unstable. Ghana was just waking up from her economic doldrums. Jerry Rawlings could not keep track of the vagaries of his economic maladministration until he quit office late last year. The new head of state has an uphill task. How may he restore some strength to the Cedi? Should he go aborrowing to the IMF and the World Bank with their slavish conditionalities? Togo had just managed to survive from a not-too-recent political uprising, yet the chances for free and fair elections fell on deaf ears in that land. Eyadema is heading the OAU today. One wonders what magic wand he has to turn the fortunes of the African continent around for better profits at the world market in the wake of increasing globalization currently being foisted on African nation states whose concept of the "village" is far different from those of the G8. Reports of election rigging had nearly capsized the boat of good hope and peace in Senegal.

Where may one speak of stability and human promotion on the west coast of the Atlantic? Is it in the République du Bénin where child slavery is still the order of the day? If the parents have enough to feed their God-given offspring, why would they sell them off to agents and dealers across the boarders to Nigeria and Niger? Is it in Sierra Leone where a gruesome war is being fought which has mesmerized the West

African Peace-Keeping Force (ECOMOG) and turned the fortunes of the democratically elected head of state into gloom? How may one explain the carnage, rape, destruction, and uncontrolled trafficking in arms from that war-land to most of the cities of the subregion?

In most of these countries, the army has assumed an elitist position and arrogates to itself a dominant role in politics to the detriment of the flowering of democratic political culture. The economy is generally in shambles. Human development, education, and the promotion of the people's well-being are neglected in favor of massive arms buildup and the favoritism of their cronies. From a West African observation post, it seems correct to argue that our age has become increasingly dominated by a leadership steeped in political error that exults in the arrogance of power and privilege. While our people grope for meaning and existence, the Bible remains their source of hope and solace. It speaks to our people in their situation. The West African sociopolitical realities urge us on to develop newer methods and make them fully operational to ensure that our reading of the Bible is relevant and responsive to the West African experience. The specific West African sociopolitical state of affairs must be considered as useful critical resources for our interpretation of the Bible. Like other interpretative enterprises, the West African nations, the sociocultural ethos, the interpreter, and the text must all be taken together. Social scientists like Peter Berger, Thomas Luckmann, and others keep reminding us that the sociocultural contexts shape both text and interpreter; hence there is need to read scripture in the light of the various host cultures.

> An opinion consensus has emerged today where it is no longer possible to equate the results of historical criticism with the full reality of the Biblical texts. New directions are wanted and a pluralist theoretical perspective seems increasingly possible[5]

Many themes, typologies, and life experiences in our host cultures must be allowed to influence the methodological principles of our contemporary exegetes. Our earliest biblical scholars, whose work we have reviewed in this study, interpreted the Bible based on the need to compare biblical customs with African life patterns in order to strengthen Christian praxes and doctrines. The younger generation of exegetes are seeking inculturational antecedents and cultural categories for their Christological portraits. All these interpretative approaches are quite significant and bring rich diversity in our quest for the Christ of Africa. But what about the form and the state of contemporary West

African life? Can our methods of biblical interpretation still afford to ignore the possibility of grounding our exegetical findings in favor of the region's social political predicament, especially in the light of God's liberating love which remains a cardinal message in the Bible? Can we continue to allow Western approaches to inhibit West African genius from reading the Bible quite independently? It is my suggestion that viable contextual biblical hermeneutics as are being outlined in this study must be perceived as our only ways of letting the Bible speak to the suffering masses, the dangers of the HIV/AIDS epidemic, political instability in most of the states of the subregion, the hardships and the severe economic realities of West African Christians as citizens of the Economic Community of West African states (ECOWAS).

According to W. Amewowo, and rightly so, the peoples of West Africa see the Bible as the Word of God and history of the actions of the Almighty God (Amewowo 1986:16). As the Word spoken by God, it must possess power and "divine authority" which must be addressed to West African conditions which have become so increasingly bedeviled not only by the retrogressive Structural Adjustment Programs foisted on the hapless peoples of our countries but also by the stultifying economic consequences of the IMF, the World Bank loans, and now the theories of globalization and its effect on the lives of men and women in the region. As a culturalist method, contextual exegesis implies reading the Bible stories through the lens of the West African people's own sociopolitical and religious experiences. This choice of reading the Bible in the light of the overt and systematic injustices arising from the misguided economic and political planning of the subregion seeks to redress and to reaffirm the otherness of humanity against the destructive evils, agents of death, of greed, nepotism, corruption, ethnic and religious conflicts, and undemocratic governance. It is therefore an existential interpretation of the Bible focused for the future in order to awaken Christian consciousness and responsibility in both the religious and political spheres of life. It is existential because the interpreted Word of God speaks to the hearer as well as to the reader.

For me, letting the Word of God challenge the people is the real kernel of a sociocultural methodology. It is aimed at understanding and interpreting the faith which West African Christians have come to embrace as members of the People of God inserted into the cultural milieu of the subregion. As indicated much earlier, it is a vision which invites biblical exegetes to move beyond the classical diachronic method that has so far dominated Western biblical interpretation to more synchronic reading of the sociohistorical factors operative in a given nation/region in the light of the scriptural message. In this approach, the biblical narratives will have been put into contact with the daily realities of the region's state of underdevelopment and economic malaise, even when caused by our leaders' ineptitude, lack of vision, and bad governing.

The sociopolitical message of the Bible is outstandingly clear. From Moses through the classical prophets to Jesus of Nazareth, messianism had been associated with the ways that the reign of God breaks into history. This message must continue to be heard by the West African leaders as well as their people. The West African biblical scholar who is mindful of the sociopolitical ills of the subregion these past twenty-two years since the formation of the block, called ECOWAS, would be expected to interpret the Bible in favor of the historical emancipation of his or her peoples. Therefore, as Jesse Mugambi, the East African theologian, has said (Mugambi 1995), a restoration paradigm is expected of the OT exegetes while a reconstruction Christology is required of the NT scholars in order to provide theological grounding for the raison d'être of the Anti-Corruption Bill, poverty alleviation programs, National Rebirth and Renaissance, which are currently being proclaimed as part of their political agenda by West African leaders like Chief Olusegun Obasanjo of Nigeria, Mathieu Kerekou of Bénin, and the newly elected President of Ghana, Mr. John Kufour.

Prof. Chris Ukachukwu Manus
Dept.of Religious Studies, Obafemi Awolowo University
Ile–Ife, Nigeria.

NOTES

[1] See Onwu, n. 8. In the seventies, there appeared two nonbiblical but relevant studies which delineated the theme, salvation by West Africans. These are the work of Harry Sawyerr, a Sierra Leonian, and E. Enang, a Nigerian. While Sawyerr in his article, "Salvation Viewed for African Situation" (1972), investigated the concept in its African anthropological background, Enang in his book, *Salvation in a Nigerian Background* (1979), exhaustively treated the subject in its Nigerian context, illustrating his insight from the Anang experience, an Ibibio subethnic group in southeast Nigeria. Both authors affirm the fact that salvation for the African implies healing from sin, sicknesses, poverty, and deliverance from the clutches of both seen and unseen forces. When the evil forces are destroyed by the power of Jesus Christ, salvation is believed to have been achieved. For the African, both agree, salvation guarantees robust health, fecundity, and longevity, thus making the salvation which Jesus offers to man liberating and total. Healing is, in the African situation, explained by these theologians as salvation par excellence.

[2] W. Amewowo et al. (eds.), *Les Actes des Apotres et les Jeunes Eglises*, 2nd Congress, Kinshasa, 1990; W. Amewowo et al (eds.), *Communautés Johanniques/Johannine Communities*, 4th Congress, Kinshasa, 1991, and L. Nare, C.U. Manus et al. (eds.), *Universalisme et Mission dans la Bible/Universalism and Mission in the Bible*, 5th Congress, Nairobi, 1993.

[3] Done to respond to this appeal, see my "Jn 6:1–15 and Its Synoptic Parallels: An African Approach Toward the Solution of a Johannine Critical Problem," *The Journal of the Interdenominational Theological Center*, Atlanta, GA, USA, Vol XIX, Nos. 1&2, 1991/1992, pp. 47–71.

[4] This fact is borne out in a number of journal publications and a book-length work in which Jesus is portrayed as King. My "King–Christology" highlights the manner in which African Christians do image the Lordship of Jesus as King in their lives, churches and communities (Manus 1992:545). See, for example, C.U. Manus, "Jesu Kristi Oba: A Christology of "Christ the King" among the Indigenous Christian Churches in Yorubaland, Nigeria" *AJT* 5(1991)311–330; idem, "'King–Christology': The Result of a Critical Study of Matt 28, 16–20 as an Example of Contextual Exegesis in Africa," *Scriptura Journ. of Bible and Theol. in Southern Africa*, 39(1991)25–42; idem., "'King–Christology': Reflections on the Figure of the Endzeit Discourse Material (Matthew 25, 31–46) in the African Context," *Acta Theologica* 11(1991)19–41; idem., "'King–Christology': The Example of Some Aladura Churches in Nigeria," *Africana Marburgensia*, Vol. 24, No.1, 1991, pp. 28–46; idem., *Christ the African King. New Testament Christology*, Frankfurt/Main, Berlin, Bern, New York, Paris, Wien, Verlag Peter Lang, 1993.

[5] Quote is taken from SCM Press advert flier of Francis Watson (ed.), *The Open Text. New Directions for Biblical Studies*, London, SCM Press, April 1993.

SELECTED BIBLIOGRAPHY

Abogunrin, S.O. 1986. "Biblical Research in Africa: The Task Ahead," AJBS 1 (1, 1986), 9–24

———. 1987. "The Synoptic Gospel Debate: A Reexamination in the African Context," *AJBS* 2 (1–2, 1987), 25–54.

Amewowo, A. 1986. "Experiences and Discoveries with the Bible in West Africa," *Mission Studies*, Vol. III, No. 1, pp. 12–24.

Atal sa Angang, D., et al (ds.), 1980. Christianism et Indentité Africaine. Point de vue exegetique. *Actes du 1er Congrès des Biblistes Africains*, Kinshasa.

Bediako, K. 1983. "Biblical Christologies in the Context of African Traditional Religions" in S. Vinay & C. Sugden (eds.), *Sharing Jesus in the Two Thirds World: Evangelical Christologies from the Contexts of Poverty, Powerlessness and Religious Pluralism*, Bangalore, Brilliant Printers, pp. 155–166.

Dickson, K.A. 1968. *The History and Religion of Israel*, 3 Vols, London, Darton, Longman & Todd.

Dickson, K.A. & Ellingworth, P. (eds.), 1969. *Biblical Revelation and African Beliefs*, London, Lutterworth Press.

Dickson, K.A. 1972. "African Tradition and the Bible" in Mveng M. et al. (eds), *Black Africa and the Bible*, Jerusalem, pp. 115–175.

———. 1975. "Research in the History of Religions in West Africa," *Religion: Journal of Religion and Religions*, August, pp. 91–93.

———. 1979. "Continuity and Discontinuity Between the Old Testament and African Life and Thought," *BAT* Vol 1, No. 2, pp. 179–193; also in K. Appiah–Kubi & S.

Torres (eds.), *African Theology en Route*, New York, Maryknoll, Orbis Books, 1983, pp. 95–108.

Hanks, P. 1979. *Collins Dictionary of the English Language*, London, Glasgow, Collins.

Igenoza, A.O. 1985. "African Weltanschauung and Exorcism: The Quest for the Contextualization of the Kerygma," *ATJ* 14, 3, pp. 179–194.

ma Mpolo, M. 1983. "Jesus Christ—Word of Life. An African Contribution to the Theme of the Sixth Assembly," *The Ecumenical Review* (EcuRev) 35, 2, pp. 213–219.

Manus, C.U. 1985. "The Centurion's Confession of Faith (Mk 15,39): Reflections on Mark's Christology and Its Significance in the Life of African Christians," *BAT* 7, pp. 261–278.

———. 1985. "Contextualization: Theology and the Nigerian Social Reality," *NJTH*, 1, 1. pp. 21–42.

———. 1992. "Contextual Theology in Africa Today: Introduction, Recent Approaches and Representatives," *Hirschberg*, 45, 7/8, pp. 537–548.

Mugambi, J.N.K. *1995. From Liberation to Reconstruction: African Christian Theology After the Cold War*, Nairobi, East African Educational Publishers.

Ngally, J, 1975a. "Bible Studies from an African Perspective" Bulletin of All Africa Conference of Churches (BAACC), January–February.

———. 1975b. Jesus and Liberation in Africa: A Bible Study", EcuRev 3, 5, pp. 213–219.

Nkwoka, A.O. 1991. "Jesus as Elder Brother (Okpara): An Igbo Paradigm for Christology in the African Context," *AJT* 5, pp. 87–103.

-Nyamiti, C. 1993. "A Critical Assessment of Some Issues in Today's African Theology" in Manus, C.U. et al. (eds.), *Healing and Exorcism: The Nigerian Experience*, Enugu, Snaap Press, pp. 129–145; also in *AfricChrStud* 5 (1989), 5–18.

Okeke, G.E. 1980. "The Mission of Jesus and Mans Sonship with God", *ATJ* 9, 3, pp. 9–17.

Okure, T. 1989. "Inculturation in the New Testament: Its Relevance for the Nigerian Church," in *Inculturation in Nigeria. Proceedings of the Catholic Bishops' Study Session*, November, 1988, Lagos, Catholic Secretariat, pp. 39–62.

Onwu, A. N. 1984/85. "The Current State of Biblical Studies in Africa," *JRT* 41, pp. 35–46.

Osei–Bonsu, J. 1990. "The Contextualization of Christianity: Some New Testament Antecedents," *Irish Biblical Studies (IBS)* 12, pp. 129–148.

Sarpong, P.K. 1990. "Evangelization and Inculturation," *WAJES* 2, 1, pp. 1–9.

Schineller, P. 1990. *A Handbook on Inculturation*, New York, Paulist Press.

Schreiter, Robert J., 1981. *Faces of Jesus in Africa*, Orbis Books.

Ukpong, J.S. 1987a. "Contextualization: Concept and History," *RAT* 2, 22, pp. 149–163.

———. 1987b. "Contextualizing Theological Education in Western Africa: Focus on Subjects," *AfricChrStud* 3, 3, pp. 59–76.

———. 1992. "The Immanuel Christology of Matthew 25:31–46 in African Context", in Pobee, J.S. (ed.), *Exploring Afro-Christology*, SIHC 79, Frankfurt/Main, Verlag Peter Lang, pp. 55–67.

Uzukwu, E.E. 1985. *Church and Inculturation. A Century of Roman Catholicism in Eastern Nigeria*, Spiritian Booklets No. 1, Obosi, Pacific College Press.

Williams, J.J. 1930, *Hebrewisms of West Africa: From Nile to Niger with the Jews*, New York, Lincoln MacVeach/The Dial Press.

CHAPTER 2

Negotiating with "The White Man's Book": Early Foundations for Liberation Hermeneutics in Southern Africa[1]

Gerald West

> When the white man came to our country he had the Bible and we (Blacks) had the land. The white man said to us "let us pray." After the prayer, the white man had the land and we had the Bible.

This familiar anecdote, told all around Africa, is recounted with particular hermeneutical force in South Africa. Although the anecdote remains essentially the same, the biblical hermeneutics implicit in its retellings shifts from context to context and teller to teller. My purpose in the first part of this essay is to explore three interpretations of this story as a guide to the place of the Bible and biblical interpretation in South African black theology. The interpretations I have chosen to represent each come from a particular phase of South African black theology, though they are not confined to that phase. In other words, the distinctive features of a particular biblical hermeneutics are not confined to a particular sociohistorical period, though their formative impulses will have been forged in and by particular sociohistorical realities. In the second part of the essay, a sort of flashback, I trace the emergent hermeneutical moves implicit in the earliest encounters of indigenous South Africans with the Bible, attempting to track lines of connection between third-phase black theology and its ancestors who transacted with the Bible-bearing missionaries.

THE PRESENT: THE BIBLE AND SOUTH AFRICAN BLACK THEOLOGY

South African Black (Liberation) Theology

In a recent concept paper, Tinyiko Maluleke categorizes three phases of South African black theology. Though Maluleke's phases follow a chronological periodisation, he stresses the continuity between the phases:

23

The first phase starts with the formation of the Black Theology Project by the University Christian Movement in 1970, while the second starts in 1981 with the establishment of the Institute for Contextual Theology. In phase one, Black Theology, though acknowledging Blackness to be a state of mind, nevertheless took objective Blackness as its starting point in such a way that all Black people were the focus of liberation and the whole Bible (Christianity) could be used for liberation. In phase two, objective Blackness, in and of itself, is no longer sufficient. Not all Black people are the focus of Black Theology. Not all theology done by Black people is Black Theology and not all of the Bible (Christianity) is liberating. Furthermore, while phase one Black Theology was closely linked to the Black Consciousness philosophy, phase two Black Theology recognized a wider ideological ferment within the Black Theology movement. Most distinctive of the second phase has been the increasing introduction of Marxist historical materialism in the hermeneutic of Black Theology. (Maluleke 1998:61)[2]

The contours of the third phase are more difficult to discern, says Maluleke, because "we are living in and through it" (61). Nevertheless, he does offer a tentative sketch of the third phase. Repudiating allegations of black theology's death, Maluleke argues that the third phase of black theology draws deeply on resources within earlier phases of black theology, and elaborates these formative impulses into the future.

First, while the plurality of ideological positions and political strategies in the construction of black theology has been acknowledged since the early 1980s, the ideological and political plurality within black theology in the 1990s is more marked and brings with it a new '90s temptation that must be refused, suggests Maluleke.[3] Ideological and political plurality in post-apartheid (and post-colonial)[4] South Africa must avoid both the temptation of an uncommitted play with pluralism and the temptation of a despairing paralysis (perhaps even an abandonment) of commitment. Despite the pressures of ideological and political plurality, commitment remains the first act in black theology, whatever the particular brand (61).

Second, if race was the central category in the first phase of black theology, and if the category of class was placed alongside it in the second phase of black theology, then gender as a significant category has joined them in the third phase of black theology. But, once again, the tendency to minimize the foundational feature of black theology, namely, race, must be resisted. Gender, like class, in South Africa always has a racial component. Furthermore, warns Maluleke, in a context "where race is no longer supposed to matter" (61), racism often takes on different guises and becomes "more 'sophisticated'" (62).

The third and final feature of phase three black theology has three related prongs, each of which might be considered as a separate element. Here, however, I want to stress their connectedness, as does Maluleke, and so will treat them as subelements of a formative feature of the third phase of South African black theology. The formative feature of phase three black theology is the identification of African Traditional Religions (ATRs) and African Independent/Instituted/ Initiated Churches (AICs) as "significant" (perhaps even primary?) dialogue partners (62).[5]

Subsumed under this general feature, the first of the three prongs has to do with culture. Whereas phase one black theology "ventured somewhat into cultural . . . issues," phase two "became more and more concerned with the struggle of black people against racist, political and economic oppression" (Maluleke 1998:133). However, "At crucial moments connections with African culture would be made—provided that culture was understood as a site of struggle rather than a fixed set of rules and behaviours" (133). Culture remains problematic in phase three, but the envisaged rapprochement with ATRs and AICs that characterizes phase three foregrounds culture in a form not found in phase two.

The second prong has to do with solidarity with the poor. In each of its phases, black theology "has sought to place a high premium on *solidarity with the poor* and not with the state or its organs—however democratic and benevolent such a state might be."[6] While such a position "must not be mistaken with a sheer anti-state stance . . . Black Theology is first and foremost not about the powerful but about the powerless and the silenced." And—and I stress this conjunction— "serious interest" in ATRs and AICs affords black theology in phase three "another chance of demonstrating solidarity with the poor–for ATRs is [sic] the religion of the poor in this country" (Maluleke 1998:62).

Closely related to the first and second prongs, but particularly to the first, is a third. By making culture a site of struggle, black theology "managed to relativize the Christian religion sufficiently enough to encourage dialogue not only with ATRs but with past and present struggles in which religions helped people to take part, either in acquiescence or in resistance" (133). If, as Itumeleng Mosala has argued

(Mosala 1986), African culture can be a primary site of a hermeneutics of struggle for African theology, supplemented only with a political class-based hermeneutics, then Christianity is not a necessary component in a black theology of liberation (Maluleke 1998:133). A key question, therefore, for the third phase of South African black theology is, "Have black and African theologies made the necessary epistemological break from orthodox or classical Christian theology required to effect 'a creative reappropriation of traditional African religions'"? (Mosala 1986: 100) (135).

Generally, Maluleke responds to his own question, South African black theology has tended to use "classical Christian tools, doctrines and instruments—for example the Bible and Christology" for its purposes. Black theology has used Christianity (and what follows is Itumeleng Mosala's take on the anecdote I began the essay with) to "get the land back and get the land back without losing the Bible" (Mosala 1987:194).

> Realizing that Christianity and the Bible continue to be a "haven of the Black masses" (Mofokeng 1988:40), black theologians reckoned that it would not be advisable simply "to disavow the Christian faith and consequently be rid of the obnoxious Bible." Instead the Bible and the Christian faith should be shaped "into a formidable weapon in the hands of the oppressed instead of just leaving it to confuse, frustrate or even destroy our people" (Mofokeng 1988:40). Preoccupation with Christian doctrines and ideas was, for black theology therefore, not primarily on account of faith or orthodoxy considerations, but on account of Christianity's apparent appeal to the black masses. (Maluleke 1998:134)

Given this analysis, Maluleke goes on to argue,

> What needs to be reexamined now [in phase three] however, is the extent to which the alleged popularity of Christianity assumed in South African black theology is indeed an accurate assessment of the religious state of black people. If it were to be shown that ATRs are as popular as Christianity among black South Africans then in not having given much concerted attention to them, black theology might have overlooked an important resource. There is now space for this to be corrected by making use of alternative approaches. (Maluleke 1998:134)

These brief comments, exegeting as they do the framework proposed by Maluleke, provide a provisional sketch of black theology, and do probably just enough to situate my analysis of the Bible and biblical hermeneutics in South African black theology.[7]

A Hermeneutics of Trust

When the white man came to our country he had the Bible and we (blacks) had the land. The white man said to us "let us pray." After the prayer, the white man had the land and we had the Bible. To which, having retold the anecdote, Desmond Tutu has on occasions responded, "And we got the better deal!"[8] This response is typical of a hermeneutics of trust with respect to the Bible that characterizes the first phase of South African black theology and persists into the present in the biblical hermeneutics of black theologians like Tutu and Allan Boesak.[9]

I have discussed the biblical hermeneutics of Tutu and Boesak in detail elsewhere, both from an emic approach–using the categories and concepts internal to the discourse of black theology—and from an etic approach—using concepts and categories from discourses outside of black theology (West 1995). Here I will briefly delineate some of the key characteristics of this particular orientation to the Bible and biblical interpretation in South African black theology, again using both emic and etic concepts and categories.

The overall interpretative orientation toward the Bible is one of trust. A hermeneutics of trust is evident in a number of respects. First, as in much of African theology (and African American black theology and Latin American liberation theology), the Bible is considered to be a primary source of black theology (see Mbiti 1977). The Bible belongs to black theology in the sense that doing theology without it is unthinkable. Second, the Bible is perceived to be primarily on the side of the black struggle for liberation and life in South Africa. The Bible belongs to black theology in the sense that the struggle for liberation and life is central to them both (see Tutu 1983:124–129).

While there is definitely an awareness that there are different, sometimes complementing and sometimes contradicting, theologies in the Bible, this is understood as evidence of the thoroughly contextual nature of the Bible, and, because the pervasive theological trajectory is one of liberation, the plurality of theologies in the Bible is unproblematic for black theology (Tutu 1983:106). Those who use the Bible against black South Africans are therefore misinterpreting the Bible, because the Bible is basically on the side of black theology.

In terms of interpretative interests (Fowl 1990), the dominant interests among black theologians who work within a framework of a hermeneutics of trust can be characterised as a combination of a focus on the text itself and a focus on the central symbolic and thematic semantic axis (or trajectory) of the final canonical form. A careful and close reading of particular texts is used in conjunction with a generally accepted sense of the liberatory shape of the final Christian canonical form, culminating as it does in Jesus, "the ultimate reference point" (see Tutu 1983:106; West 1995:64–70, 146–173; Draper 1996).

Although race may not be an obvious dimension of biblical texts—and South African black theology has not shared the same passion as black theology in the USA for recovering an African presence in the Bible or of bringing racial analysis to bear on the Bible itself (see Felder 1991)—the first phase of black theology found numerous lines of connection between their struggle and the struggle of God's people in the pages of the Bible. Even Takatso Mofokeng, a proponent of phase two black theology, makes the claim that

> when many Black Christians read their history of struggle carefully, they come upon many Black heroes and heroines who were inspired and sustained by some passages and stories of the Bible in their struggle, when they read and interpreted them in the light of their Black experience, history and culture. They could consequently resist dehumanization and the destruction of their faith in God the liberator. It is this noble Black Christian history that helps to bring out the other side of the Bible, namely, the nature of the Bible as a book of hope for the downtrodden. (Mofokeng 1988:38)

But this is not the whole story.

A Hermeneutics of Suspicion
When the white man came to our country, he had the Bible and we (blacks) had the land. The white man said to us "let us pray." After the prayer, the white man had the land and we had the Bible. To which, having recounted the anecdote, Takatso Mofokeng responds by saying that this story expresses more precisely than any statement in the history of political science or Christian missions the ambiguity of the Bible and "the dilemma that confronts black South Africans in their relationships with the Bible."

> With this statement, which is known by young and old in South Africa, black people of South Africa point to three dialectically

related realities. They show the central position which the Bible occupies in the ongoing process of colonization, national oppression and exploitation. They also confess the incomprehensible paradox of being colonized by a Christian people and yet being converted to their religion and accepting the Bible, their ideological instrument of colonization, oppression and exploitation. Thirdly, they express a historic commitment that is accepted solemnly by one generation and passed on to another—a commitment to terminate exploitation of humans by other humans. (Mofokeng 1988:34)

That the Bible is both a problem and a solution is a central characteristic of second-phase black theology. The dominant orientation is one of suspicion toward the Bible. Again, I can only sketch the contours of the biblical hermeneutics of this phase (for more detail, see West 1995), using wherever possible the emic categories and concepts of black theology itself.

While the "external" problem of the misuse of the Bible by oppressive and reactionary white South African Christians remains, phase two black theology identifies a more fundamental problem—the "internal" problem of the Bible itself. Mofokeng is critical of those who concentrate only on the external problem, those who accuse "oppressor-preachers of *misusing* the Bible for their oppressive purposes and objectives" and "preachers and racist whites of not practising what they preach." It is clear, Mofokeng maintains, that these responses are "based on the assumption that the Bible is essentially a book of liberation." While Mofokeng concedes that these responses, so characteristic of phase one–type biblical hermeneutics, have a certain amount of validity to them, the crucial point he wants to make is that there are numerous "texts, stories and traditions in the Bible which lend themselves to only oppressive interpretations and oppressive uses because of their inherent oppressive nature." What is more, he insists, any attempt "to 'save' or 'co-opt' these oppressive texts for the oppressed only serve the interests of the oppressors" (Mofokeng 1988:37–38). Young blacks in particular, Mofokeng continues, "have categorically identified the Bible as an oppressive document by its very nature and to its very core" and suggest that the best option "is to disavow the Christian faith and consequently be rid of the obnoxious Bible." Indeed, some "have zealously campaigned for its expulsion from the oppressed Black community," but, he notes, with little success (Mofokeng 1988:40).

Unfortunately, particularly given Maluleke's question of the place of the Bible in phase three black theology, Mofokeng does not offer further reflection on those who would "be rid of the obnoxious Bible"; instead he focuses on the reason for their lack of success, which, he argues, is

> largely due to the fact that no easily accessible ideological silo or storeroom is being offered to the social classes of our people that are desperately in need of liberation. African traditional religions are too far behind most blacks while Marxism, is to my mind, far ahead of many blacks, especially adult people. In the absence of a better storeroom of ideological and spiritual food, the Christian religion and the Bible will continue for an undeterminable period of time to be the haven of the Black masses par excellence.

Given this situation of very limited ideological options, Mofokeng continues, "Black theologians who are committed to the struggle for liberation and are organically connected to the struggling Christian people, have chosen to honestly do their best to shape the Bible into a formidable weapon in the hands of the oppressed instead of leaving it to confuse, frustrate or even destroy our people" (Mofokeng 1988:40).

But on just how the Bible is to become "a formidable weapon in the hands of the oppressed" Mofokeng is not too clear. For this we will have to turn to the work of Itumeleng Mosala. Mosala is the clearest of phase two black theologians on this matter. In an early essay on "The Use of the Bible in Black Theology," he is the first black theologian to question in print the ambiguous ideological nature of the Bible itself (Mosala 1986; 1989:1–42). Mosala's basic critique is directed at black theology's exegetical starting point which "expresses itself in the notion that the Bible is the revealed 'Word of God'" (Mosala 1989:15). He traces this view of the Bible as "an absolute, non-ideological 'Word of God'" back to the work of James Cone.[10] He finds it even in the work of the "most theoretically astute of [African American] black theologians," Cornel West. Whatever the origin, what matters to Mosala is that "South African black theologians are not free from enslavement to this neo-orthodox theological problematic that regards the notion of the 'Word of God' as a hermeneutical starting point" (Mosala 1989:17). Mosala underlines the pervasiveness of this view of the Bible by subjecting South African black theologians Sigqibo Dwane, Simon Gqubule, Khoza Mgojo, Manas Buthelezi, Desmond Tutu, and Allan Boesak to a similar critique (Mosala 1989:17–42). More recently, Tinyiko Maluleke has extended this critique to African theologians north of the Limpopo River,[11] including Lamin Sanneh, Kwame

Bediako, John Mbiti, Byang Kato, and Jesse Mugambi (Maluleke
1996:10–14).

Mosala's contention is that most of the Bible "offers no certain
starting point for a theology of liberation within itself." For example, he
argues that the biblical book of Micah "is eloquent in its silence about
the ideological struggle waged by the oppressed and exploited class of
monarchic Israel." In other words, "it is a ruling class document and
represents the ideological and political interests of the ruling class." As
such there "is simply too much de-ideologization to be made before it
can be hermeneutically straightforward in terms of the struggle for
liberation" (Mosala 1986:196; 1989:120–121). The Bible, therefore,
cannot be the hermeneutical starting point of black theology. Rather,
those committed to the struggles of the black oppressed and exploited
people "cannot ignore the history, culture, and ideologies of the
dominated black people as their primary hermeneutical starting point"
(Mosala 1986:197).

However, this does not mean that Mosala totally rejects the Bible.
While the Bible cannot be the primary starting point for black theology
"there are enough contradictions within the book [of Micah, for
example] to enable eyes that are hermeneutically trained in the struggle
for liberation today to observe the kin struggles of the oppressed and
exploited of the biblical communities in the very absences of those
struggles in the text." Because the Bible is "a product and a record of
class struggles" (Mosala 1986:196), black theologians are able to detect
"glimpses of liberation and of a determinate social movement
galvanized by a powerful religious ideology in the biblical text." But,
he continues, the "existence of this phenomenon is not in question;
rather, the problem here is one of developing an adequate hermeneutical
framework that can rescue those liberating themes from the biblical
text" (Mosala 1989:40).

Mosala goes on in his work to offer an adequate hermeneutical
framework for black theology, proposing a dialectic between an
appropriation of black culture and experience and an appropriation of
the Bible (Mosala 1986:119). "Black Theology has roots in the Bible
insofar as it is capable of linking the struggles of oppressed people in
South Africa today with the struggles of oppressed people in the
communities of the Bible," but because the oppressed people in the
Bible "did not write the Bible," and because their struggles "come to us
via the struggles of their oppressors," "Black Theology needs to be
firmly and critically rooted in black history and black culture in order

for it to possess apposite weapons of struggle that can enable black people to get underneath the biblical text to the struggles of oppressed classes." However, black theology must also be "firmly and critically rooted in the Bible in order to elicit from it cultural-hermeneutical tools of combat" with which black people can penetrate beneath both the underside of black history and culture and contemporary capitalist settler colonial domination to the experiences of oppressed and exploited working-class black people (Mosala 1986:120).

While the forms of black theology inherited by Mosala and others from phase one are "firmly . . . rooted in the Bible," they are not "critically rooted in the Bible." This is the fundamental problem of black theology for Mosala, and because his understanding of what it means to be "critically rooted in the Bible" is so important in its contribution to South African black theology (and because it ought to be clearly heard by all forms of African theology) I will discuss his contribution in some detail.

Mosala contends that the impotence of black theology as a weapon of struggle comes from the enslavement of black theology "to the biblical hermeneutics of dominant ideologies" (Mosala 1989:4). More specifically, black theology's impotence comes from embracing "the ideological form of the text"[12]—"the oppressors' most dangerous form" (Mosala 1989:28). Existential commitment to the struggle against apartheid in South Africa was no substitute "for scientific analysis of the valence of a tradition in the class struggle" (Mosala 1989:34). While Mosala accepts that "texts that are against oppressed people may be coopted by the interlocutors of the liberation struggle," he insists that "the fact that these texts have their ideological roots in oppressive practices means that the texts are capable of undergirding the interests of the oppressors even when used by the oppressed. In other words, oppressive texts cannot be totally tamed or subverted into liberative texts" (Mosala 1989:30).

Mosala rejects a "fundamentalism of the Left"[13] that "attempts to transplant biblical paradigms and situations into our world without understanding their historical circumstances." Like Norman Gottwald, and using his analysis, Mosala criticises liberation theologians who invoke biblical symbols of liberation but who "seldom push those biblical symbols all the way back to their socio-historic foundations" and consequently are not able to "grasp concretely the inner-biblical strands of oppression and liberation in all their stark multiplicity and contradictory interactions." Not only does this "picking and choosing" of biblical resources by some liberation theologians "not carry sufficient structural analysis of biblical societies to make a proper comparison with the present possible," a lack of interest in and knowledge of "the history of social forms and ideas from biblical times to the present" results in the risk that "unstructural understanding of the Bible may simply reinforce and confirm unstructural understanding of the present" (Gottwald, cited in Mosala 1989:31–32). It is "a risky business," says Gottwald, "to 'summon up' powerful symbolism out of a distant past unless the symbol users are very self-conscious of their choices and applications, and fully aware of how their social struggle is both like and unlike the social struggle of the architects of the symbols" (Gottwald 1979:703).[14] Efforts to draw "religious inspiration" or "biblical values" from, for example, early Israel "will be romantic and utopian unless resolutely correlated to both the ancient and the contemporary cultural-material and social-organizational foundations" (Gottwald 1979:706).

Mosala agrees with Gottwald; he is concerned at "a thinness of social structural analysis and a thinness of biblical analysis" in black theology (Gottwald, cited in Mosala 1989:31). His fundamental objections against the biblical hermeneutics of black theology are that not only does it suffer from an unstructural understanding of the Bible, but, both as a consequence and as a reason, it also suffers from an unstructural understanding of black experience and struggle. Central to Mosala's hermeneutics of liberation is the search for a theoretical perspective that can locate both the Bible and the black experience within appropriate sociohistorical contexts. Historical-critical tools (to delimit and historically locate texts), supplemented by sociological resources (including a historical-materialist understanding of struggle), provide the theoretical perspective for Mosala's treatment of texts; historical materialism, particularly its appropriation of "struggle" as a key concept, provides the categories and concepts necessary to read and critically appropriate both black history and culture and the Bible. "The category of struggle becomes an important hermeneutical factor not only in one's reading of his or her history and culture but also in one's understanding of the history, nature, ideology, and agenda of the biblical texts" (Mosala 1989:9).

In order to undertake this kind of analysis, Mosala argues, black interpreters must be engaged in the threefold task of Terry Eagleton's "revolutionary cultural worker": a task that is projective, polemical, and appropriative. While Mosala does not doubt that black theology is "projective" and "appropriative" in its use of the Bible, it is "certainly *not* polemical—in the sense of being critical—in its biblical hermeneutics" (Mosala 1989:32). Black theology has not interrogated the text ideologically in class, cultural, gender, and age terms. Black theology has not gauged the grain or asked in what code the biblical text is cast and so has read the biblical text as an innocent and transparent container of a message or messages (Mosala 1989:41). By not using socio-historical modes of interpretation, black theology continues to spar "with the ghost of the oppressor" in its most powerful form—the ideological form of the text (Mosala 1989:28).

The Bible, according to Mosala's analysis, is a complex text best understood as a "signified practice." "It cannot be reduced to a simple socially and ideologically unmediated 'Word of God.' Nor can it be seen merely as a straight forward mirror of events in Ancient Israel. On the contrary it is a *production*, a remaking of those events and processes" (Mosala 1989:3). Using the language of redaction criticism, Mosala argues that the different "layers" that historical-critical work detects each have a particular ideological code. Some layers of the Bible are cast in "hegemonic codes," which represent social and historical realities in ancient Israel in terms of the interests of the ruling classes. Other parts of the Bible are encoded in "professional codes," which have a relative autonomy, but which still operate within the hegemony of the dominant code. Then there are layers that are signified through "negotiated codes," which contain a mixture of adaptive and oppositional elements, but which still take the dominant codes as their starting point. Finally, there are a few textual sites that represent "oppositional codes" which are grounded in the interests and religious perspectives of the underclasses of the communities of the Bible (Mosala, 1989:41–42).

A critical and structural analysis of the biblical text requires that black theology identify the ideological reference code in which a particular text is encoded. For it is only by recognizing the particular ideological encoding of a text that an interpreter can prevent herself or himself from colluding with the dominant and hegemonic. Moreover, it is only by recognizing the particular encoding of a text that the interpreter can then interpret the text against the grain. In other words, the polemical task of the interpreter is vital because it enables the appropriative task. A critical analysis of the biblical text ensures that black theology is able to appropriate the text against the grain. Such an approach would not be selective, nor would it engage in "proof-texting."

Rather, a critical and structural ideological mode of reading "advocates an analytic approach to the text of the Bible that exposes the underlying literary and ideological plurality in the text without denying the hegemonic totality or shall we say unity of the final product" (Mosala 1989:4).[15]

This phrase of Eagleton's, "against the grain," seeks to remind us, Mosala argues, "that the appropriation of works and events is always a contradictory process embodying in some form a 'struggle.'" The interpretive struggle consists of, depending on the class forces involved, "either to harmonize the contradictions inherent in the works and events or to highlight them with a view to allowing social class choices in their appropriation" (Mosala 1989:32).[16] The concern of Mosala is not that black theologians *cannot* read any text, no matter what its encoding, against the grain, but that they *ought not* to do this without *recognizing* what they are doing.

The Bible "is the product, the record, the site, and the weapon of class, cultural, gender, and racial struggles. And a biblical hermeneutics of liberation that does not take this fact seriously can only falter in its project to emancipate the poor and the exploited of the world. Once more, the simple truth rings out that the poor and exploited must liberate the Bible so that the Bible may liberate them" (Mosala 1989:193). "One cannot," Mosala maintains, "successfully perform this task by denying the oppressive structures that frame what liberating themes the texts encode" (Mosala 1989:41). So, only a *critical* appropriation of the Bible along socio–historical and ideologically socialist lines, systematically and critically (re)located in the broad black working-class struggle (Mosala 1989:190–192), will enable the Bible to be a resource with which black theology will be to "get the land back and get the land back without losing the Bible" (Mosala 1987:194).

Ancestral Hermeneutics

> When the white man came to our country he had the Bible and we (Blacks) had the land. The white man said to us "let us pray." After the prayer, the white man had the land and we had the Bible.

To which, having retold the anecdote,[17] Tinyiko Maluleke poses the question of what precisely it means to say that black people "have the Bible." Although Maluleke does not formulate the question in this way, his frequent and insightful reflections on the Bible and biblical interpretation in South African black theology (and African theology) push in this direction.

As I have shown, via Maluleke's analysis, one of the important features of phase three black theology is the recognition, recovery, and revival of its links with ATRs and AICs; and in so doing renewing its dialogue with African theology in its many and various forms.[18] This rapprochement raises the question, as we have already noted, of the place of Christianity in black theology (and African theology). Starkly articulated, in the words of the African theologian Gabriel Setiloane, "Why do we continue to seek to convert to Christianity the devotees of African traditional religion?" (Setiloane 1977:64, cited in Maluleke 1997:13). "This," says Maluleke, "is a crucial question for all African theologies [including South African black theology] as we move into the twenty–first century" (13).

Alongside this question, of course, comes the related question of whether black theology can be done without the Bible. If it is true, as is claimed by both Mofokeng and Mosala, that the Bible is primarily of strategic, not substantive (see Cady 1986; West 1995: chapter 5), importance to black theology, a claim that is vigorously rejected by Tutu (see above), Boesak (see Boesak 1984), Simon Maimela (Maimela 1991), and many other black theologians, then there are good grounds for a black theology without "the Book." Before we too quickly dismiss the claim made by Mofokeng and Mosala, we would do well to hear their claim clearly. Remember Mofokeng's argument:

> the Bible is important to Black Theology because besides the Bible there is no easily accessible ideological silo or storeroom being offered to the social classes of our people that are desperately in need of liberation. African traditional religions are too far behind most blacks while Marxism, is to my mind, far ahead of many blacks, especially adult people. In the absence of a better storeroom of ideological and spiritual food, the Christian religion and the Bible will continue for an undeterminable period of time to be the haven of the Black masses par excellence. (Mofokeng 1988:40)

In other words, ideologically contested though it is, there are good strategic and pragmatic reasons for continuing to use the Bible, so long as it remains the most readily available resource for social trans- formation. "Preoccupation with Christian doctrines and ideas [and the Bible] was, for black theology therefore, not primarily on account of faith or orthodoxy considerations, but on account of Christianity's apparent appeal to the black masses" (Maluleke 1998:134). But, Maluleke continues,

> What needs to be reexamined now [in phase three] however, is the extent to which the alleged popularity of Christianity [and the Bible] assumed in South African black theology is indeed an accurate assessment of the religious state of black people. If it were to be shown that ATRs are as popular as Christianity among black South Africans then in not having given much concerted attention to them, black theology might have overlooked an important resource. (Maluleke 1998:134)

However, Maluleke doubts whether "pragmatic and moral arguments can be constructed in a manner that will speak to masses without having to deal with the Bible in the process of such constructions" (Maluleke 1996:14). The Bible remains in the 1990s, and probably into the millennium, "a 'haven of the Black masses'" (14). And as long as it is a resource, it must be confronted, "precisely at a hermeneutical level" (14). Quite what Maluleke means by this is not clear, but he does offer some clues, which emerge in his dialogue with the biblical hermeneutics of African theology (Maluleke 1997:14–16).

He agrees with Mercy Amba Oduyoye, who speaks with many African women,[19] when she says that the problem with the Bible in Africa is that "throughout Africa, the Bible has been and continues to be absolutized: it is one of the oracles that we consult for instant solutions and responses" (Oduyoye 1995:174, cited in Maluleke 1997:15). "However," continues Maluleke, while many African biblical scholars and theologians are locked into a biblical hermeneutics that makes "exaggerated connections between the Bible and African heritage," "on the whole, and in practice, [ordinary] African Christians are far more innovative and subversive in their appropriation of the Bible than they appear" (Maluleke 1997:14–15). They "may mouth the Bible-is-equal-to-the-Word-of-God formula, they are actually creatively pragmatic and selective in their use of the Bible so that the Bible may enhance rather than frustrate their life struggles" (Maluleke 1996:13). The task before black theology, then, is "not only to develop creative Biblical hermeneutic methods [such as those forged in former phases of Black Theology], but also to observe and analyze the manner in which African Christians 'read' and view the Bible" (15).

Indeed, an important task confronting black and African theologies in South Africa is "to observe and analyze the manner in which African

Christians 'read' and view the Bible." As the work of phase two black theologians has hinted at, ordinary black South Africans have adopted a variety of strategies in dealing with an ambiguous Bible, including rejecting it (Mofokeng 1988:40) and strategically appropriating it as a site of struggle (Mosala 1986:184; Mofokeng 1988:41). But, as I have argued (West, 1999:88–89), neither Mofokeng nor Mosala provide the kind of detail required for Maluleke's project. Even my own attempts to reflect on and conjure concepts that elucidate the way in which ordinary black South Africans "read" the Bible are not detailed enough (West 1999:89–107). And we have all been concentrating on the *present*, as we should, given the daily realities of our struggle against apartheid and the lack of leisurely space to do anything different. With the space that liberation has afforded, we must now, I would suggest, not only deepen our analysis of current stances toward the Bible in our context, but we must also follow Maluleke's gaze to the past, to our interpretative ancestors. We cannot do justice to Maluleke's task, I would argue, unless we also observe and analyze the manner in which African Christians *have "read"* and *have viewed* the Bible. Implicit in Maluleke's summoning of (or being summoned by) African traditional religion and the African independent churches, is the pull of the past.

The Past: Historical and Hermeneutical Dimensions of African Biblical Hermeneutics

> In the early years, the evangelists watched Southern Tswana intently for signs that they were hearing the Word; for evidence, as Mary Moffat (Moffat and Moffat 1951) put it, that they would "come out and be separate." Such signs were not often forthcoming, at least in a form discernible to the Europeans (Comaroff and Comaroff 1991:73).

Historical accounts of the early encounters between missionaries and indigenous Africans are plentiful and rich in detail and analysis. But they are pretty thin when it comes to documenting the reception and early interpretation of the Bible. There is much talk of "the Word" (Landau 1995), but on closer examination this tends to stand for the missionaries' message in general and not the Bible in particular. That the Bible is seldom treated separately from the arrival and reception of Christianity is not surprising, particularly as it can be argued that the Bible is analytically (in the philosophical sense) bound up with Christianity (Barr 1980:52). I do not want to dispute the interconnectedness of the Bible and Christianity, but I do not want to conflate them either. We assume too much too quickly if we do not pause to analyze the nature of their interconnectedness more carefully.

Heuristic Help from African American Encounters with the Bible

We should not assume, for example, that the reception of Christianity and the reception of the Bible are about receiving the same thing. While there is a paucity of work on indigenous receptions of the Bible in Africa, Vincent Wimbush's interpretative history of the Bible among African Americans provides compelling reasons for analyzing the reception of the Bible as distinct from but related to the reception of Christianity.

Wimbush proposes five major types and phases of biblical interpretation among African Americans. His research has both a hermeneutical and a historical dimension in that he correlates each major type of reading with a particular historical period. His research identifies, delineates, and analyzes the major types of African American readings of the Bible from slavery to the present (Wimbush 1991:84). While there are many significant differences between African American and indigenous African transactions with the Bible, there are also many striking similarities which make Wimbush's analysis heuristically valuable.

An analysis of the transactions between Africa and the Bible, particularly the early encounters, is not only of historical value. The early African American encounters with the Bible have functioned, according to Wimbush, "as phenomenological, sociopolitical and cultural foundation" for subsequent periods (Wimbush 1993:131). If Wimbush is right in asserting that the array of interpretative strategies forged in the earliest encounters of African Americans with the Bible are foundational, in the sense that all other African American readings are in some sense built upon and judged by them, then such analysis has tremendous hermeneutical significance for our current context.

African slaves' initial encounter with the Bible is characterized, according to Wimbush, by a combination of rejection, suspicion, and awe of "Book Religion." During this period the story of European colonization and conquest of "the New World" as told by Wimbush is remarkably similar to the story that indigenous South Africans tell about the coming of European colonization to Southern Africa.

They conquered native peoples and declared that European customs, languages, and traditions were the law. The Europeans' embrace of the Bible helped to lend this process legitimacy. Since many of them through their reading of and reference to the Bible had already defined themselves as dissenters from the dominant social, political, and religious traditions in their native countries, they found it a rather natural resource in the context of the New World. The Bible functioned as a cultural image-reflector, as a road map to nation-building. It provided the Europeans justification to think of themselves as a "biblical nation," as God's people called to conquer and convert the New World to God's way as they interpreted it. (Wimbush 1991:84)

While the Bible did play a role in the missionizing of African slaves, in the earliest encounters its role was not primary and so its impact was indirect. "It was often imbedded within catechetical materials or within elaborate doctrinal statements and formal preaching styles" (Wimbush 1993:130). When African slaves did encounter the Bible itself, this was done from the perspective of cultures steeped in oral tradition, so the notion of religion and religious power circumscribed by a book was "at first frightful and absurd, thereafter, . . . awesome and fascinating" (Wimbush 1993:131). As illiterate peoples with rich, well-established, and elaborate oral traditions the majority of the first African slaves were suspicious of and usually rejected "Book religion." However, as Wimbush notes, "It did not take them long to associate the Book of 'Book religion' with power." So early in their encounter with "the Book," before they began to appropriate the Bible in an empowering and affirmative manner, their "capacity and willingness to engage 'the Book' were significant, for they demonstrated the ability of African slaves to adapt themselves to different understandings of reality," and in so doing to survive (Wimbush 1991:85).

During what Wimbush classifies as the second period of encounter with the Bible, African slaves began to appropriate and own the Bible. With the growth of the non-establishment, evangelical, camp meeting revivalist movements, Africans "began to encounter the Bible on a large and popular scale." As significant numbers of Africans converted to Christianity, even establishing their own churches and denominational groups, they began to embrace the Bible.

What did not go unnoticed among the Africans was the fact that the white world they experienced tended to explain its power and authority by appeal to the Bible. So they embraced the Bible, transforming it from the book of the religion of whites—whether aristocratic slavers or lower class exhorters—into a source of (psychic-spiritual) power, a source of inspiration for learning and affirmation, and into a language world of strong hopes and veiled but stinging critique of slave-holding Christian culture. (Wimbush 1993:131)

The point Wimbush is making here is that African slaves, like their missionized, colonized, and conquered cousins in Africa, adopted and adapted the hermeneutic moves of the European "masters." African slaves would have noted the diversity of readings the Bible could inspire, including cultural, political, and denominational (religious) readings. They would also have observed the selective way in which the missionaries and preachers read the Bible; they read certain parts and ignored others. The various forms in which readings of the Bible could be articulated were appropriated and amplified: "in song, prayers, sermons, testimonies, and addresses" (Wimbush 1991:86). If the missionaries and masters could interpret the Book under the guidance of the Spirit, then so could they.

And interpret they did. They were attracted primarily to the narratives of the Hebrew Bible dealing with the adventures of the Hebrews in bondage and escaping from bondage, to the oracles of the eighth-century prophets and their denunciations of social injustice and visions of social justice, and to the New Testament texts concerning the compassion, passion, and resurrection of Jesus. With these and other texts, the African American Christians laid the foundations for what can be seen as an emerging "canon." In their spirituals and in their sermons and testimonies African Americans interpreted the Bible in the light of their experiences. Faith became indentification with the heroes and heroines of the Hebrew Bible and with the long-suffering but ultimately victorious Jesus. As the people of God in the Hebrew Bible were once delivered from enslavement, so, the Africans sang and shouted, would they be delivered. As Jesus suffered unjustly but was raised from the dead to new life, so, they sang, would they be "raised" from their "social death" to new life. So went the songs, sermons, and testimonies. (Wimbush 1991:86–87)

These various forms—spirituals, sermons, and testimonies— embody the hermeneutical processes whereby African slaves appropriated the Bible as their own property. They "reflect a hermeneutics characterized by a looseness, even playfulness, vis–à–vis the biblical texts themselves"; a looseness and playfulness toward the text which included the following strategies: interpretation "was not controlled by the literal words of the texts, but by social experience"; texts were heard and retold more than read; texts "were engaged as stories that seized and freed the imagination"; biblical texts were usually interpreted collectively; biblical stories "functioned sometimes as allegory, as parable, or as veiled social criticism" in a situation where survival demanded disguised forms of resisting discourse; certain texts in the canon were read and others ignored (Wimbush 1991:88–89).

In addition to offering a preliminary description of these formative hermeneutical processes, Wimbush also wants to argue that the array of interpretative strategies forged in this period of African American encounter with the Bible are foundational: all other readings would in some sense be built upon and judged by them. The beginning of the African American encounter with the Bible has functioned, according to Wimbush, "as phenomenological, sociopolitical and cultural foundation" for subsequent periods (Wimbush 1993:131). The Bible, understood as "the white folk's book," "was accepted but not interpreted in the way that white Christians and the dominant culture in general interpreted it" (Wimbush 1991:89).

In the absence of a careful analysis and history of the early encounters of indigenous South Africans with the Bible, the first two phases of Wimbush's interpretative history are suggestive, especially in two respects. His characterization of the hermeneutics of encounter as "a looseness, even playfulness" toward the biblical text and his claim that such a hermeneutics is foundational for and constitutive of the hermeneutics of subsequent phases in the ongoing appropriation of the Bible are particularly insightful and significant, and resonate with my own preliminary research and reflections on the Southern African context, and find echoes in the work of some South African black theologians (West, 1999, #3387:86–107). But before we allow such resonances to return us to the place of the Bible in the present, I want to use the impetus of Wimbush's work to push us back into the past, to the earliest encounters between indigenous South Africans and the Bible.

Early Indigenous Southern African Encounters with the Bible

Following the death of Dr van der Kemp, "that valuable man who [pioneered and] superintended the African missions" on behalf of the London Missionary Society (Campbell 1815 [Reprinted 1974]:v), the Directors thought it expedient to request one of their own body, the Rev. John Campbell, to visit the country, personally to inspect the different settlements, and to establish such regulations, in concurrence with Mr. Read and the other missionaries [already in Southern Africa], as might be most conducive to the attainment of the great end proposed–the conversion of the heathen, keeping in view at the same time the promotion of their civilization. (Campbell 1815 [Reprinted 1974]:vi)

The complex and protracted processes that constitute missionary notions and practices of conversion and civilization in Southern Africa have been carefully analyzed by many others, but with particular insight by Jean and John Comaroff (Comaroff 1985; Comaroff and Comaroff 1991; Comaroff and Comaroff 1997). Their thorough and theoretically astute work on missionary (and colonial) activity among the Southern Tswana provides a detailed backdrop to my own contribution, an attempt to probe the place of the Bible in the transactions that take place between indigenous Africans and the missionaries. While their work does take note of the Bible in the "long conversation," a recurring metaphor of the Comaroffs, between the Nonconformists and the Southern Tswana, I want to praise the Bible from the Christian missionary package if I can. I may not be able to, but the attempt is important to me as a socially engaged biblical scholar who is trying to understand the role of the Bible in the struggles of indigenous South Africans for survival, liberation, and life. I do not want to too easily assume that the Bible appeared to Africans as it did to the missionaries who brought it.[20]

Another way in which I have managed the available material for the purposes of this essay is to limit my analysis to one of the very earliest accounts of a Southern Tswana encounter with the Bible that I can find. Unfortunately, this requires that I am largely dependent on missionary narrative constructions of such encounters, but socially engaged biblical scholars (and anthropologists [see Comaroff and Comaroff 1991:171, 189]) have become adept at "reading against the grain," particularly in contexts like South Africa where, Mosala reminds us, "the appropriation of works and events is always a contradictory process embodying in some form a 'struggle'" (Mosala 1989:32).

And so I come, with John Campbell, who was, as the Comaroffs say, an astute observer (Comaroff and Comaroff 1991:178), to see what his narrative of such an encounter might have to offer to the scrutinizing gaze of the Tlhaping, the southernmost group of Southern Tswana

("Bechuana") peoples. For their gaze was no less penetrating and discriminating than that of the missionaries who marched into their lives. And gaze they did; and listen, touch and taste: "the very first exchanges were visual, aural, and tactile, a trade of perceptions" (Comaroff and Comaroff 1991:181).

John Campbell, a director of the London Missionary Society, had been commissioned and sent to the Cape in 1812 in order "to survey the progress and prospects of mission work in the interior" (Comaroff and Comaroff 1991:178). Campbell made his way from mission post to mission post in the Colony, and when he came to Klaarwater, which was then some distance north of the boundary of the Cape Colony, though the boundary was to follow him some years later (in 1825) almost as far as Klaarwater, he heard that Chief Mothibi of the Tlhaping people a hundred miles further to the north had expressed some interest in receiving missionaries (Comaroff and Comaroff 1991:178). With barely a pause in Klaarwater, spending no more than a week there, Campbell and his party set off for Dithakong ("Lattakoo"), then the capital of Chief Mothibi, on the 15th June 1813.

Though not the first whites or missionaries to make this trek (see below), I pick up their trail and tale as they arrive on the outskirts of Dithakong in the afternoon of 24th June 1813. Having crested a hill, "Lattakoo came all at once into view, lying in a valley between hills, stretching about three or four miles from E. to W." (Campbell 1815 [Reprinted 1974]:180). But as they descended the hill toward "the African city," they were "rather surprised that no person was to be seen in any direction, except two or three boys," and the absence of an overt presence continued even as the wagons wound their way between the houses, save for a lone man who "made signs" for them to follow him. The stillness continued, "as if the town had been forsaken of its inhabitants," until they came "opposite to the King's house," at which point they "were conducted" into the Chief's circular court (*kgotla*), "a square, formed by bushes and branches of trees laid one above another, in which," for this space was not forsaken, "several hundreds of people assembled together, and a number of tall men with spears, draw[n] up in military order on the north side of the square." And then the silence was broken! "In a few minutes the square was filled with men, women, and children, who poured in from all quarters, to the number of a thousand or more. The noise from so many tongues, bawling with all their might, was rather confounding, after being so long accustomed to the stillness of the wilderness" (Campbell 1815 [Reprinted 1974]:180).

Signed upon and conducted into a dense symbolic space (Comaroff 1985:54–60; Landau 1995:xvii, 20–25)[21] not of their choosing or understanding, Campbell and company become the objects of Tswana scrutiny. With a feeling of being "completely in their power," Campbell confesses in a letter written some days later, "They narrowly inspected us, made remarks upon us, and without ceremony touched us."[22] The Tlhaping "see," "feasting their eyes," they "examine," and they "touch."[23] Having been momentarily "separated," and having "lost sight of each in the crowd," the missionaries soon gathered themselves, though they "could hardly find out each other," and devised "a scheme, which after a while answered our purpose; we drew up the wagons in the form of a square, and placed our tent in the center" (Campbell 1815 [Reprinted 1974]:180). Being led into a round "square" not of their own making, they construct a square which they (only partially) control.[24] From this site of some control they plot and execute "the real object" of their visit, which they explain in the following terms to the nine local leaders (who represent Chief Mothibi in his absence from the city) who gather in their tent "a little after sunset" (Campbell 1815 [Reprinted 1974]:181).

> Through three interpreters, viz. in the Dutch, Coranna, and Bootchuana languages, I informed them that I had come from a remote country, beyond the sun, where the true God, who made all things known—that the people of that country had long ago sent some of their brethren to Klaar Water, and other parts of Africa, to tell them many things which they did not know, in order to do them good, and make them better and happier . . . [that] I had come to Lattakoo to inquire if they were willing to receive teachers—that if they were willing, then teachers should be sent to live among them. (Campbell 1815 [Reprinted 1974]:182).

The leadership reply that they cannot/may not give an answer until Mothibi returned, after which there is an informal, it would appear, exchange of gifts: tobacco and milk (Campbell 1815 [Reprinted 1974]:182). A number of observations, interactions, and transactions are recorded over the next few days as Campbell (impatiently) waits for the arrival of Mothibi. But in the evening of the 27th, when the uncle of the Chief, "Munaneets," comes to their tent with an interpreter, there was "much interesting conversation," during which the Bible is explicitly designated in discourse. On the first morning after their arrival (the 25th June), Campbell and his party hold worship in their kitchen, a house in "the square, used by them for some public purpose" but assigned to them for a kitchen (Campbell 1815 [Reprinted 1974]:181), which is attended by "some of the people" (Campbell 1815 [Reprinted 1974]). It is hard to imagine the Bible not being present and not being used as either an unopened sacred object or an opened text. Similarly, during worship in the afternoon of the 27th, at which "About forty of the men sat round us very quietly during the whole time" (Campbell 1815 [Reprinted 1974]:191), the Bible too must have been present. But the first explicit reference to the Bible in this narrative, where it is separated out from the normal practice and patterns of the missionaries, is in the discussion with the Chief's uncle.

In their constant quest for information and opportunities to provide information, scrutinizing as they are scrutinized, the missionaries "enquired of him their reason for practicing circumcision." It is not clear what prompts this question, but quite possibly what appear to be a series of ritual activities each day involving women, perhaps the initiation of young women (Campbell 1815 [Reprinted 1974]:185–186, 188, 191, 194–195; Comaroff 1985:114–118), may, by association, have generated a question to do with male initiation (see Comaroff 1985:85–115). The Chief's uncle replies that "it came to them from father to son." Sensing, no doubt, an opportunity "to instruct," the missionaries persevere, asking "Do you not know why your fathers did it?" To which the Chief's uncle and his companions answer, "No." Immediately the missionaries respond, Campbell reports, saying: "We told them that our book informed us how it began in the world, and gave them the names of Abraham, Ishmael, and Isaac, as the first persons who were circumcised" (Campbell 1815 [Reprinted 1974]:191–192). The elocutionary intent of this information is clearly to establish an earlier, and therefore superior, claim of origin. Origins were becoming increasingly important to the emerging modernity of missionary England, and so the Bible was seen as particularly potent, containing as it did "the Origin" of all origins.[25] However, what impressed the Chief's uncle and his colleagues was this claim to an all-encompassing origin, and the naming of the missionaries' ancestors, Abraham, Ishmael, and Isaac, which is why "This appeared to them very interesting information, and they all tried to repeat the names we had mentioned, over and over again, looking to us for correction, if they pronounced any of them wrong. Munaneets, and the others who joined the company, appeared anxious to have them fixed on their memories" (Campbell 1815 [Reprinted 1974]:192). The Book—the Bible—appeared, from the perspective of the Tlhaping, to contain the names of the missionary ancestors, and perhaps, if they picked up the illocutionary force of the missionaries' proclamation, the ancestors of their ancestors. This was, indeed, interesting, and potentially powerful, information.

Impressed, but probably also a little perplexed by this response, the missionaries persist, asking next "if they knew any thing of the origin of mankind, or when they came." The people reply, "saying they came from some country beyond them, pointing to the N., which is the direction in which Judea lies.[26] That two men came out of the water; the one rich, having plenty of cattle, the other poor, having only dogs. One lived by oxen, the other by hunting. One of them fell, and the mark of his foot is on a rock to this day." With no apparent attempt to probe this origin story in more detail, but with a clear indication of its (and the circumcision story's) inadequacy, the missionaries immediately "endeavoured to explain to them how knowledge, conveyed by means of books, was more certain than that conveyed by memory from father to son" (Campbell 1815 [Reprinted 1974]:192). The Chief's uncle, "Munaneets," is quick to realize the source of this "knowledge," knowing long before Michel Foucault theorized it, the articulations of power and knowledge on each other;[27] for he asks "if they should be taught to understand books." The use of the modal "should" perhaps conveys, as it often does in English, a sense of asking permission; Campbell's reconstruction and representation of this dialogue (via three other languages!) may accurately capture a concern on the part of the Chief's uncle that, given the evident power of the book(s), so openly exhibited by the missionaries, they may not be granted access to the book(s). That the missionaries and the Chief's representatives have in mind 'the Book,' in particular, is clear from missionaries' answer: "We answered they would; and when the person we should send (provided Mateebe consented), had learned their language, he would change the Bible from our language into theirs" (Campbell 1815 [Reprinted 1974]:192).

One of the local participants was clearly worried about outside instruction, and may also have been worried about the Bible, a new (outside) site and source of power/knowledge, though this is less clear, for during the conversation, Campbell reports, "an old man who is averse to our sending teachers, asked how we made candles, pointing to that which was on our table. He also said," Campbell continues, "he did not need instruction from any one, for the dice which hung from his neck informed him of every thing which happened at a distance; and added, if they were to attend to instructions, they would have no time to hunt or to do any thing" (Campbell 1815 [Reprinted 1974]:193). This fascinating exchange, representing as it is a complex exchange, seems to suggest a profound grasp by this "old man," possibly a *ngaka* (doctor/diviner/healer), with "dice," probably divining bones/materials, of the dangerousness of non-indigenous instruction. The context of the discussion, and the centrality of the Bible in the discussion, if not also centrally positioned in the meeting space, makes it likely that he assumes that the missionaries' book(s) is their equivalent of his "dice." My conjecture finds some support from Robert Moffat's account of an incident in which he says, "My books puzzled them." "They asked if they were my 'Bola,' prognosticating dice" (Moffat 1842 [Reprinted 1969]:384; see Comaroff and Comaroff 1991:345). Whether his aversion to "instruction" is an aversion to both the source and the interpreter of the source is not clear, but is a question that sits at the center of my study. We must not assume that this "old man" shares the assumption of the missionaries that the book and its instruction are one and the same thing. His concern that "if they were to attend to instructions, they would have no time to hunt or to do any thing" may reflect rumors of the time schedules and modes of production of established mission station church and school routines to the south (see also below), in which case the focus of his aversion is the instruction regime rather than the source of power/knowledge itself, the Book.

But I may be imagining a fissure where there is none, for this insightful "old man" may be making a simpler point; by pointing to the candles, and asking how missionaries made them, he may be demonstrating an important difference between knowledge that he and his people would find useful—how to make candles—and knowledge that is potentially damaging and dangerous—instruction about what happens "at a distance," such as circumcision, ancestors, and origins. The book, the source of the latter, but not, it would seem from his analysis, of the former, is as much a problem as the instruction.

Some days later (30th June), with the city still awaiting the arrival of Mothibi, and with many significant interactions transacted each day, including the constant gathering and giving of information, the Bible is again foregrounded. Campbell's major preoccupation during this time is seeking permission to "instruct the people." The local leadership consistently insists that he wait for Mothibi's return, and when Campbell and his men indicate an interest in using the time until Mothibi's return "to visit a large village about a day and a half's journey "higher up the country," they receive a visit that evening—after a busy day full of formative transactions, including Campbell's showing "a person his own face in the looking glass," another missionary brought objects saturated with symbolic significance (Comaroff and Comaroff 1991:170–197)—from Mmahutu, "the queen," Mothibi's senior wife (see Campbell 1815 [Reprinted 1974]:200, 207). She entered their tent and said that she "was averse" to their "going any where till Mateebe came," and that at the very least they should leave part of their wagons and party behind. Using this as a lever, the missionaries claim that they would never have thought of leaving Dithakong "even for a day before Mateebe's return" had they "been permitted to instruct the people; but that having nothing to do," they wished to visit that village and hunt. However, they are persuaded not to leave, and once this matter is settled, the missionaries "endeavoured to convey some information" (Campbell 1815 [Reprinted 1974]:199).

What follows is a remarkable exchange, signifying as it does a range of possible appropriations of the Bible:

> We explained to her the nature of a letter, by means of which a person could convey his thoughts to a friend at a distance. Mr. A. showed her one he had received from his wife, by which he knew every thing that had happened at Klaar Water for two days after he left it. This information highly entertained her, especially when told that A. Kok, who brought it, knew nothing of what it contained, which we explained by telling her the use of sealing wax. The bible being on the table gave occasion to explain the nature and use of a book, particularly of that book—how it informed us of God, who made all things; and of the beginning of all things, which seemed to astonish her, and many a look was directed towards the Bible. (Campbell 1815 [Reprinted 1974]:199)

Returning to a theme already raised, the reliability of text over oral transmission from father to son (see above), the missionaries draw Mmahutu's attention to the power of the letter as text in at least two respects. First, text can represent "every thing" that happened in a place in a person's absence. Second, text can be made to hide its message from the bearer and reveal its contents only to the intended receiver. Turning from the letter, to a quite different genre of text (for the perspective of the missionaries), the Bible, but a text nevertheless, the missionaries use the interest generated in their exposition of the letter to return to their preoccupation with the contents of the Bible, particularly the matter of origins.

Mmahutu is astonished, but what she is astonished at may not be what the missionaries imagine. Clearly, from her perspective text has power, with some appearing to have more power than others, hence "many a look" at the Bible. Text can reveal and text can hide; text can be manipulated by the people who transact with it. Clearly too, text contains knowledge/power; its contents, for those who have the power to make it speak, has to do with matters of importance to a community. This becomes clearer in a letter written by Campbell to a friend, Mr David Langton, some days later (27th July) in which he elaborates on this episode. Immediately following the final sentence in the quotation above, the following is added: "Mr Read's eye caught a verse very suitable to our situation in the page that was lying open, viz. Math. 4–16."[28] If this text was read, and the literary context suggests it would have been, Mmahutu would have heard this: "The people which sat in darkness saw great light; and to them which sat in the region and shadow of death light is sprung up." This then makes some sense of Mmahutu's questions, recorded in the next paragraph of the journal entry: "'Will people who are dead, rise up again?' 'Is God under the earth, or where is he?'" (Campbell 1815 [Reprinted 1974]:199). But only some sense, for her questions do not seem to deal directly with the passage read. The passage clearly makes sense to the missionaries, being made to bear the full weight of English missionary images of Africa (see Comaroff and Comaroff 1991:86–125). However, such allusions are probably absent from Mmahutu's hearing of this sentence from the Bible. What she does hear, and it may be the word "death," prompts here to bring her own questions to the text/missionaries, disturbed as she and others have become by talk of people rising from the dead, worrying especially that their slain enemies might arise (Moffat, 1842 [Reprinted 1969]:403–405; Comaroff, 1997, #3449:342).

Already we see emerging evidence from this very early encounter of a recognition that the Bible is power/knowledge, that as power/ knowledge it can be manipulated by those who control it, that it is beginning to be pried from the hands of the missionaries by indigenous questions, and, most significantly, that the bearer, like the bearer of the letter, might not know the power/knowledge it contains.

A Pause, Not a Conclusion

The story of the Bible's arrival among the Southern Tswana does not end here, but to tell the story fully requires more space than is available in this essay, so I pause here, allowing this final thought to linger and do its subversive work. What if early in their complex transactions with missionaries (and their colonial cousins), indigenous people like the Tlhaping already detected the missionaries' partial grasp on this book of power/knowledge? What if Mmahutu already saw signs of opportunities for appropriating the Bible for the purposes of her community (and women in particular)? What if it was already becoming apparent that the missionaries only had a partial (incomplete) understanding of this book's power/knowledge, and that their use of the Bible was partial (biased) to their agenda? Such questions drip with potential, and in themselves provide clear cause to Wimbush's claim that early encounters with the Bible may be foundational for and constitutive of the biblical hermeneutics of subsequent phases in the task of appropriation of the Bible as an African book. But I show my hand here, forgetting for a moment Maluleke's question with which I began and which structures my study: Has the Bible become an African book, or have Africans engaged with it strategically, though not substantively, as a matter of survival through the long periods of domination that the missionaries heralded and helped institute? This is a good question with which to close this part of my study, echoing as it does the question posed by Maluleke with which I began; the longer version must, of course, follow these early encounters through the establishment of missions among the Tswana, the translation of the Bible into the Tswana vernacular, the rise of various African independent churches, the emergence of black theology, and into the current post-apartheid and post-colonial theological crisis and the challenges it poses.

Gerald West
School of Theology
University of Natal
Pietermaritzburg
South Africa

NOTES

[1] The first part of this essay is based on a paper presented at the EFSA and University of Stellenbosch Department of Old and New Testament International Workshop on "Old and New Testament Studies in Africa: Learning from the Past and Planning for the Future." An earlier form of this first part has been published (West 2000).

[2] For a more detailed discussion of notions of blackness in South African black theology and of phases one and two of black theology, see (Frostin 1988: 86–103; Kritzinger 1988: 91–95; West 1995: chapter 4).

[3] The paper of Maluleke referred to here is a brief concept paper, and so I am sometimes making fairly bold inferences from the available clues. Wherever possible, I have used

Maluleke's other published work to enhance my understanding of the moves he makes in the concept paper.

[4] Talk of the post-colonial has been slow to find a foothold in the fields of theology and biblical studies in South Africa (and indeed to the north of us); the reasons for this deserve some attention (see West 1997; Dube 1996, 1997, 1999).

[5] Implicit in this formulation is my tentative analysis which locates ATRs and AICs along a continuum. At one end of the continuum ATR as a distinct "faith" would be located. I am not sure what would stand at the other end of the continuum, but along the way would be various manifestations of what we call AICs, gradually becoming less and less (primally) African. My play on "primal" here is deliberate, alluding to the "translation" trajectory in African theology (see below) and the high place they accord ATR as primal religion.

[6] Implicit here is a period of emergence of phase three black theology which includes the context of a postapartheid state; Maluleke would not use this formulation to address the relationship between black theology and the apartheid state.

[7] The sources cited in this essay provide a richer texture to black theology than I have offered here and their combined bibliographies do not leave much out; my purpose here is to give enough of a feel for black theology as a form of South African theology in order to get to the stuff of my essay, which is biblical hermeneutics.

[8] I have been unable to find a published source for this comment, but I personally have heard him make the comment on two public occasions.

[9] I have shifted here from "Black" to "black" because I am not sure that either Tutu or Boesak would still refer to themselves as "Black" theologians, that is, proponents of black theology.

[10] For a discussion of the role of James Cone in South African black theology see the important book by Per Frostin (Frostin 1988: 89–90).

[11] This is the boundary, it has been argued, especially before South Africa's liberation, between what have been called "theologies of bread" and "theologies of being" (Balcomb 1998).

[12] The question of whether texts can have ideologies, while not directly relevant to this discussion, is an important one and properly nuances discussions of textual ideology (see Fowl 1995; West 2000). Fowl's careful analysis charts the terrain of such discussions, and is particularly illuminating for this tangential discussion because he deals directly with Mosala's claim above. My article joins the discussion by accepting Fowl's analysis, but then goes on to show what is at stake in Mosala's position.

[13] The phrase is Hugo Assmann's (Assmann 1976: 104).

[14] Gottwald gives considerable space to developing this point (703–706).

[15] Elisabeth Schüssler Fiorenza makes a similar point when she argues that "The failure to bring a critical evaluation to bear upon the biblical texts and upon the process of interpretation within Scripture and tradition is one of the reasons why the use of the Bible by liberation theologians often comes close to 'prooftexting.'" Later she adds, "a critical hermeneutic must be applied to *all* biblical texts and their historical contexts" (Fiorenza 1981: 101–102, 108).

[16] David Tracy notes that "the particular form of 'correlation' [between the tradition and contemporary situation] that liberation and political theologies take will ordinarily prove to be a form not of liberal identity nor one of the several forms of analogy or similarity but rather one of sheer confrontation." "The confrontations will be demanded by both the retrieval of the prophetic tradition's stand for the oppressed and by the suspicions

released by the prophetic ideology-critique embedded in that retrieval" (Tracy 1981: 2–3).

[17] In his retelling of the anecdote Maluleke uses inclusive language, referring to "White people," thereby implicitly capturing the role white women (madams) played in missionary and colonial enterprises (see Comaroff and Comaroff 1991: 67–70, 135–138, 144–146; Comaroff and Comaroff 1997: 236–239, 276–277, 292–293, 299–300, 320–322, 374).

[18] Each of Maluleke's publications cited articulates forms of a dialogue between black theology and its three related interlocutors: ATRs, AICs, and African theologies.

[19] See for example (Dube 1997; Mbuwayesango 1997; Masenya 1997; Sibeko and Haddad 1997).

[20] My project is similar, but with a twist of perspective, to that proposed by Paul Landau, when he argues that historians of religion have too readily subsumed indigenous practices into religious categories that make sense to European researchers generally and missionary Christianity in particular (Landau 1999).

[21] The "square" would have been round (see references cited above); that it is described as "a square" demonstrates both some recognition of the political space into which they had been brought and the desire to revision what they found (see Comaroff and Comaroff 1991: 182–183).

[22] J. Campbell, Klaarwater, 26 July 1813 [CWM. Africa. South Africa. Incoming correspondence. Box 5–2–D].

[23] J. Campbell, Klaarwater, 26 July 1813 [CWM. Africa. South Africa. Incoming correspondence. Box 5–2–D].

[24] Campbell never quite copes with the way in which local people, mainly the leadership, just walk into "our tent" (Campbell 1815 [Reprinted 1974]: 181, 184).

[25] The English were, of course, about to have their views on origins thoroughly shaken and stirred by an English explorer and naturalist (Darwin 1963 [1859]); the beginnings of this paradigm shift (in the Kuhnian sense [Kuhn 1970]) can be detected in the missionary message (see below).

[26] This is a puzzling reference; could it mean biblical Judea, and if so, might the missionaries have seen this as confirming the origin of all peoples, even these "sons of Ham," from this distant land in and of the Bible?

[27] I use the term power/knowledge deliberately, realizing the hardworking hyphen (in the French *pouvoir-savoir*) and slash (in the English) bear a heavy load of theory. Accepting Foucault's invitation "to see what we can make of" his fragments of analysis (79), my use is intended to allude to this theory, especially to the fragmentary nature of Foucault's theory (79), to the implicit contrast of "idle knowledge" (79) with local forms of knowledge and criticism, subjugated knowledges (81–82), and their emergence as sites of contestation and struggle against "the tyranny of globalizing discourses" (83) and their appropriation as genealogies which wage war on the effects of power of dominant discourses (84), whether scientific (Foucault's focus) or other forms of dominating discourse. In particular, my use picks up on Foucault's analysis of the articulation of each on the other, namely, that "the exercise of power itself creates and causes to emerge new objects of knowledge and accumulates new bodies of information," that the "exercise of power perpetually creates knowledge and, conversely, knowledge constantly induces effects of power," and that it "is not possible for power to be exercised without knowledge, it is impossible for knowledge not to engender power" (52) (Foucault 1980).

[28] J. Campbell, Klaar Water, 27 July 1813 [CWM. Africa. South Africa. Incoming correspondence. Box 5–2–D].

SELECTED BIBLIOGRAPHY

Assmann, Hugo. 1976. *Theology for a nomad church.* Maryknoll, NY: Orbis.

Balcomb, Anthony. 1998. From liberation to democracy: theologies of bread and being in the new South Africa. *Missionalia* 26:54–73.

Barr, James. 1980. *The scope and authority of the Bible.* London: SCM.

Boesak, Allan. 1984. *Black and Reformed: apartheid, liberation, and the Calvinist tradition.* Johannesburg: Skotaville.

Cady, L. E. 1986. Hermeneutics and tradition: the role of the past in jurisprudence and theology. *Harvard Theological Journal* 79:439–463.

Campbell, John. 1815 (Reprinted 1974). *Travels in South Africa: undertaken at the request of Missionary Society.* Third Edition, Corrected ed. London (Reprint, Cape Town): Black, Parry, & Co. (Reprint, C. Struik).

Comaroff, Jean. 1985. *Body of power, spirit of resistance: the culture and history of a South African people.* Chicago: University of Chicago Press.

Comaroff, Jean, and John L. Comaroff. 1991. *Of revelation and revolution: Christianity, colonialism and consciousness in South Africa.* Vol. 1. Chicago: University of Chicago Press.

Comaroff, John L., and Jean Comaroff. 1997. *Of revelation and revolution: the dialectics of modernity on a South African frontier.* Vol. 2. Chicago: University of Chicago Press.

Darwin, Charles. 1963 [1859]. *The origin of species: by means of natural selection of the preservation of favoured races in the struggle for life.* New York: Washington Square Press.

Draper, Jonathan A. 1996. "Was there noone left to give glory to God except this foreigner?": breaking the boundaries in Luke 17: 11–19. In *Archbishop Tutu: prophetic witness in South Africa,* edited by L. Hulley, L. Kretzschmar, and L. L. Pato. Cape Town: Human and Rousseau.

Dube, Musa W. 1996. Reading for decolonization (John 4: 1–42). *Semeia* 75: 37–59.

———. 1997. Toward a post-colonial feminist interpretation of the Bible. *Semeia* 78: 11–26.

———. 1999. Consuming a colonial time bomb: translating *badimo* into "demons" in the Setswana Bible (Matthew 8: 28–34; 15: 2; 10: 8). *Journal for the Study of the New Testament* 73:33–59.

Felder, Cain Hope, ed. 1991. *Stony the road we trod: African American biblical interpretation.* Minneapolis: Fortress.

Fiorenza, Elizabeth Schussler. 1981. Towards a feminist biblical hermeneutics: biblical interpretation and liberation theology. In *The challenge of liberation theology: a First World response,* edited by B. Mahan and L. D. Richesin. Maryknoll, NY: Orbis Books.

Foucault, Michel. 1980. *Power/knowledge: selected writings and other interviews 1972–1977.* Edited by C. Gordon. New York: Pantheon.

Fowl, Stephen E. 1990. The ethics of interpretation; or, what's left over after the elimination of meaning. In *The Bible in three dimensions: essays in celebration of the fortieth anniversary of the Department of Biblical Studies, University of Sheffield,* edited by D. J. A. Clines, S. E. Fowl, and S. E. Porter. Sheffield: JSOT Press.

Fowl, Stephen. 1995. Texts don't have ideologies. *Biblical Interpretation* 3: 15–34.

Frostin, Per. 1988. *Liberation theology in Tanzania and South Africa: a First World interpretation.* Lund: Lund University Press.

Gottwald, Norman K. 1979. *The tribes of Yahweh: a sociology of the religion of liberated Israel, 1250–1050 B.C.* Maryknoll, New York: Orbis.

Kritzinger, J.N.J. 1988. *Black Theology: challenge to mission,* University of South Africa, Pretoria.

Kuhn, Thomas S. 1970. *The structure of scientific revolutions.* Second Edition. Chicago: University of Chicago Press.

Landau, Paul Stuart. 1995. *The realm of the Word: language, gender, and Christianity in a Southern African kingdom.* Portsmouth: Heinemann.

Landau, Paul. 1999. "Religion" and Christian conversion in African history: a new model. *Journal of Religious History* 23 (1): 8–30.

Maimela, Simon. 1991. Black Theology and the quest for a God of liberation. In *Theology at the end of modernity: essays in honor of Gordon D. Kaufman,* edited by S. G. Devaney. Philadelphia: Trinity Press.

Maluleke, Tinyiko S. 1996. Black and African theologies in the New World Order: a time to drink from our own wells. *Journal of Theology for Southern Africa* 96:3–19.

———. 1997. Half a century of African Christian theologies: elements of the emerging agenda for the twenty-first century. *Journal of Theology for Southern Africa* 99: 4–23.

———. 1998. African Traditional Religions in Christian mission and Christian scholarship: reopening a debate that never started. *Religion and Theology* 5: 121–137.

———. 1998. Black theology as public discourse. In *Constructing a language of religion in public life: Multi-Event 1999 Academic Workshop papers,* edited by J. R. Cochrane. Cape Town: University of Cape Town.

Masenya, Madipoane. 1997. Proverbs 31: 10–31 in a South African context: a reading for the liberation of African (Northern Sotho) women. *Semeia* 78:55–68.

Mbiti, John S. 1977. The biblical basis for present trends in African theology. In *African theology en route: papers from the Pan-African conference of Third World theologians, Accra, December 1977,* edited by K. Appiah-Kubi and S. Torres. Maryknoll, NY: Orbis.

Mbuwayesango, Dora Rudo. 1997. Childlessness and women-to-women relationships in Genesis and in African patriarchal society: Sarah and Hagar from a Zimbabwean woman's perspective (Genesis 16: 1–16; 21: 8–21). *Semeia* 78: 27–36.

Moffat, Robert. 1842 (Reprinted 1969). *Missionary labours and scenes in Southern Africa.* London (Reprint, New York): John Snow (Reprint, Johnson Reprint Corporation).

Moffat, Robert, and Mary Moffat. 1951. *Apprenticeship at Kuruman: being the journals and letters of Robert and Mary Moffat, 1820–1828.* London: Chatto & Windus.

Mofokeng, T. 1988. Black Christians, the Bible and liberation. *Journal of Black Theology* 2: 34–42.

Mosala, Itumeleng J. 1986. Ethics of the economic principles: church and secular investments. In *Hammering swords into ploughshares: essays in honour of Archbishop Mpilo Desmond Tutu,* edited by B. Tlhagale and I. J. Mosala. Johannesburg: Skotaville.

————. 1986. The relevance of African Traditional Religions and their challenge to Black Theology. In *The unquestionable right to be free: essays in Black Theology*, edited by I. J. Mosala and B. Tlhagale. Johannesburg: Skotaville.

————. 1986. The use of the Bible in Black Theology. In *The unquestionable right to be free: essays in black theology*, edited by I. J. Mosala and B. Tlhagale. Johannesburg: Skotaville.

————. 1987. Biblical hermeneutics and black theology in South Africa. PhD, University of Cape Town, Cape Town.

————. 1989. *Biblical hermeneutics and black theology in South Africa*. Grand Rapids: Eerdmans.

————. 1989. Black theology: Unpublished paper.

Oduyoye, Mercy Amba. 1995. *Daughters of Anowa: African women and patriarchy*. Maryknoll, NY: Orbis.

Setiloane, Gabriel. 1977. Where are we in African Theology? In *African Theology en route: papers from the Pan-African Conference of Third World Theologians, Accra, December 17–23, 1977*, edited by K. Appiah-Kubi and S. Torres. Maryknoll, NY: Orbis.

Sibeko, Malika, and Beverley G. Haddad. 1997. Reading the Bible "with" women in poor and marginalized communities in South Africa (Mark 5:21–6:1). *Semeia* 78:83–92.

Tracy, David. 1981. Introduction. In *The challenge of liberation theology: a First World response*, edited by B. Mahan and L. D. Richesin. Maryknoll, NY: Orbis.

Tutu, Desmond Mpilo. 1983. *Hope and suffering: sermons and speeches*. Johannesburg: Skotaville.

West, Gerald O. 1995. *Biblical hermeneutics of liberation: modes of reading the Bible in the South African context*. Second Edition. Maryknoll, NY, and Pietermaritzburg: Orbis Books and Cluster Publications.

————. 1997. Finding a place among the posts for post-colonial criticism in biblical studies in South Africa. *Old Testament Essays* 10: 322–342.

————. 1999. *The academy of the poor: towards a dialogical reading of the Bible*. Sheffield: Sheffield Academic Press.

————. 2000. Gauging the grain in a more nuanced and literary manner: a cautionary tale concerning the contribution of the social sciences to biblical interpretation. In *Rethinking context, rereading texts: contributions from the social sciences to biblical interpretation*, edited by D. M. Carroll and R. Sheffield: Sheffield Academic Press.

————. 2000. White men, Bibles, and land: ingredients in biblical interpretation in South African black theology. *Scriptura* 73: 141–152.

Wimbush, Vincent L. 1991. The Bible and African Americans: an outline of an interpretative history. In *Stony the road we trod: African American biblical interpretation*, edited by C. H. Felder. Minneapolis: Fortress.

CHAPTER 3

Rereading the Bible:
Biblical Hermeneutics and Social Justice

Musa W. Dube

Introduction: Reading the World and the Text

In 1997, when I returned from my graduate studies, I had just completed my dissertation in which I struggled to reread the Bible as a postcolonial subject. In this work I revisited the Exodus text, and the mission passages of Matthew 15:21–28 and John 4:1–42, asking what made the Biblical readers of colonial times work hand in hand with other colonial agents of their time (Dube 2000a). I reexamined these texts for an ideology that may have appealed to the colonial readers and struggled with issues of re-presenting the mission in such a way that it does not become cultural imperialism. To guide a reader to read for decolonization and liberation, I suggested the following hermeneutical questions:

1. Does this text have a clear stance against the political, cultural, and economic imperialism of its time? How are readers reading the test as colonizers, the colonized, or collaborators?
2. Does this text encourage travel to distant inhabited lands? If so, how does it justify itself? Who travels and shy? Which side of the text am I journeying on as a reader? (see also Dube 1996)
3. How does this text find difference: is there dialogue and mutual interdependence between the involved parties or condemnation of all that is foreign? (see also Dube 1996)
4. Does this text use gender representations to construct relationships of subordination and domination? If so, which side am I reading from: the colonizer, the colonized, or the collaborator? If I read as a decolonizing reader, does this translate into a depatriarchalizing act or vice versa. (see also Dube 2000b)
5. How does imperialism affect men and women? (see also Dube 1997b)

6. How can I reread this text to grasp the interdependence between nations, gender, races, and other social categories of our world as a liberating force? (see also Dube 1996:54–57)

This struggle to reread as a postcolonial subject, who is also a black African woman, on my part was/is a search for social justice. It was and is a resistance to the injustice of colonial Christian gospel and the international relations that have and still characterize our world.

African Rereadings

In my attempt to reread as a postcolonial subject I am not a pioneer. My voice is one among many who have been and are still struggling to hear or read the Biblical text in such a way that it does not endorse or legitimate international evils and exploitation of any other form. For example, African theologians have been involved in a hermeneutics of inculturation—one which went through many stages, and is still evolving (Martey 1992). Inculturation is a search for the mating point between the Biblical text/religions and African cultures. This rereading of the Biblical text followed or even started during colonial times and continues to this day as a form of resistance and search for justice (Maluleke 1997c: 4–23). From its beginning it resisted the colonial readings/interpretations of the Bible that began by dismissing all aspects of African culture as pagan, exotic, evil, savage, ungodly, or childish.

The inculturation Biblical readers adopted different levels of response, but they all reread their Bible in the light of their own culture—insisting there is nothing savage or ungodly in their African culture. Inculturation approach compared the two cultures and argued that they find a great deal of similarities between their own cultures and the Bible; some argued that, in fact, their cultures are the base through which the Biblical gospel must be transmitted to the African people. Others held (in what has now became a classic statement) that Christianity only found a fertile ground in the African continent because African people are "notoriously religious." Some studied the linguistic forms of Hebrew language and compared it with some African languages. Many more compared Jesus with the various holy figures of African cultures.

Inculturation approaches sought to read the Biblical text with and through the African cultures and contexts. It departed from the "mainstream Biblical studies" that sought to read Biblical texts through the ancient context of the Middle East. Inculturation hermeneutical approach(es) was an act of resistance, seeking decolonization and liberation. It was sparked by a former reading; a colonial one that rendered all cultures invalid before the Biblical ones. The inculturation readers were therefore seeking for social justice by insisting on their right to be Africans and Christians. They were seeking for the social justice that recognizes differences and strengths in different cultures, by making hermeneutical attempts to cultivate a new sacred space—a hermeneutical space where both African religions and cultures can kiss and mate with Biblical faith rather than dwell in the apartheid territory of separate spaces. Inculturation has received many criticisms and, like any hermeneutical approach, it has its own weaknesses. Its greatest weakness is its search through love for a commonality between Biblical and African faith, while searching for social justice through hate. This search for social justice is seen as something that must constantly pursue a just world, one where different cultures exchange their cultural contributions rather than suppress their cultural differences—a suppression that is closely tied into economic and political oppression.

Asian Rereadings

That building cultural diversity is a search for social justice and a cause for rereading the Bible is also evident amongst Asian Biblical scholars and theologians (Kwok 1995 & Sugirtharajah 1993). Resisting the presentation of Biblical religion among the multiple-faith context as if Christian faith is the only faith, Asians are rereading the Biblical text to find and to build a context that nurtures multiple religions rather than attempts to suppress differences. Thus in his effort to reread the Bible for diversity, Wesley Ariarajah begins by asking the question: "Is the Bible tolerant of plurality, especially religious plurality?" (1999:5). Ariarajah's rereading of the Bible indicates that the Bible is not as exclusive as interpreters sometimes make it out to be. He argues that when we read the Bible from a "pluralistic perspective" we will realize that "the Bible sets the story of the people of Israel and of the church in the context of God's love and concern for the whole creation. The Bible begins with creation (Genesis 1) and ends with new creation, a new heaven and earth"(7).

Latin American Rereadings

In Latin America the urge to reread was prompted by the encounter with economic injustice, which disfigures all other aspects of people's lives. Latin Americans began to reread the Bible in search for a just world, which identifies economic exploitation and suppressors of the other as inconsistent with God's will for God's people (Santa Ana 1979; Torres & Eagleton 1984; Sobrino 1985). Their approach to the Biblical texts notably departed from the mainstream Biblical interpretation, by refusing to regard the ancient context of the Biblical text as the normative interpretative background. Latin Americans insisted on reading the Bible from their own context; holding that their own context is closer to the context of Jesus' time, hence gives them a better understanding of the text. The rereading of Latin Americans marked the beginning of what became largely known as liberation theology (Gutierrez, 1974). The approach openly acknowledged its advocacy and search for justice. By so doing, it revealed that there is no neutral reading; we are either reading for or against the powers of oppression. Its option for the poor showed that the neutral and objective Biblical approach is a high-class, white male Biblical reading/s, which was fully engaged in authorizing structures of oppression and exploitation in the world (Segovia 1995:1–32).

Black Rereadings

Other groups that were impelled by a search for social justice to reread the Bible included the black people of the U.S. (Felder 1991; Wimbush 2000). Living with a history of slavery and continued racism, they developed a hermeneutical approach that foregrounded freedom as its core starting point. God of the Bible was seen as the God who sets slaves free (Massey 1994:154–160). The Biblical text was read to prophetically denounce the society that still embraced racial discrimination. This rereading against a history of slavery and racism led to the emphasis on reading for liberation. Rereading for their full dignity, some readers' approach was to select and skip the text that endorses their oppression (Weems 60–65). Black South Africans, confronted by the same evil, also developed a black hermeneutical approach that sought to understand the basis of apartheid and to articulate a rereading that affirmed people of different colors. Black theology used Marxist theories to understand the economic and class issues that necessitate apartheid (Mosala 1989).

Women Rereadings

But one cannot talk of rereading and searching for social justice without mentioning feminist Biblical readers (Newsom & Ringe 1992; Schussler Fiorenza 1983 & 1999; Osiek 1994:181–187). The scholarship and the church were for centuries an exclusively male arena. Go rena barena. Only lords ruled! The injustice of this exclusion and its consequences became evident. That is, male Biblical interpretations did not advocate gender justice in the church, academy, and society at large. Instead, male readers read for their own interests—they endorsed the disempowerment of women advocated by the text and the society. This denial of gender justice in the society sparked one of the earliest recorded feminist rereadings, that of Elisabeth Cady Stanton 1895. The story of Stanton, the woman who brought together a group of women to write what became called *The Woman's Bible* in 1895, is a story of the encounter with injustice in the society, in Biblical interpretation, and a quest for social justice. It was her encounter with injustice that led to a rereading. She sought to reread the Biblical texts in such a way that they would empower women to become recognized members of the society with human rights—the right to vote and to go to school, etc.

Stanton's rereading for gender justice was suppressed by forces of oppression that identified her work as outrageous and blasphemous—leading many women supporters to distance themselves from her. The legacy of Stanton received its full revival in the sixties, about forty years ago, when women entered the theological studies in big numbers. Instead of reading the Bible as neutral subjects, they insisted on reading the Bible as women and for women. This rereading entailed many angles such as examining the text itself for an oppressive gender ideology, highlighting the positive portrait of women agents in the text, rereading the negative women characters for feminist uses, exposing misogist texts and interpreters, and rereading the text for the full dignity of women and men. As Stanton's project of rereading attests, current feminist rereadings, in their various methods of reading, are a call and search for social justice against the oppression authorized by the text, the readers alike and the society. Feminist reinterpretations challenge us to move away from endorsing the oppression of women in the text and in the society. Feminist rereadings invite us to become architects of gender justice in our work and world.

Let me return to where I started: that is, the point when I first returned from my graduate school three years ago. I had spent my five years agonizing about how to reread the Bible in such a way that it does not continue to endorse the colonizing of any nation or people. My rereading was, and continues to be, a search for a space of international and national interaction, which would be liberating to all the parties involved, that is different genders, races, ethnic groups, nations, cultures, and the like. My hermeneutical practice revolves around a dream world of liberating interdependence between our diversities.

Rereading for Social Justice in the Global Village

As any returning student, I had a cultural shock, or should I say hermeneutical shock, in my intellectual journey. I was immediately struck by the change in national and international politics. The buzz word was globalization. It was everywhere: in the national budget speech, in the parliament, and financial policymakers were grappling with liberizing our policies, to create a conducive national space for the age of globalization. Our president was flying from one continent to another, trying to whore foreign investors to come and invest in our country, in our land. The argument held and still holds that "we need foreign investors to come and create jobs for us in Botswana." What?

I felt like I was a million years old. I could not believe how history had slipped by so fast! Why did it seem like yesterday when we were singing songs of resistance and liberation? It was only yesterday when we chanted, "*Aluta Continua, Phambere ne handa . . . Amandla nga wethu?*" Why does it seem just like yesterday when we sang the songs of liberation and now we are talking of a new phenomenon: globalization? Now our presidents are going back to our former colonizer and asking them to come back. Something is wrong somewhere.

While I was still digesting this cultural shock, I met a colleague of mine, Barolong Seboni, who is a writer. We had been together in the WABO, Writers Association of Botswana, during the years of the struggle for independence. We wrote poetry of resistance. I remember one of my poems entitled "Africa oh Africa, Tell me Africa, what happened to you, speak Africa . . ." (Dube 1989). One time one of our government ministers listened to our writer's corner radio program. He was reportedly struck by this warring poetry—full of screams, pleas, and songs of resistance. He reportedly complained that the writers hardly wrote any romantic poems about flowers and the ever blue skies of Botswana. We were in the wars for liberation and war hardly smells or sees flowers in the war zones. And so when I met Barolong Seboni, this fellow writer in the struggle for liberation and decolonization, and I said to him, "Barry what's this talk about relaxing policies to whore foreign investors here; what is this all about our President going away to beg and invite them back here? This globalization thing, how is it different from the colonialism that we have been fighting against." "Man," he said to me, shrugging his shoulders as one who has resigned himself to the fate of the situation, "I do not know. But yes it sounds like we are now voluntarily seeking and asking to be colonized."

Indeed, when it comes to globalization, many of us are still on the "I do not know" plane. But certainly globalization is propounded from some centers, sold to many worlds in the margins, who must respond and prepare the ground for it to nest. For example, the talk about globalization was where I had been studying, but the difference was that this was the center, where globalization is being propounded and sold to others, unlike in most Two-Thirds World, where most people must adjust, not by choice, but by international pressure, to welcome globalization wherever and whenever it wants to arrive.

Nonetheless, the international maps of power and powerlessness had changed! Speaking of the colonizer, the colonized and pride in independence seemed outdated. The new map of the world was being drawn not by the sprit of independence, but by the spirit of globalization, regionalization, and liberation of financial policies. Globalization and not independence is now being proclaimed as our redeemer and our savior. One writer, evaluating its brilliant benefits, noted in an intriguing phrase, "even Africa will gain from globalization over the next 15 years" (Oberhansli 1999:107). That is, globalization is so good that even the African continent can/will benefit! As a Biblical reader who reads for social justice, I was compelled to reread the Biblical text in the light of this new world map called the global village. For while the praise singers of globalization raise a song that tells us that even Africa can/will benefit, those who are on the receiving end point to a system that is competitive, profit driven, and unethical (Lind 1995:27–43). While the praise singers of globalization sing its blessings, those on the receiving end are pointing to its curses: increased marginalization of the powerless and loss of control over one's destiny. They point out that power is increasingly concentrated in few hands; that multinational companies control everything and impose their interest everywhere; they point to "increasing" problems of poverty, unemployment, social exclusion, and other forms of marginalization (Petrou 1999:125). The global village, they tell us its not what we are led to believe, a haven of justice where all shall equally reap their fields and those of others.

This led me to another rereading. I wrote a paper entitled "Praying the Lord's Prayer in the Global Era" (Dube 1997a: 439–450). My struggle here was to examine what made the past global relations oppressive to others. I wanted to know if the text gives us any models for a better global village. My question was: How can we imagine a global village that is a true village, a place that is home for all; a place where everyone knows everyone else and cares about their well-being; a place where we are all the children of the same parent and grandparent. I wondered how we can pray saying our Father and Mother who is in our village! Let your village Spirit come and reign forever. My struggle here was: How could the Lord's prayer help us imagine terms of trade that build a world, or should I say a "global village," that embraces social justice for all its members and trading partners? In short, globalization is one of those phenomenon that I still have to fully understand, but I am increasingly aware that I should revisit the text in its light, or should I say, "its heart of darkness," and try to strike a spark of light.

Rereading in the Social Context of HIV/AIDS

Not only was I hit by the cultural shock of globalize or die, reigning in the air upon my return home, I was also immediately under the shadow of death: Botswana was and still tops the world statistics of HIV/AIDS infection. We, the young and productive people, are dying or dead. If I do not see a friend for a long time, I cannot rule out two things: that this friend is sick and closed up somewhere or downright dead. One goes to burials every weekend, so often that worship no longer takes place in church, but by the graveyard. In spite of all this, the stigma for the infected and the sick in the society remains high. They are feared, because they carry an incurable, communicable disease. It was and is in this social context, where people are suffering and dying lonely and helpless, where I started/am teaching the synoptic gospels. In these texts, Jesus is a maverick healer. He heals every type of disease, and touches even the contagious lepers, who are feared and discriminated against by the whole society for their incurable and contagious diseases.

As I went about with business as usual, teaching the SG from a feminist, narrative, historical, or redactional criticism and the like, there came a point that this academic approach began to become artificial and strange even on my tongue. I began to ask myself: Why am I talking about the historical context of Jesus, redactional criticism, narrative, and all this stuff and skirting the main issue in this context and the gospels; namely, sickness and healing? I began to ask myself a question, which every student also had in mind; namely, If Jesus can heal this much, why can't Jesus heal us of HIV/AIDS in our nation and the world? With the HIV/AIDS death scare, stigma, suffering, and fear of dying or contacting a disease, how do you read the Synoptic gospels? The social setting of illness, fear, and discrimination against the sick and orphans demanded a rereading.

My position of inhabiting the HIV/AIDS front zones has impelled me to undertake a different rereading of the miracles of Jesus. I am impelled to ask such questions as: What is the meaning of the miracles of healing in the Synoptic Gospels? Are they still relevant? Can Jesus' healing and touching of lepers speak to our fear and secure justice for the sick and discriminated? How does one propound a theology of healing where there is no healing? In this rereading of the healing miracles of Jesus, I have no point of reference, save the society which is itself confronted by this situation. A theology of healing where there is no healing; a theology of living with the contagiously sick in the society must rise—and it can only rise when I read from, with, and for the affected and the infected people of my nation (Dube 2001). One of the issues that I will be focusing on this academic year, which is related to HIV/AIDS, is the position of widows and orphans, who are growing in number.

The Nomadic Reader

In these broad strokes of rereading the Bible and social justice, a few things have emerged. Rereading for social justice seems to rise against a history of oppressive

1. dominant structures
2. context
3. biblical readers and readings

It also rises out of
1. changing social circumstances
2. The response of a socially engaged scholar to the social changes and circumstances

Clearly rereading the Bible for social justice demands that one should read both the text and the society. Since society is dynamic, a reader for social justice never arrives. One cannot say, I am a narrative critic, a feminist reader, a postcolonial reader, period. Rather, one is constantly forced to delve into completely new reading strategies in search for social justice. One who reads the text and the society will just have to reread as new challenges arise. Such a scholar is better seen as a nomadic reader, who will have to use and develop different methods and new theories of reading. Social justice readers also challenge those readers who are not concerned with reading for liberation to reexamine their reading and how it authorizes the oppression of the other. They challenge many scholarly readers whose reading strategies are informed and invigorated by fellow scholars rather than the society in general.

Conclusion: Heal the World

To conclude, my brief narration seems to suggest that rereading for social justice is the business of the oppressed groups such as the colonized, Two–Thirds World masses, women, the sick, blacks, and other marginalized groups. Indeed, many times when I present my papers on postcolonialism I have encountered an audience that says to me, "That's your social location and your experience. It's not my experience." What this usually means is that "I cannot speak with you on this subject: it's your business." This always shocks me, not only because colonialism/imperialism affected the whole world, First and Two Thirds World Readers, but also because to reread the Bible in the light of social justice is to invite dialogue and self-examination among different groups. It is an act of saying, "Let's reason together. Let's imagine a better world that is fair to all of us." If I could use the words of Michael Jackson's song, "Heal the world. Make it a better place for you and me and the entire universe. There are people dying, if you will remember." To reread the Bible for social justice is, therefore, a quest for coexistence that is not built on exploiting the other. It is a search for ways of building a just society and world. This must involve all of us. If we realize that we are not just reading the text, but rereading it in the light of social justice, then no audience should say, "That's your social location and your experience. Its not my experience," for as long as we are in the world we are interconnected.

Yet with a brief look at the groups that I have tabulated above and those who are largely known to read for social justice, it is clear that it is largely the marginalized groups who are actively involved in the search for a just world. In a way, it is explainable that it is the most oppressed groups who have pioneered the struggle for social justice rather than those whose worlds are slightly comfortable—for one who has trampled on a hot charcoal cannot help but scream and jump out of his/her pain and need for help. Nonetheless, I believe that the 20th Century has distinguished itself in the quest for social justice. It is in the 20th Century that we have seen the nations pass the Human Rights

Charter; The Children's Charter, The CEDAW, Environmental Awareness, etc. All these legal instruments that we have set for ourselves as policy guidance should go a long way to inform every Biblical scholar to become a seeker and builder of social justice. As we enter the age of globalization, I would propose that we should reread the Bible in the light of United Nations charters to build a better village globe.

Musa W. Dube
University of Botswana.
P/Bag 0022, Gaborone, Botswana

SELECTED BIBLIOGRAPHY

Ariarajah, Wesley. S., "Reading the Bible in Pluralistic Context." The Ecumenical Review 51/1 (1999) 5–10

Boff, L. *Ecclesiogenesis: The Base Communities Reinvent the Church*. Maryknoll: Orbis Books, 1986.

Dube, M. W. Africa, p. 30, In *Kutlwano Magazine*. Gaborone: Botswana Government Printers, 1989.

————. Reading for Decolonization (John 4:1–42), 37–59 Semeia 75. Atlanta: Scholars Press, 1996.

————. "Praying the Lord's Prayer in a Global Economic Era," *The Ecumenical Review* 49/4 (1997a) 439–456

————. "Towards Postcolonial Feminist Interpretation of the Bible," 11–26 Semeia 78. Atlanta: Scholars Press, 1997b.

————. "Storytelling Feminist Interpretation of Mark 5:24–43,"11–17. In *The Ecumenical Review* 51/1 (1999) 11–17.

————. *Postcolonial Feminist Interpretation of the Bible*. St Louis: Chalice Press, 2000a.

————. "Rahab Says Hello to Judith: Postcolonial Feminist Hermeneutics of Liberation," A paper presented in Feminist Biblical Interpretation and the Hermeneutics of Liberation Ascona, Switzerland 1–7 July 2000b.

————., "Healing Where There Is No Healing: Reading the Miracles of Healing in a HIV/AIDS Context." (Forthcoming in Gary Phillips and Nicole Wilkinson, eds., *Essays in Honour of Daniel Patte*, Trinity, Winter 2001)

Fall, Yassine ed., *Africa: Gender, Globalisation and Resistance*. New York: AAWord, 1999.

Felder, Cain Hope, *Stony the Road We Trod: African American Biblical Interpretation*. Minneapolis: Fortress Press, 1991.

Gutierrez, G, *A Theology of Liberation*. London: SCM Press, 1974.

Kwok, Pui Lan, *Discovering Jesus in the Non-Biblical World*. Maryknoll: Orbis, 1995.

Lind, Christopher, *Something Is Wrong Somewhere: Globalization, Community and the Moral Economy of the Farm Crisis*. Halifax: Fernwood, 1995.

Maluleke, T.S. "A Letter to Job From Africa, *Challenge Magazine* No 43. (1997a) 14–15.

————. What Africans Are Doing to Jesus: Will He Ever Be the Same Again? 187–205. In *Images of Jesus*. Pretoria: University of African Identity, 1997b.

————."Half a Century of African Theologies," in *Journal of Theology for Southern Africa* 99 (1997c) 4–23.

Massey, E. J., "Reading the Bible As African Americans," 154–160. In *The New Interpreters Bible* Vol 1. Nashville: Abingdon Press, 1994

Mosala, I., *Biblical Hermeneutics and Hermeneutics and Black Theology In South Africa*. Grand Rapids: Eerdmans, 1989.

Newsom, C. A, and Sharon H. Ringe, eds., *The Women's Bible Commentary*. London SPCK, 1992.

Oberhansli, Herbert, "Globalisation and Sustainable Prosperity," 107–110. In *Santa Ana, Julio, Sustainability and Globalisation*. Geneva: WCC, 1998.

Okure, Teresa, ed. *To Cast Fire Upon the Earth: Bible and Mission Collaborating in Today's Multicultural Global Context*. Natal: Cluster, 2000.

Osiek, C. "Reading the Bible as Women," 181–187. In *The New Interpreter's Bible* Vol. 1. Nashville: Abingdon Press, 1994.

Petrou, Joannes, "Sustainability and Globalization: Demystifying the Single Thought and Single Structure," 123–129. Julio de Santa Ana, ed. *Sustainability and Globalisation*. Geneva: WCC, 1998.

Santa Ana, Julio. *Good News to the Poor: The Challenge of the Poor in History of the Church*. Maryknoll: Orbis Books, 1979.

Schussler Fiorenza, E. *In Memory of Her: A Feminist Theological Reconstruction of Christian Origins*. New York: Crossroad, 1993.

————. *Rhetoric and Ethic: Politics of Biblical Studies*. Minneapolis: Fortress Press, 1999.

Segovia, F. F., "And They Began to Speak in Different Tongues: Competing Modes of Interpretation in Contemporary Biblical Criticism," 1–32. In F. F. Segovia and Mary Ann Tolbert, eds., *Reading from This Place*, Vol. 1: *Social Location and Biblical Interpretation in the United States*. Minneapolis: Fortress Press, 1995.

————. eds. *Reading From this Place*, Vol 2: *Social Location and Biblical Interpretation in the Global Perspective*. Minneapolis: Fortress Press, 1995.

Sobrino, J. *The True Church and the Church of the Poor*. London: SCM Press, 1985.

Sugirtharajah, R.S. ed., *Voices from the Margin: Interpreting the Bible in The Third World* (2nd ed). London: SPCK, 1995,

————. ed., *Asian Faces of Jesus*. Maryknoll: Orbis, 1993.

————. ed., *The Postcolonial Bible*. Sheffield: Sheffield Academic Press, 1998.

Torres, S. and J. Eagleson, eds. *The Challenge from Basic Christian Communities: Papers From International Ecumenical Congress of Theology*. Maryknoll: Orbis Press, 1980.

Weems, Renita, "Reading Her Way Through the Struggle: African American and the Bible," 57–77. In Cain Hope Felder, ed. *Stony the Road We Trod*. Minneapolis: Fortess Press, 1991.

Wimbush, Vincent L, ed. *African Americans and the Bible: Sacred Text and Social Texture*. New York: Continuum, 2000.

CHAPTER 4

African Approaches to the Trinity

Mika Vähäkangas

Introduction

C hristology is at the center of African theology today. The majority of writings on African theology that could be classified as doctrinal theology deal with Christology. Perhaps the topic which has been written about the most after Christology is -ecclesiology. The Holy Trinity has not gained much attention among African academic theologians. Even in those cases when it has been discussed, it has sometimes been briefly mentioned almost as if it were a necessary evil or in other cases the Trinitarian dogma, or at least its traditional form, has been rejected.[1] This is done on the grounds that the vocabulary of the doctrine of the Trinity is based on hellenistic metaphysical thinking and that the entire idea of three persons in one God is totally incomprehensible according to African patterns of thought. On the other side there are those African theologians who have been eager to find *vestigia trinitatis* in African traditional cultures, wishing to prove that the doctrine of the Trinity is compatible with traditional African ways of thinking. However, the vast majority of African theologians seem to prefer writing on Christology if they focus on doctrinal matters at all.

The Need for African Theological Reflection on the Trinity

While it is advisable that Christology would serve as the focus of theological enterprise, one must realize that any complete work on Christology inevitably serves as a prolegomena for reflection on the Trinity. This is so even in the case in which the divinity of Jesus of Nazareth is denied, because such a contention logically leads to the denial of the doctrine of the Trinity. This is all the more the case when Christ's divine character is not denied, which is the actual case in practically all African writings on Christology. If Christ is divine as well as human, it is natural that the theological inquiry has to proceed to the doctrine of the Trinity. Attempts to build genuine African

69

Christologies are left half finished if one does not proceed to the treatment of the Trinity. It is not possible to maintain that there would be a genuine African Christology if the doctrine of the Trinity is inherited from the West without original African reflection. African Christology would then be dependent on Western trinitology, which endangers the originality of the Christology and runs the risk of becoming only a Western Christology decorated with African ideas. Thus, the emergence of genuine African reflection on the doctrine of the Trinity is not only needed but is a logical outcome of African Christologies.[2]

There is also a pressing practical need for fresh African approaches to the Trinity. This is partly manifested by the above-mentioned rejection of this doctrine by academic theologians and by some African Independent Churches.[3] If the problem with the Trinitarians' dogma (at least with the academic theologians) is that the teaching is expressed within a foreign philosophical frame of reference, does it follow that the reality one strives to convey by using foreign philosophy has to be rejected as well? Could it not rather be understood as a challenge to an independent theological reflection on the Trinity? Furthermore, that the idea of a triune God is perhaps difficult for Africans is nothing new since this has been the case in every culture.[4] The idea of a triune God was not easy for the Greeks either even though the vocabulary to express this teaching was borrowed from their cultural sphere.[5] Thus, the Africans' difficulties in understanding the doctrine of the Trinity need not necessarily be understood as a deficiency on either side, that of the Africans or the doctrine, but can be seen as a consequence of God's being the ultimate Mystery.

Western patterns of understanding the Trinity, however ingenious they might be, are not always felt to be adequate in Africa. Furthermore, even the biblical language and testimony to the Trinity may be seen as a difficulty. This feeling of inadequacy. is another path toward an indigenous African reflection on the Trinity. Thus the Zulu independent church leader Isaiah Shembe found the teaching of the trinitarian persons as the Father, the Son, and the Holy Spirit so disturbing that he decided to use different expressions for the Persons. This was so because for the Zulu a father is always superior to his son. Shembe decided thus to abandon the orthodox vocabulary in order to save the orthodox doctrine. To avoid the monarchianist heresy, Shembe calls the persons of the Trinity as God the Creator, God the Redeemer, and God the Consoler.[6] This move is naturally not without its problems, like that of the danger of separating the work of the Trinity *ad extra* according to the persons of the Trinity, yet it shows that there is a felt need for fresh African approaches to the Trinity. The Trinity is a problem for African Christians, and will remain such, if the topic remains ignored by African theologians.

The majority of African reflections on the Trinity are social analogies to the family or familial relations, but the possibility of building trinitology on the basis of an entire worldview has also been realized, albeit to a lesser extent.

The Trinity and the African Family

In addition to the general idea of communality,[7] the concept of family is a natural point of departure for African trinitarian speculation. For Africans, family always traditionally means the extended family, or clan. Most often when family had been discussed in African theology, the doctrinal topic corrected with it had been the Church.[8] When African ecclesiology began to proceed further, the Holy Trinity was discussed more than before in this connection. This is perhaps due to the fact that African theology has tended to be more praxis oriented than theory oriented, just as the African traditional religions have been. The Church is a tangible reality directly affecting Christians' lives, but the Trinity enters the picture only when one needs a more profound view of the Church as a family.[9] It is also noteworthy that the major impetus for elaborating the connection between the image of the Church as family and the Trinity comes from the Roman Catholic hierarchy.[10]

The Bishops' Special Synod for Africa emphasizes that the Trinity is the basis and the model for the unity of the Church as well as the whole human community. The bishops remain in the framework of the traditional African understanding of the extended family and do not concentrate on the number of persons but rather on the Holy Spirit as the bond of unity.[11] However, the African concepts of family are not lifted up as the standard criterion of a proper understanding of the Trinity. Rather, the trinitarian model is left free both to influence African models of family and also to be interpreted through them. The primary view, however, is that the African family should reflect the trinitarian communion.[12]

Professor John O. Egbulefu's interpretation of the bishops' suggestion about the connection between family and the trinitarian community represents a model in which the number three gains a more special importance and the scope is shifted from the relations in an extended family to those of the nuclear family, i.e., family as understood in the West. Egbulefu draws a social analogy of the Trinity to family "since God contains all good things . . . and every good thing . . . bears the imprint of the divine inner life."[13] This means that in family there are some marks of circumincession and inner trinitarian communion as well as of God's "bilateral attention," i.e., His "internal divine dialogue" and "external contact and communication with the whole universe."[14] Egbulefu does not go into details in building this analogy and thus his observations mostly remain as hints as to how he would like to see the family concept to be used in discussing the Trinity.

One of the most fascinating references toward an African family trinitology is, however, professor Charles Nyamiti's construction, which is a kind of a "side product" of his family ecclesiology. Perhaps just the fact that the Trinity is not treated as a separate subject but as a foundational doctrine of Christianity helps Nyamiti to interweave different dimensions of theology and culture in his concept of Trinity. Nyamiti starts from a three-dimensional understanding of African family communality: the family consists of the living members, the ancestors, and it is also integrated to the tripartite cosmos of spirits, human beings, and nature. The relationship of a family to God is considered especially important here. Thus, Nyamiti concludes, African family ecclesiology draws its inspiration from this three-dimensionality of the African understanding of family.[15] At the same time, the Church, because it was founded by the trinitarian God, reflects the communality of the Trinity.[16] Also the relationship between the Church and the triune God is closely linked to the world in which the Church has the task of "trinifying the world" and "enworlding the Trinity."[17] Thus the concepts of Trinity, the Church, family, and the tripartite cosmos are ingeniously interwoven in a consistent whole strongly based on the standard Roman Catholic teaching of the Church.

The Trinity and Ujamaa

Ujamaa is a special case of an African understanding of family. The Swahili word *jamaa* means (extended) family and belongs to the basic vocabulary of the language, whereas its derivative *ujamaa* (familyhood), belongs predominantly to political rhetoric. The father and champion of ujamaa politics was Julius Nyerere, the first head of state of independent Tanganyika/Tanzania and a devout Catholic. *Ujamaa,* in his reckoning, was supposed to be the third way between capitalism and socialism, viz., a communal way of life based on the traditional African understanding of communality within the framework of the extended family. The extended family was still more extended to cover the whole nation. Some theologians greeted the new politics with enthusiasm which they considered to be in line with genuinely Christian principles.[18] The outcome was *ujamaa* theology, which, in principle, was "not meant to be a theology of *ujamaa* politics . . . [y]et, certain overtones of *ujamaa* politics [were to] prevail."[19] It was inevitable that this type of theology had a close connection with politics, since the name was already taken from political language. Some *ujamaa* theological writings became thus little more than political euphoria in the guise of theology. However, in the cases in which the writer was competent and prudent enough to work within the framework of *ujamaa,* using the terminology and ideas as an impetus for genuine theologizing, the writings still have validity in spite of the fall of *ujamaa* in the political arena.

Catholic bishop Cristopher Mwoleka confessed: "I am dedicated to the ideal of Ujamaa because it invites all men . . . to imitate the life of the Trinity which is a life of sharing."[20] Mwoleka considers that *ujamaa* could serve Christians in understanding the mystery of the Trinity because in the Trinity the question is not of an "intellectual puzzle" but of a concrete life of sharing.[21] Mwoleka, true to his message, does not enter into theological subtleties nor into drawing analogies between the Trinity and *ujamaa.* The emphasis of his trinitarian-modeled communality shifted later to ecclesiology.[22]

Another Roman Catholic, Camillus Lyimo, does not contrast intellectual reflection on the Trinity with practical reflection of the Trinity but wants to draw an analogy between the *ujamaa* communality and the communion within the Trinity. Thus, from his point of view, the notion of communal life is not the only correct alternative for a true understanding of the mystery of the Trinity but rather a way which could provide insights for a better intellectual understanding of that mystery.[23] However, the topic of the Trinity has never been thoroughly examined in the light of *ujamaa;* the *ujamaa* theologians' concerns seemed to be of a more practical type.

Ujamaa, if understood less in connection to a particular political ideology, points toward deep structures of African traditional thinking,[24] as professor Charles Nyamiti seems to think. For Nyamiti the point in *ujamaa* is not material development or sharing as such but rather the deeper values or structures of African thinking that *ujamaa* (or at least some given aspect of it) represents. The family is at the center of

African life and is thus connected to the axis of the worldview. *Ujamaa,* understood as familyhood in the sense connected to the traditional family, serves as a key deeper into African thought. When Nyamiti combines the notion "union is strength"[25] *(umoja ni nguvu)* with the Trinity, he does not deal with a political slogan (as it was also used) but with a statement penetrating toward the core of Bantu thought. Instead of *ujamaa* politics, Nyamiti finds another approach to the African concept of family more fruitful: that of the ancestors.

Ancestral Relations in the Trinity

Professor Charles Nyamiti is the African theologian who has penetrated deepest both into the idea of ancestors as a theological point of departure and into the doctrine of the Trinity. Even though he has written on the Trinity from the point of view of African concepts of responsibility,[26] naming ceremony,[27] personality, and fecundity,[28] as well as from an African relational worldview,[29] ancestral relations remain the point of departure most elaborated by him.

Nyamiti defines ancestorship by listing five main elements: "kinship between the ancestor or ancestress and his or her earthly kin," "superhuman or sacred status of the ancestor," "mediation . . . between his earthly kin and the Supreme Being," "exemplarity of behaviour in community," and finally the idea that "the ancestor enjoys right to regular sacred communication with his earthly kin."[30] All of these qualities are more or less relational, and only sacred status could be understood predominantly as essential in the sense that it represents more what the ancestor is rather than the ancestor's manner of being-with-the-others. However, this status is linked to kinship in the sense that as a progenitor of living relatives, the ancestor is often considered as the *"source of life* of his terrestrial relatives"[31] Sacred status, in turn, is interpreted by Nyamiti to include "superhuman vital force obtained through special nearness to the "Supreme Being,"[32] which facilitates the ancestor's being a mediator. The first three elements are based on the relative positions in the Bantu hierarchy of vital force.[33] This hierarchy is a web of relations in which vital force is transmitted from on high downward and in which transmitting force down to one's own dependents also increases the force of the transmitter. Thus, the first three elements are essentially relational. Furthermore, it is noteworthy that for Nyamiti exemplarity of behavior is a communal measure because exemplarity is manifested in community. Finally, the right to regular communication emphasizes the fact that the relations sought after are not only potential or theoretical but real. Ancestorship is thus not basically an entity in itself to be observed in isolation but rather it is a relation, comparable to parenthood.

According to Nyamiti, all the ancestral characteristics save mediation can be found in God[34] even if only in an analogous sense, since "no human term or category can apply univocally to God and His creatures."[35] Therefore, for Nyamiti, it is legitimate to maintain that ancestral relations exist within the Trinity.[36] It has to be noted that even though Nyamiti rules out the possibility of univocal application of ancestral terminology to the Trinity, he does not consider the terminology to apply only in a figurative or metaphorical sense. According to Nyamiti, ancestral relations really exist in the Trinity, and the reality to which ancestral terminology refers in the created and uncreated order is basically the same even if the proportion is different. The question is thus about an analogy of proper proportionality.[37]

Thus, in ancestral terminology, the Father is the Ancestor of the Son who is the Descendant. The Holy Spirit is the mutual Oblation of the two. Is this but a play with Words rehearsing Augustinian mutual love theory[38] under an African guise? Nyamiti is convinced that this is not the case. According to him, in the traditional Western models of the Trinity, the Holy Spirit remains an outsider for the Trinity because fatherhood as such does not imply that there is a communion between the Father and the Son, whereas this communion would naturally belong to ancestorship.[39] What makes this statement problematic, however, is that today Nyamiti speaks clearly of an ancestor's enjoying a "title to sacred ritual communication"[40] instead of tending to speak of actual communication as he used to.[41]

If ancestorship does not imply actual communication, the situation does not differ from the traditional model, since it is possible to maintain that just as the ancestral relation ideally implies communication, so does the father–son relationship. Nyamiti also points out that his model would create an intrinsic link between fatherhood/sonship and sanctity because ancestor and descendant are by definition holy. Furthermore, according to him, the trinitarian exemplarity would be ⁻better understood by Africans if expressed through an ancestral terminology. This would be so because the Western approaches concentrate easily on the *imago Dei* as an essential question, whereas what counts for an African is not essentiality but exemplarity in the practical communal life.[42] However, what adjudges the validity of theological constructions, according to Nyamiti, in addition to their orthodoxy, is the practical outcome for the Christian life.[43] For Nyamiti, the outcome is positive: a proper understanding of sanctification, a balanced view of God's mercy and anger, sound submission to the ecclesiastical authorities, and a living missionary spirit.[44]

This construction, Nyamiti believes, is not only inculturated local theology but a major theological innovation which is valid in all countries of the world, regardless of whether there exist ancestral cults in those countries or not. This conviction is based on the proposal that ancestorship is an existing universal entity which can be found both in God and men.[45] To be able to maintain this, Nyamiti needs to subscribe to the concept of ancestors' being entitled to ritual communication instead of actual communication.[46] Were it not so, the universality of ancestorship would be highly questionable because of the widespread modern neglect of the ancestors.

The Trinity and African Worldviews

Nyamiti's ancestral trinitology might not be his last word about the Trinity seen in the light of African cultures. It seems rather that he has used ancestorship as a tool to elaborate some more abstract and perhaps more deep-going principles of a Bantu worldview. It is of a great significance that Nyamiti defines ancestorship in a relational rather than an essentialistical way. Furthermore, the chief gain ideally to be achieved through the ancestral trinitarian theory is the fact that the spiration of the Holy Spirit is logically and intrinsically demanded by the generation of the Son. This means that the compactness of the trinitarian relations would be strengthened. At the same time, it is interesting to notice that Nyamiti has attempted to arrive at the same conclusion by means other than ancestorship.

In African understandings of reality, according to Nyamiti, being is always being-with-the-others; purely individual nonrelational existence is out of the question.[47] Furthermore, the quality or strength of being is defined by one's relations to the others. The deeper and more harmonious the union one has with others, the stronger he or she will be. The Trinity is the deepest possible communion of persons and this means that God is the most powerful Being, in fact, Being as such or the source of the power to be of all of the rest of the cosmos.[48] Unlike in the traditional models which attribute the distinctions between Persons to their relative opposition, Nyamiti's approach maintains that the three Persons' personality comes from communication. The deeper one's communion is with others, the more fully he or she will be a person.[49]

This is no contradiction to the traditional views but presents the other side of the coin; without relative opposition or any kind of a distinction, there can be no communion. The role of the Holy Spirit is again emphasized as the crown and seal of God's being; without communion in the Holy Spirit neither the Father nor the Son could exist.[50] The outcome is practically the same as should have been of the ancestral approach. Unfortunately Nyamiti has not yet continued further with this reflection. However, one easily sees the vast possibilities to proceed in pneumatology, with the Holy Spirit as the Vivifer and the bond of love in the cosmos.[51]

In fact, the seeds of this kind of a trinitarian theory based on the African relational worldview can be found already in Vincent Mulago's dissertation of the early 1960s. Even though he does not enter deeply into a discussion about the Trinity from the African theory of relations point of view, all material that would have been needed for this elaboration is already present.[52] Mulago's work was on ecclesiology and thus the question of the Trinity remained relatively peripheral. Especially promising for the treatment of the Trinity was Mulago's development of Tempels' ideas of vital force into an idea of vital participation. Unlike the notion of vital force, that of vital participation can be applied directly to the trinitarian relations and the constitution of being in-the-world. In fact, later Mulago worked briefly on this issue. Mulago's trinitarian view, however, must be seen mostly as little more than a presentation of the Augustinian mutual love theory in which the concept of substance is replaced with "Life."[53] Mulago moves quickly from the philosophical heights of Bantu cosmology to the common analogy between the Trinity and family/human communality.[54] Nyamiti's views come close to those of Mulago concerning the Bantu traditional worldview and Mulago's influence on Nyamiti seems probable.[55]

Éfoe Julien Pénoukou begins from the Togolese Ewe-Mina worldview, analyzing some of their myths in order to build a relevant Christology. As a by-product he also has to elaborate on the Trinity to a limited extent. Unlike most other African theologians dealing with the doctrine of the Trinity, he does not begin from the traditional *depositum fidei* trying to see how best to adapt it to an African reality but attempts to start from the mystery of the Trinity without any ready Western theological commentaries. The point of departure is the encounter with the trinitarian God in faith.[56] The concrete outcome, however, does not go further than concluding that God's being a communion of three is in accord with the Ewe-Mina conception of being as always being-with.[57] However, this conclusion is earned somewhat further by indicating that speculation about God's essence is not fruitful, but that one should rather concentrate on finding out how the triune God communicates Himself to us.[58] Namely, the Triune God turned in on Himself would not fulfill the ideal of communal being since the communion would ultimately be a closed one.

A hint toward the possibility of using an African worldview for elaborating the Trinity in a way other than that of communality or relationality is made by Egbulefu, who mentions that "the God one and three is the God of equilibrium."[59] This statement reflects the tendency of many African cultures (just like many other archaic cultures) to seek an equilibrium. In this view consensus is of great importance and harmony is the central characteristic of the cosmos. Equilibrium could thus also be used as a point of departure in viewing the Trinity from an African cosmology point of view. Egbulefu does not proceed in a trinitarian direction in dealing with the idea of equilibrium and thus also this possibility remains only on the level of a hint toward an African approach to the Trinity.

Conclusion

Genuinely African thinking about the doctrine of the Trinity can be said to be still generally, in the germinal stage. The most common starting point for African theologies of the Trinity have been social analogies based on different aspects of (extended) family relations. Some attempts toward a trinitarian theology based on the principles of these social relations have also been conducted in striving to combine the doctrine of the Trinity directly with deepseated cultural structures.

If African theology is to continue to develop toward a more mature group of genuinely Christian theologies which cover the whole field of Christian doctrine, deeper elaboration of the doctrine of the Trinity must take place, or otherwise African theology will run the risk of becoming a curious branch of theology of a more practical type dependent on Western doctrinal theologies. If the doctrine of the Trinity is neglected or even denied, the quality of African theology as Christian theology will become highly questionable. Efforts at a renewed understanding of the doctrine of the Trinity should not be seen either as a threat to authentic African thinking or to the orthodox Christian understandings of the faith. The churches of today face crises concerning the credibility and vitality of the doctrine of the Trinity, and African theologians must be welcomed to bring their own contribution to the common faith of the Christians in Africa as well as all over the world.

Dr. Mika Vähäkangas is a lecturer at Makumira University College (Tanzania) teaching Systematic Theology. He is the managing editor of the *Africa Theological Journal.*

NOTES

[1] Gabriel Setiloane, "Where Are We in African Theology?" in *African Theology en Route: Papers from the Pan-African Conference of Third World Theologians, December 17–23, 1977, Accra, Ghana,* eds. Kofi Appiah-Kubi and Sergio Torres, (Maryknoll, NY: Orbis Books, 1979), 64–65: "I used to think that the theme of God the Holy Spirit needed to be treated from an African theological perspective. Often now I fear that such a treatment would be an endorsement of the Hellenistically-originated trinitarianism of the early church . . . Pneumatology, so-called, should, from an African perspective, be prepared to look squarely at and even dismantle the western trinitarian formula of Divinity."

    Jesse N.K. Mugambi is not in favor of dismissing the whole doctrine but proposes that it should be presented so that the concept of person would be totally avoided because it is unfit for Africa: *African Heritage and Contemporary Christianity* (Nairobi: Longman Kenya Ltd., 1989), 75. Thus also, from an Afro-American point of view, Robert Hood, *Must God Remain Greek? Afro Cultures and God-Talk,* (Minneapolis: Fortress Press, 1990), xi, 109–110, 124.

    See also Cristopher Mwoleka, "Trinity and Community," *African Ecclesiastical Review* 17 (1975), no. 4, 203: "It is a pity that many people find it very difficult to understand what this mystery [of the Trinity] is all about. Many Christians do not know what to do with it except that it must be believed."

[2] See Efoé Julien Pénoukou, "Christologie au village" in *Chemins de la christologie africaine,* 95–96. This is also the case with Charles Nyamiti, who has to proceed to Trinitology in order to provide a solid basis for his speculation on Christology. Thus Nyamiti criticizes Bénézet Bujo for not including discussion on the doctrine of the Trinity in ancestral approach: "Teología de la inculturación: Una perspectiva africana," *Scripts Teologica* 24, no. 3, 805, footnote 54. See also Hood, *Must God Remain Greek?* 105. J. Vonkeman defends the Africans' right for a genuine reflection on the doctrine of the Trinity also without superimposed Western concepts: "The Doctrine of the Trinity in Africa," 147–148. See also David Bosch, "God in Africa: Implications for the Kerygma," *Missionalia* 1 (1973), no. 1, 20.

[3] Adam Wolanin, *Alcuni aspetti dells realtà religiosa africana: "Chiese indipendenti" e teologia africana* (Roma: Editrice Pontificia Università Gregoriana, 1993), 63, 68, 77; Malcom J. McVeigh, "Theological Issues Related to Kenyan Religious Independency" in *Kenya Churches Handbook: The Development of Kenyan Christianity, 1498–1973,* eds. David B. Barrett et al. (Kisumu, Kenya: Evangel Publishing House, 1973), 136. Compare Inus Daneel, *Quest for Belonging: Introduction to a Study of African Independent Churches,* Mambo Occasional Papers-Missio-Pastoral Series No. 17 (Gweru, Zimbabwe, Mambo Press 1987), 263.

    Bengt Sundkler maintains in his book *Bantu Prophets in South Africa* (Second edition [London: Oxford University Press, 1961], 244, 280–281, 323–330) that in some cases Black Messiahs usurp the role of Christ and that "Zionist churches" misinterpret the Holy Spirit so that the concept is no more Christian. See also Clive and Margaret

Kileff, "The Masowe Vapostori of Seki: Utopianism and Tradition in an African Church" in *The New Religions of Africa,* ed. Bennetta Jules-osette (Norwood, NJ: Ablex Publishing Corporation, 1979), 153. These kind of views naturally clash with the trinitarian dogma, at least in the orthodox form. Allan Anderson disagrees with Sundkler about the misinterpretation of the concept of the Spirit (*Moya: The Holy Spirit in an African Context,* Manualia didactica 13 [Pretoria: UNISA, 1991]).

[4] Thus also Vonkeman, "The Doctrine of the Trinity in Africa," 155.

[5] Mubabinge Bilolo stems to think quite to the contrary, namely that (many) Africans would have less difficulties in accepting and understanding the doctrine of the Trinity because (many of) their cultures have ideas which are similar to the trinitarian doctrine. This, he suggests, would be based on the connections to ancient Egyptian thinking, which, in turn, would have been the breeding ground for Christian teaching on the Trinity ("Die Begriffe 'heiliger Geist' und 'Dreifaltigkeit Gottes,'" 1–23).

[6] Hans–Jürgen Greschat,"Das Christusbild und die Heilserwartung in 'nichtorthodoxen' christlichen Kirchen" in Ist Christus der einzige Weg zum Heil?, eds. Karl Müller and Werner Prawdzik, Veröffentlichungen des Missionspriesterseminars St. Augustin bei Bonn Nr. 40 (Nettetal: Steyler Verlag, 1991), 178, referring to a lecture of Elphas Ngobese in NERMIC Symposium 28–29. June 1989, UNISA, Pretoria under the title "The Concept of the Trinity among the Amanazaretha." On the same problem, see also Vonkeman, "The Doctrine of the Trinity in Africa," 155.

[7] See, for example, Mosha, "The Trinity in the African Context," 44–45; Mercy Amba Oduyoye, *Hearing and Knowing: Theological Reflections on Christianity in Africa* (Maryknoll, NY: Orbis Books, 1986), 141–142.

[8] See Sankey, "The Church as Clan"; Robert Kaggwa, "Koinonia: The Triune God and Mission, A Critical Study of Jürgen Moltmann and John Zizioulas' Trinitarian Theologies and an Inquiry into their Possible Relevance to Contemporary African Situations" (Rome: Pontificia Universitas Gregoriana, facultas theologiae, unpublished dissertation, 1995), 322, footnote 52.

[9] This was already the case with Vincent Mulago, who worked mainly on ecclesiology, but since he considered the Church as the prolongation of the Incarnation, he moved via Christology to Trinitology: *Un visage africain de christianisme: l'union vitale bantu face a l'unité vitale ecclesiale* (Paris: Présence africaine, 1965), 167–169. On the Church as a family, see also, for example, Mosha, "The Trinity in the African Context," 45; Leonard Namwera, "Personal Liberation through Communication" in Leonard Namwera et al., *Towards African Christian Liberation,* Christian Leadership in Africa Series (Nairobi: St. Paul Publications Africa, 1990), 123.

[10] This view was expressed by the Roman Catholic hierarchy in Burkina Faso in 1977 according to Kaggwa, "Koinonia," 317–318.

[11] "Message of the Synod," *Synodus Episcoporum Bulletin* 06.05.1994, no. 35 (Holy See Press Office: English Edition), art. 20, art. 25. The family to which the Message refers is the extended one (see art. 27).

[12] "Message of the Synod," art. 27.

[13] "In the African Synod the Image of a Young Church in Increasing Maturity," *Omnis Terra* (English edition), Jan. 1995, 31. Thus also Muzunqgu, "*Je ne sais pas venu pour abolir mais accomplir,*" 181.

[14] In the African Synod," 31.

[15] "The Trinity as Source and Soul of African Family Ecclesiology," *African Christian Studies,* vol. 15, no. 1 (1999), 34–39.

[16] *Ibid.,* 64.

[17] *Ibid.*, 81.

[18] Such theologians are, for example, Per Frostin, Peter Kijanga, Camillus Lyimo, Laurenti Magesa, Thomas Musa, and Christopher Mwoleka. Far more numerous are, however, those who paid lip-service to *ujamaa* politics and added the theme in their writings.

[19] Camillus Lyimo, "An Ujamaa Theology" in *African Christian Spirituality*, ed. Aylward Shorter (Maryknoll, NY: Orbis Books, 1980), 126.

[20] "Trinity and Community," 203.

[21] "Trinity and Community," 203–205.

[22] "Trinity and Community," 203–205. In a similar vein, also Vonkeman, "The Doctrine of the Trinity in Africa," 155. See Christopher Mwoleka: *Do This! The Church of the Third Millennium—What Face Shall It Have?* (Peramiho, Tanzania: Benedictine Publications Ndanda, 1988), 43–49.

[23] See "An Ujamaa Theology," 128. Lyimo suggests that *ujamaa* (politics) reflects the Trinity, whereas Mwoleka seems to suggest that through *ujamaa* human beings are called to imitate the Trinity and only in that manner can *ujamaa* become a reflection of the Trinity. This difference in emphasis results in a great difference: unlike Lyimo, Mwoleka need not sacralize *ujamaa* even if he views the Trinity through it.

[24] Here I do not suggest that there would be a single Pan-African culture. Rather, here "African culture" is used in the sense of the cultural background of *ujamaa* (and Nyamiti's thought), i.e., the Bantu cultural family.

[25] *African Tradition and the Christian God*, Spearhead no. 49 (Eldoret, Kenya: Gaba Publications, s.a. ca. 1977), 54.

[26] Especially "Divine Immanent Responsibility: An African Approach to the Trinity," *African Christian Studies*, vol. 14, no. 4 (1998), 1–45.

[27] "The Naming Ceremony in the Trinity: An African Approach to the Trinity," Essays on African Theology 7 (Kipalapala, Tanzania: unpublished, 1980), later published as "The Naming Ceremony in the Trinity," *African Christian Studies* 4 (1988), no. 1, 41–74; "The Naming Ceremony in the Trinity," *African Christian Studies* 4 (1988), no. 3, 55–83.

[28] Especially "Personality and Fecundity: The Trinity in the Light of Some African Views." Essays on African Theology 10 (Kipalapala, Tanzania: unpublished, 1981).

[29] For example, *African Tradition and the Christian God*, 53–70.

[30] "The Trinity from an African Ancestral Perspective," *African Christian Studies* 12 (1996), no. 4, 41.

[31] *Ibid.*, 41.

[32] *Ibid.*, 41.

[33] Nyamiti is heavily influenced here by the sketch of the Bantu worldview of Placide Tempels, which he presented in the famous book *La philosophie bantoue*, trans. A. Rubbens (Elisabethville, Belgian Congo: Lovania, 1945).

[34] "The Trinity from an African Ancestral Perspective," 46–48.

[35] *Ibid.*, 46.

[36] Nyamiti suggested this for the first time in a published form in *African Tradition and the Christian God*, 47–50.

[37] Teología de la inculturación", 773: "Pero uno toma el término >antepasado< con todas sus implicaciones africanas y lo aplica, por ejemplo, a Cristo (el Antepasado) o a la gracia (la gracia es >ancestral<) —y esto no es un sentido metafórico o figurado, sino según la analogía de proporcionalidad . . ."

[38] See "The Trinity from an African Ancestral Perspective," 55–56.

[39] *African Tradition and the Christian God*, 49: "[T]he relationship of Fatherhood and Sonship is, as such, not so apt as Ancestorship and Descendancy to show the *intrinsic* link they have with the Spirit. Without the idea of ancestorship, the Holy Spirit appears as a 'stranger' to the Father and the Son and, as it were, extraneous to their relationship."

[40] "The Trinity from an African Ancestral Perspective," 41.

[41] *African Tradition and the Christian God*, 46. Compare, however, ibid., 49.

[42] "The Trinity from an African Ancestral Perspective," 51: "[W]herever the African speaks of his ancestors as his exemplars, he sees them more as models of his conduct or way of life in community, rather than as prototypes of his natural human structure. The African is little concerned with the latter kind of exemplarity, because for him it has little relevance for practical life."

[43] *The Scope of African Theology*, Gaba Pastoral Papers no. 30 (Kampala: Gaba Publications, 1973), 39: "[The African theologian's] vocation is in the first place to the welfare of his people—their problems, needs and aspirations, as well as confronting Christianity with their culture."

[44] "The Trinity from an African Ancestral Perspective," 67–69.

[45] *African Tradition and the Christian God*, 45: "[T]he particular relationship between an ancestor and his or her offspring is not a matter of pure convention. It is based on the natural constitution of man." See also *Christ as Our Ancestor: Christology from an African Perspective*, Mambo Occasional Papers— Missio–Pastoral Series no. 11 (Gweru, Zimbabwe: Mambo Press, 1984), 17.

[46] Thus, neither of the choices, actual communication or right to communication, can provide for Nyamiti's needs of keeping both the universality of ancestorship and a more compact communion within the Trinity.

[47] God in African and Christian Contexts," Essays on African Theology 1 (Kipalapala, Tanzania: unpublished, 1977), 115: "Power, life, holiness and solidarity point finally to communication or participation as their fundamental source. Lack of communication means lack of all these factors, i.e. it means weakness, egoism and death."

[48] *African Tradition and the Christian God*, 62: "The Trinity reveals God as essentially communicative. Of his very nature he is *the immanently communicating and communicated independent Vital Force* . . . He is the only One who is totally and fully shared, and the only one who is fullness of life, power and love, for that very reason."

[49] "God in African and Christian Contexts," 155: "Since personality is nourished by communication, the more we communicate to others, the more we deepen and discover our personality."

[50] *African Tradition and the Christian God*, 54: "[T]he Father cannot be what he is (and thus have his power) unless he begets the Son; and the power of the Father and the Son cannot be had without 'spirating' the Holy Spirit in oneness of love. Hence we may conclude that in God, power is based on the intrinsic unity and plurality of shared life. Without this the divine Persons can do nothing, they cannot even exist. . . Thus the African philosophy of power applies also to God in his inner life." "An African Theology of God's Perfection," Essays on African Theology 4 (Kipalapala, Tanzania: unpublished, 1978), 22: "Holy Spirit. . . is the personification of God's absolute perfection seen as sanctity and love."

[51] See *African Tradition and the Christian God*, 54–55: "God's power is the source of their being and existence, and is their ultimate goal in as much as they naturally tend towards and achieve their perfection in this divine Vital Power."

[52] See *Un visage africain de christianisme*, 173–194. Also Kisimba Nyembo brings together the Trinity and ecclesiology in Mulago's footsteps but does not proceed any

further in his "L'Église–famille et ministères" in *Église famille; église fraternité: Perspectives post–synodales: Actes de la XXe semaine théologique de Kinshasa du 26 novembre au 2 décembre 1995*, Semaines théologiques de Kinshasa (Kinshasa: Facultés .catholiques de Kinshasa 1997), 271–272.

[53] "Le problème d'une théologie africaine revu à la lumière de Vatican II," *Revue de Clergé Africain* 24 (1969) no. 3–4, 308. According to Vonkeman, Mulago tries to fuse Greek philosophy and African cosmology together in an unacceptable manner. Furthermore, according to him, concentrating on vital participation leaves no room for *sola fide*. ("The Doctrine of the Trinity in Africa," 152–153). Mulago's exposition of the basic compatibility between scholastic and Bantu philosophies seems, in fact, quite artificial (see "Le problème d'une théologie africaine," 296–298). As to Vonkeman's criticism of vital participation usurping the place of faith, it seems that the basic problem here is not in Mulago's personal views but confessional differences between Reformed and Roman Catholic views. Specifically, Mulago has no intention to let grace sink into the all-embracing natural vital participation (see "Le problème d'une théologie africaine," 309–310).

[54] "Le problème d'une théologie africaine," 308–310.

[55] Both Mutago and Nyamiti are influenced by Tempels, which explains part of the similarities between them. It is also noteworthy that already Mulago used the ancestral approach in his dissertation even though he did not use it as a point of departure for elaborating the whole of Christian doctrine as does Nyamiti (see *Un visage africain*, 191–192). For Mulago the central issue is vital participation, or *union vitale*, which, however, gives similar results as Nyamiti's ancestral approach.

[56] "Christologie en village," 95–96: "Point n'est besoin de ressasser ici les données classiques et tenues pour acquises, des discours trinitaires propres a l'Occident, ni de se complaire daps des considérations abstraites qui embrouillent plus qu'elles n'éclairent l'ineffable mystère de la sainte Trinité. Il s'agira plutôt de poser des donnes anthropologiques évoquées jusqu'à présent comme capables d'accueillir *dons la foi* un tel mystère, et donc de l'interpréter de façon pertinenete pour le chrétien Ewe–Mina." However, one may question whether it is possible at all to start directly from faith and to leave the burden of centuries of theological traditions aside.

[57] *Ibid.*, 96.

[58] *Ibid.*, 96–97.

[59] "Mistero trinitario a contesto africano," in *Trinità in contesto*, ed. Angelo Amato, Biblioteca di scienze religiose 110 (Rome: Libreria Ateneo Salesiano, 1994), 198: "[I]l Dio uno e trino, è il Dio dell'equilibrio."

CHAPTER 5

The Church as a Family Model:
Its Strengths And Weaknesses

Aidan G. Msafiri

Introduction

In this article I shall present a critical analysis and reevaluation of *The Church as Family of God* model against today's ever-changing African understanding of family. Hopefully, this will highlight both the excellence (strengths) and limitations (weaknesses) of the family model in contemporary Africa. Although I do not intend to discuss other related Church models, particularly those advocated by contemporary and outstanding ecclesiologists or theologians such as A. Dunes, Yves Congar, Charles Nyamiti, it should be understood right from the outset that no model is exhaustive. Each model plays a complementary role with other models to give a deep or full understanding of the Church, which is a mystery.

Part one shows the Biblical and Magisterial foundations of the family model. Among other documents, the Pauline *Letters of Ephesians* and *Colossians, Vatican II's, Lumen Gentium,* John Paul II's *Familiaris Consortio* and *Ecclesia in Africa* are given unique and special prominence. Part two highlights both the positive and negative aspects as well as implications of the model in relation to today's situation and understanding of the African family. The article ends with a critical reevaluation of the limitations (weaknesses) of the family model.

Need for further reflection on the Church as Family of God model

The *raison d'etre* of *The Church as Family of God* model is succinctly encapsulated in article 25 of the *Intrumentum Laboris*:

> Among the biblical images of the Church enumerated in the Dogmatic Constitution on the Church, *Lumen Gentium,* that of the Church as the House of God (cf. I Timothy 3:15), the Household of God in the Spirit (cf. Ephesians 2:19–22) is particularly relevant for Africa . . . In many answers to the *Lineamenta,* there is a strong emphasis on the notion of the Church as the family of God among human beings.[1]

85

According to the Synodal Fathers, the *family model* is fitting and appropriate for Africa because there is a correlation between the African understanding of *family* and the Church as *family of God*. Consequently, the *family model* has very enriching theocentric, Trinitarian, Christological, sacramental, ecclesiogenetic, pastoral, and communitarian imcations to the life and mission of the Church in Africa during the third millennium.

But, the traditional African understanding of family is subject to multiple and constant changes because of, among other factors, the modern cultural Euro-American (Western) as well as Asian influences. These affect the contemporary understanding of the African family. Such inevitable circumstances may have negative implications on the ever-changing African concept of family and *The Church as Family of God* model. This is a challenge which cannot simply be ignored or overlooked by contemporary African ecclesiologists, theologians and scholars: There is, therefore, need for an in-depth analysis, scrutiny, and rethinking of the family model, if Africa is to develop a sound African ecclesiology as a useful and effective means toward inculturation and evangelization 2000.

The Biblical and Magisterial Foundations of the Family Model

A. Biblical foundation

(i) Old Testament
The Hebrew terms *mispaha* and *bet* (house) in the Old Testament embrace both the narrow and broader notions of family. These could either mean a single family unit or a wider circle of consanguinity (cf. Genesis 24:38), a clan, an ethnic group (a tribe), or even a nation (cf. Amos 3:1–2). The family concept in the Old Testament represented one of the most commonly used models, metaphors, or analogies to expiate in a human way the unique relationship between God and Israel.[2]

(ii) New Testament
The Greek term *oikia,* which means house or a household, is usually used to refer to a family. There is a profound theological and ecclesiological growth of the concept of *family* in the New Testament literature. Such evolution is marked by continuity and discontinuity. Thus, in the New Testament, particularly in the Pauline ecclesiological *Letters (*Ephesians, I Timothy, and Colossians), the family metaphor or image expresses the relationship between the Church and the human

family. Paul calls the Church a "household of God" (I Timothy 3:15) or "Part of God's household" (Ephesians 2:19–22). The latter expression is also used by Peter (I Peter 4:17).[3] Other New Testament passages or allusions to the *household* metaphor include: John 4:53, Acts 11:14; 16:15; Colossians 3:18–21; Romans 16:3–5; and I Corinthians 16:19. The *household* image is tantamount to the *family* concept.

B. Magisterial foundation

Basically, the family model or image has always been one of the most central themes of *post–Vatican II* magisterial teachings. Among others, the following teachings from the Magisterium highlight the understanding of the Church as family of God.

(i) Vatican II

In the Dogmatic Constitution of the Church *(Lumen Gentium)* the Conciliar Fathers employ different images such as the "household of God" metaphor to describe the Church. *Lumen Gentium* article 6 states, "This edifice has many names to describe it: the house of God in which dwells His family: the household of God in the spirit"[4]

(ii) Familiaris Consortio (1981)

In this Apostolic Exhortation, Pope John Paul II describes the family as a Church:

> We must examine the many profound bonds linking the church and the Christian family and establishing the family as "church in miniature" *(Ecclesia domestica)* in such a way, the family is a living image and historical representation of the mystery of the church.[5]

In a very special way, this Exhortation contains references and allusions to the role and mission of present-day Christian families, both in the Church and the world.

(iii) Christifideles Laici (1988)

The family image or model is not very explicit in *Christifideles Laici* as in *Familiaris Consortio*. However, there are some passages in the former *(Christifideles Laici)* which offer some allusions to the family. In one of the passages, John Paul II maintains that, "Jesus is concerned to restore integral dignity to the married couple and solidarity to the family (Matthew 19:3–9), St. Paul shows the deep rapport between marriage and the Church (cf. Ephesians 5:22; 6:4, Colossians 3:18–21; I Peter 3:1–7)."[6]

(iv) Instrumentum Laboris (1993)

In this working document prior to the *Special Assembly for Africa of the Synod of Bishops* (10 April–8 May, 1994), the family model is given special attention. According to this preparatory document:

> It is felt that Africans can be more easily enabled to experience and to live with the mystery of the church as communion by utilizing to good advantage the Africans' understanding of the family especially as regards the values of family unity and solidarity.[7]

(v) Ecclesia in Africa (1994)

This is the most recent magisterial document which speaks specifically on "The Church as a Family of God." According to the Synodal Fathers, the "Church as God's Family" model "emphasizes care for others, solidarity, warmth in human relationships, acceptance, dialogue and trust."[8] It is quite evident, therefore, that the family model highlights the unique and rare human values characteristic of a typically traditional African family.

An African Perspective of the Family of God Model

A. Its excellence (strengths)

(i) The model is theocentric

The family model is profoundly God-centered. It highlights God's central position in terms of the Church's divine origin, mission, continuity, and care. It also brings to the fore the connection and similarity between the invaluable roles played by a committed traditional African father to his family and God the Father to the Church. Definitely, this can serve as an important factor toward creating deep-rooted confidence and esteem in Christians.

(ii) It is Trinitarian

The tripartite relationship and intercommunication between the three Persons of the Blessed Trinity demonstrates the profound inner life of the Triune God in terms of perfect unity and the harmonious diversity of persons. According to Professor Charles Nyamiti:

> The Son is the perfect image of the Father His exemplar.
> Each of them is entitled to the uninterrupted and eternal

> sacred communication in the Holy Spirit whom they breathe
> out their mutual love and communicate Him to each other in
> token of their reciprocal love.[9]

Many traditional African families and clans, especially those in the rural areas, still enjoy close interpersonal ties and relationships. This definitely serves as a useful and effective means to promote and enhance sincere relationships and responsibility at various levels of Church life in Africa, thereby accentuating the current theological struggle toward a practical African ecclesial Trinitology. According to Bakole wa Ilunga, the Archbishop of Kananga, Zaire:

> The close bond between members of the same family and solidarity
> that unites a clan are undoubtedly important values of the African
> tradition . . . This solidarity is undoubtedly a powerful force and the
> dynamism that pervades it is of fundamental importance for
> communal life . . . The need is to take the attitudes and energies
> traditionally embodied in familiar relationships and to redirect them
> in broader perspective of present day society.[10]

(iii) It is Christologico-Sacramental

Jesus founded and established a Church. In his book, *Ecclesiogenesis: The Base Communities Reinvent the Church,* Boff states that, "The Christological foundation of the Church is born of the complex Christological event, with the resurrection and the activity of the Holy Spirit."[11] From the Pauline viewpoint, particularly, in his *Letter to the Ephesians,* Paul depicts Christ as the "Head of the Church." He further portrays Christ as God's instrument of reconciliation and grace. The sacramentality of the Personhood of Christ is a very central idea in Scillebecky's Christological and ecclesiological enterprise. According to him, "The church is the visible expression of Christ's grace and redemption realized in the form of a society which is a sign *(Societas signum)*."[12] Such Christology shares certain common aspects with Nyamiti's "African Christology" inculturated in African milieu and encapsulated in his famous formula "Christ Our Ancestor." In the same line of thinking, Professor Bujo's "Proto-Ancestor Christology" echoes and develops the same Christologico-Sacramental understanding by maintaining that:

> . . . many Black African ethnic groups, the presence of the ancestor
> is visually represented by means of a special tree, the ancestor tree.
> The tree in question is an ever verdant tree, such as Ficus, which

symbolizes the life that never dies. Among the Bahema of Eastern
Zaire the Ficus is planted on the grave of the family father. The father
lying in the grave is not dead at all but shoots forth to new life as a
Ficus tree so that he now becomes shelter and vivifying "spirit." The
branches and the leaves of this tree symbolize the numerous
descendants of the deceased . . . Separated from him they cannot
survive . . . The church as the proto-ancestor is sacrament par
excellence in which the faithful encounter Christ as the sacrament of
God.[13]

Like the Bahema of Zaire, the Chagga of northeastern Tanzania
(whom I hail from) have a very special robust and evergreen *ancestral*
tree called *Isale*. This is usually planted at the grave of the clan ancestor
(*mbuonyi*) where all the family sacrificial offerings (*mirumo*) are
performed. For the Chagga, the ancestor's grave is sacrosanct and it
plays the role of today's altar for the Eucharistic Sacrifice. According
to the Chagga, the green color signifies a vital and continuous presence
of the ancestor as a source of hope and life in the family. Moreover, as
an ancestral tree, the *Isale* is also used to reconcile people in feuds,
clashes, or quarrels. Last, but not least, the *Isale* is used to ask for
pardon for a crime (e.g., murder, theft, *et alii*) committed. Those who
know the *sacred* nature of the *Isale* will automatically grant pardon and
clemency. Thus, the *Isale* plays a unique and significant reconciliatory
role in the similar way "*mutatis mutandis* Christ reconciled humanity
with God" (Romans 11:15; Ephesians 2:13–14; Colossians 1:20). Such
a traditional African ancestral-centered understanding of the family can
strengthen the Christologico-Sacramental dimension and roles within
the Church in Africa.

(iv) It is Ecclesiogenetic

Christ commissioned His disciples to preach the Good News from
Galilee to the ends of the earth (Matthew 28:18–20). Consequently, by
its very nature and mission, the Church grew and still grows in time and
space. Its missionary role is extensively explicated in *Vatican II
Documents: Ad Gentes* and *Gaudium et Spes*. A decade later, *Evangelii
Nuntiandi* reiterated strongly the Church's missionary mandate. Such
growth does not, however, necessarily or always imply geographical
expansionism, although this dimension cannot be simply ignored. The
Church is the living "Body of Christ" (Romans 12:4–5; I Corinthians
12:12–27), and to use a Petrine metaphor, its members are "living
stones" of the same edifice (I Peter 2:5). Such an Ecclesiogenetic

dimension of the Church complies with the traditional African concept of the extended family. This can, therefore, be a very effective pastoral means toward *Evangelization 2000*, especially by and through Small Christian Communities (SCCs). Based on this traditional African concept of family, the Synod Fathers insist that, "These SCCs should be permeated by the universal love of Christ who breaks down the barriers and natural alliances of clan, tribe or other interest groups."[14]

(v) It is Eucharistic (communitarian)

During His Last Supper (Banquet), Christ founded and empowered a perpetual Eucharistic community of blood, life, and love (Luke 22:19–20, I Corinthians 11:23–27). Joseph Cardinal Ratzinger considers this as the foundation of Eucharistic ecclesiology.[15] The post-Apostolic ecclesial community translated this into *koinonia* morality. During Nyerere's presidency in Tanzania, this could have been termed *Ujamaa* morality based on the African values of hospitality and equality. The practice and concept of communal meals, festivals, or get-togethers is still quite common, particularly among the traditional African families and clans living in the rural areas. Such meals play a very significant unitive role among members. There is a great resemblance between the Christian Eucharistic Banquet and the traditional African communal meals and festivals. That is why Professor Bujo maintains that:

> The Eucharist should be seen as a proto-ancestral meal with and of Jesus Christ himself . . . a vital element in the building up of a truly African church . . . A theology of the Eucharist not only as a celebration of a proto-ancestral meal which vivifies the church, but also an ecclesiology into this African World of thought.[16]

(vi) It is Eschatologico-ecologico

There is a profound unity and interconnectedness between the human family and the cosmos. Therefore, humanity shares an integral and sacred interrelationship with the earth. According to Gerald Siegwalt:

> . . . the creation narrative of Genesis 1 is also understood eschatologically in the light if Revelation 21:5: "Behold I, make all things new" . . . The history of the earth is "becoming" as the history of Israel. In this context, the order of Gen. 1 is understood as an evolutionary historical order. The goodness God saw in creation is eschatological.[17]

The integral unity and interdependency between the human family and the cosmos suggest a holistic and all-embracing ecologico-eschatology which encompasses the traditional Catholic *one-sided* human-centered eschatological understanding. Humanity and creation are, therefore, to be considered as undergoing a transformative teleological process and a "becoming" (2 Peter 3:13, Revelation 21:1).

There is a *realized* existing unity between humanity, creation, and God journeying toward a new heaven and earth in the *not yet*. Many traditional African societies still have a *pantheistic view* of creation as clearly demonstrated in their special respect and honor for certain sacred trees, rivers, huge mountains like Kilimanjaro, volcanic mountains such as Oldonyo Lengai in Arusha, Tanzania, which literally means "the mountain of God." Contacts, communication, and communion with the ancestral community (the living dead) are sometimes performed by and through certain sacred trees which are believed to mediate life. Eschatologico-ecological worldviews are a common phenomenon in traditional African families, clans, and societies, indicating a profound redemptive and eschatological goal.[18] Such a traditional African inclusive eschatologico-ecological weltschauung could have very enriching positive effects, especially against the ever-growing environmental and ecological destruction in Africa.

B. Its limitation (weaknesses)

(i) A negative ecumenical implication

When understood or interpreted from an exclusivistic Catholic-oriented or from a Euro-American understanding, the family model can have very negative ecumenical consequences. Among others, the following deserve special attention:

1. A Catholic-oriented interpretation of the family model would run the risk of being an obstacle to attaining the target of Christian unity which involves a number of Christian churches and ecclesial communities all over the world. Jesus' prayer in John 17:11, 22 was that not only the Catholic Church but that all be "one like us."

    The post–*Vatican II* period is markedly characterized by constant striving toward Christian unity. This new ecumenical vision is particularly highlighted in the Decree on Ecumenism *(Unitatis Redintegratio)*, the Dogmatic Constitution on the Church *(Lumen Gentium, Articles 1–4), The 1993 Directory for the Application of Principles and Norms on Ecumenism,* and in the recent 1995 *Papal Encynical, Ut Unum Sint.* Feeling the need and urgency for Christian unity in Africa, the Synodal Fathers clearly expressed this view in the *Lineamenta,* the *Instrumentum Laborr's,* and in the *Post-Synodal Apostolic Exhortation (Ecclesia in Africa)* by John Paul II. Such ecumenical visions can be used against the dangers of narrow or Catholic-centered ecclesiological understanding of the family model.

2. Any exclusivistic Catholic-centered understanding of the family model runs the risk of excluding non-Christians such as Muslims and adherents of Traditional Religions from God's *family.* This danger is, however, clearly stated in the *Lineamenta,* particularly in the sub-titles: "Practice of Ecumenism in Africa" (Art. 61), "The Agenda of Dialogue" (Art. 67), and on "Problems and Hopes" (Art. 68).

3. Any Afro-centric interpretation of the family model neglects or excludes a universalistic dimension of the unity of humanity. Today, more than ever before, solidarity among humanity in its entirety is undoubtedly of paramount importance. A credible or sound humano-centric worldview has to go beyond religious beliefs (creed), race, or skin color. A balanced view of the family model should transform our mentalities to create universal perspectives and global human relationships. According to Bakole wa Ilunga:

> Jesus relativises the primacy of familial bonds or subordinates these to other and more basic values (cf., Mark 3:31–35) . . . When he says by his words and by his actions that every human being can become my neighbor and that there are therefore no boundary lines in this area (cf., Luke 10:30–37), he enables me to discover that every human being, and not just the members of my clan is my brother or sister.[19]

G. Martinez's concept and vision on "The Birth of a Global Church" suggests a universal human-centered ecclesiology. In his view:

> The Church's Social Mission requires a greater awareness . . . to form a humanistic partnership of peace and solidarity . . . Vatican II was not only a truly Catholic Council, but a potentially World Council as well. Karl Rahner saw Vatican II as the first official self-realization of Catholicism as world church.[20]

(ii) A negative implication based on "single-parent familles"

Today, there is an increasingly ever-growing number of *single-parent* families in Africa. The traditional African values and moral ethos which united marriage couples are steadily and speedily being replaced by new destructive values and lifestyles. These include among others, the Euro-American divorce revolution, sexual freedom, modernism, consumerism, feminism, unemployment, polycentrism, and the crisis of street children. Indeed, the speed is so terrific that, soon, a high percentage of African families, especially those living in big towns or cities, will be single-parent families, either physically or functionally. As a consequence of this, in some cases, for example:

> . . . early childhood experiences with a tyrannical and overly strict
> father are the roots of irrational and disproportionate guilt complexes.
> Deep-seated rebellion against a feudalistic or paternalistic "father
> image" of church often goes hand in hand with an overt rebellion
> against any despotic or outdated exercise of parental authority. [21]

Contrasts between the traditional African family and the present-day African families portray a failure in representing an authentic and correct picture of the *Divine Family*. Furthermore, the escalating parental irresponsibility not only among single-parent families but also even among families with both parents is also distorting the family model. Again, such a phenomenon displays a defective image of the *trinitarian family* which has a full and high degree of responsibility and *accountability* as evidenced in the entire salvation program.

(iii) Negative consequences of the traditional African patrilineal-matrilineal systems and the gender issue

Ninety percent of the traditional African societies are predominantly patrilineal. In these societies there is a tendency to give more favors and privileges to the father and sons at the expense of the mother and the daughters. This segregative and oppressive attitude is clearly evident among the Chagga. Here, boys are given greater opportunities and more chances in terms of education, inheritance, esteem, and in many other sociohuman rights. Such a dichotomy between patrilineal against matrilineal systems and or vice versa presents an inadequate picture of the family of God model in Africa. As a counterreaction against male chauvinism and superiority, feminist discussions, issues of women emancipation, and gender issues are increasingly becoming the most debatable current issues, particularly among Africa's female elites.

(iv) The negative implication of African witchcraft

In many African societies where there are strong beliefs and practices of witchcraft, familial or clan bonds of solidarity become an oppressive phenomenon. Among the Chagga, witchcraft is collectively known as *usawi*. In west African societies, particularly in Nigeria, *juju* is the most common word used to denote witchcraft. Bakole wa Ilunga strongly affirms that:

> . . . men, women and children fall victim to evil forces unleashed against them by members of their own family who have but one purpose: to harm or even kill others. When we see how obsessed some individuals are by this will to destroy, we may well think ourselves to be in the presence of Satan. Nor may we forget that the very fear of witchcraft paralyses many or prevents their full development and their enthusiasm for numerous understandings.[22]

Among the Ngoni of Songea and the Nyakyusa of Sumbawanga (Southern Tanzania) many educated or well-to-do people are normally reluctant to develop or even to go back home, for fear of being bewitched. They prefer to build permanent houses and initiate development projects far away from their villages, preferably in the big towns or cities such as Dar-es-salaam, Arusha, Mwanza, etc. Undoubtedly, witchcraft poses a serious problem which has far reaching moral and social negative implications and effects which distort the family model as proposed by the African Synod.

(v) African attitude toward death and its negative implication

In many traditional African societies, death is often attributed to something or someone. It is never understood as a necessary and inescapable human reality. According to Bakole wa Ilunga:

> If someone dies, there will always be reasons or causes given. Often, someone must be at fault, preferably the wife in case of a husband's death. It is as if the family had to find a victim on which it might discharge its hostility in the face of death as if the wife had to suffer and thus atone for the death of her husband. Even though Christian husbands, as death approaches, often express the desire that their wives not be abused and even though the last wishes of a dying person are sacrosanct according to all our traditions, it is not uncommon to see the family vent its fury on the surviving wife.[23]

Among the Chagga, like in many African societies, the *mfiri wo matanga* (mourning period) is usually four days. But, today some people take these days as a *golden* opportunity to eat, *feast,* and drink, regardless of the future economic needs of the bereaved. This is one of the most serious moral problems where family rights and social justice are being violated, thus highlighting the weakness of the family model.

Conclusion

In this article I have pointed out the strengths of the family model as applied in a concrete present-day African family situation, thereby highlighting the *similarities* between the traditional African family model and the Divine Family. This, to a certain degree, is a great help toward a better self-understanding of the Church in Africa. But, there is always danger to over-emphasize or exaggerate the excellence of the African family image. However, from the article it is obvious that the family model as proposed by the African Synod is subject to a number of limitations based on complex and multiple, static and ever-changing conditions which cover a large part of the African spectrum.

However, there is no image or model that is exhaustive. Therefore, the search for a more credible, balanced, and viable model which is relatively closer to Africa's present-day *Sitz im Leben* has to continue. This is not an easy or a one-day task. It calls for an in-depth and critical research of the entire African sociocultural, theological, anthropological, human, economic, and religious matrix. It has to involve many African scholars and experts from all walks of life. The purpose of this article, therefore, is to provoke African ecclesiologists and theologians to embark on immediate critical and deep reflections bearing in mind the following questions:

> With such concrete divergences and dichotomies, how does the family model really correspond to the present-day pseudo-African situation? Could there be possibilities of preserving today's African families from the devastating Euro-American and Asian influences or forces particularly in the AMECEA countries? Do African ecclesiologists and theologians foresee the pastoral moral and ecclesial implications of the family model and their negative consequences, particularly in connection to inculturation and *Evangelization 2000?*

Success toward a credible African interpretation ecclesiology should not simply be a purely humanistic endeavor. In this inquiry, the role of the Holy Spirit through prayer and sacrifice is of paramount importance.

Fr. Aidan G. Msafiri is a Diocesan Priest of the Catholic Diocese of Moshi, Tanzania. He studied at CUEA (Catholic University of Eastern Africa), Nairobi, from 1996–1998. His address is: Diocese of Moshi, P.O. Box 3041, Moshi, Tanzania.

NOTES

[1] *Intrumentum Laboris*, Article 25 (Vatican City, 1993).

[2] Metzger, B., and Coogan, D. C. (eds.), *The Oxford Companion to the Bible* (New York: Oxford University Press, 1993), s.v. "Family."

[3] The family or household model is a resonant quote in Vatican II *Lumen Gentium* Article 10 and in *Acta Apostolicae Sedis* 68 (1976): 60.

[4] Flannery, A., *Vatican Council II*, Dogmatic Constitution on the Church *Lumen Gentium* Art. 6 (Bombay, St. Paul Publications, 1975).

[5] John Paul II, Apostolic Exhortation (*"Familiaris Consortio"* on the Role of the Christian Family in the Modern World) (Nairobi: East African Graphics, 1987), No. 49.

[6] John Paul II, J., Apostolic Exhortation *"Christifideles Laici:* The Vocation and Mission of the Lay Faithful in the Church and in the World" (Meru: St. Paul Communication Africa, Kolbe Press, 1988), No. 40.

[7] *Instrumentum Laboris* (Vatican City, 1993), No. 25.

[8] John Paul II, *Post Synodal Apostolic Exhortation (Ecclesia in Africa)* (Nairobi: Pauline Publication Africa, 1995), No. 63.

[9] Nyamiti, C., "African Ancestral Veneration and Its Relevance to African Churches," *CUEA African Studies* Vol. 9, No. 3 (September 1993): 22.

[10] Wa Ilunga, B., *Paths of Liberation: A Third World Spirituality* (New York: Orbis Books, 1978), 159–160.

[11] Boff, L., *Ecclesiogenesis: The Base Communities Reinvent the Church* (New York: Orbis Books, 1986), 59–60.

[12] Scillebecky, E., *Christ the Sacrament* (London: Sheed and Ward, 1966), 56.

[13] Bujo, B. (ed.), "On the Road Towards African Ecclesiology" in *The African Synod: Documents, Reflections, Perspectives* (New York: Orbis Books, 1996), 141–142.

[14] *The African Synod: Documents, Reflections, Perspectives*, 90.

[15] Ratzinger, J., *Church, Ecumenism and Politics* (New York: Crossroad Publishing Co., 1988), 7–8.

[16] Bujo., B., *African Christian Morality at the Age of Inculturation* (Nairobi: St. Paul's Publications–Africa, 1990), 83.

[17] Siegwalt, G., "The Ecology Crisis: Challenge for Christians," *Theology Digest* Vol. 38, No. 2 (Summer 1991): 124.

[18] Bujo, B., "Eucharist in Black African Perspective," *Theology Digest,* Vol. 37, No. (Summer 1990): 127–128.

[19] Wa Ilunga, B., 160

[20] Martnez, G., "An Ecclesiology of Peace," *Theology Digest,* Vol. 38, No. 3 (Fall 1991): 237.

[21] Haring, B., *What Does Christ Want?* (London: Geoffrey Chapman, 1968): 155–156.

[22] Wa Ilunga, B., 163.

[23] *Ibid.*, 162

98   AFRICAN THEOLOGY TODAY

SELECTED BIBLIOGRAPHY

Acta Apostolicae Sedis, The Vatican gazette, 1976.

Boff, L., *Ecclesiogenesis: The Base Communities Reinvent the Church.* New York: Orbis Books, 1986.

Bujo, B., *African Christian Morality at the Age of Inculturation.* Nairobi, St. Paul Publications Africa, 1990.

———. "Eucharist in Black African Perspective," *Theology Digest,* Vol. 37: No. 2, Summer 1990.

———. (Eds.) "On the Road Towards African Ecclesiology," *The African Synod Documentary Reflections, Perspectives.* New York: Orbis Books, 1996.

Flannery, A., *Vatican Council II.* Bombay: St. Paul Publications, 1975.

Haring, B., *What Does Christ Want?* London: Geoffrey Chapman, 1968.

Ilunga, B., *Paths of Liberation: A Third World Spirituality.* New York: Orbis Books, 1978.

Instruntentum Laboris Articles 25. Vatican City, 1993.

John Paul II, J., *Post Synodal Apostolic Exhortation (Ecclesia in Africa).* Nairobi: Paulines Publications, 1995.

Martinez, G., "An Ecclesiology of Peace," *Theology Digest,* vol. 38: No. 3, Fall 1991.

Metzger, B., and Coogan M. D. (Eds.), *The Oxford Companion to the Bible.* New York: Oxford University Press, 1993.

Nyamiti, C., "African Ancestral Veneration and Its Relevance to African Churches," *CUEA African Studies,* Vol. 9, No. 3, September 1993.

Ratzinger, J., *Church, Ecumenism and Politics.* New York: Crossroads Publishing Co., 1988.

Schillebeecky, E., *Christ the Sacrament,* London: Sheed and Ward, 1966.

Siegwalt, G., "The Ecology Crisis Challenge for Christians," *Theology Digest,* Vol. 38: No. 2, Fall 1991.

CHAPTER 6

The Church's Role in Defining Genuine Democracy In Africa

Clement Majawa

Introduction

Many African countries are still being ruled by autocratic regimes even though the majority among them have already celebrated their independence. The facts on the ground indicate that *genuine democracy* has not yet been achieved, thereby raising the inevitable question: Is *democracy* in Africa real or a mirage? In spite of African politicians claiming to be champions of democracy, they neither safeguard it nor uphold the principles upon which a democratic government is founded. The Church should, therefore, play its role of ensuring that *democracy* in Africa takes root: According to *Vatican II,* it is the Church's responsibility to read and interpret the signs of the times, thereby sharing the joys, sorrows, hopes, anguish, oppression, liberation, aspirations as well as integral development of the people and society where it is established. This means that it has to work in solidarity with the human family, as is highlighted in this article in which I emphasize the Church's role in defining genuine democracy for Africa.

The Meaning of Democracy and the Need to Adapt It to Different Situations

According to some political analysts, *democracy* has a wider meaning than the one given to it in the classical treatises on the science of government. In the former's view it is, first and foremost, a general philosophy of human and political life: people's state of mind, their socioeconomic growth, and any form of recognized or legitimate government. It should be compatible with human dignity and social viability. A monarchy can, therefore, be democratic if it is consistent with the principles of this philosophy. The dynamism involved here is what Abraham Lincoln termed, "a government of the people, by the people and for the people." According to this definition, many European countries are democratic, albeit in different ways, whereas most African countries have not experienced true *democracy*. It needs to be noted, however, that the application of the reality of *democracy* in Africa and other developing countries should be different from the way it is done in Europe and North America. As John Ndlobvu states in his book, *Democracy in Africa: A Copy of European Political Philosophy:*

> Democracy in Africa will be meaningful if it is intrinsically different from political categories of the European countries. Just as the Western politics followed the European pattern of thought, African democracy should respect and follow African philosophy and worldview.[1]

The important thing is not to find new names for *democracy*, but to discover its essence and implement it in different countries. For instance, as far as some political critics are concerned, what the young democracies of Africa need is to become stable. Therefore, political, economic, and social endeavors must be subordinated to this one goal, even if doing this supports the status quo and compromises justice. This, no doubt, jeopardizes the basic principle of *democracy* as a people-centered government, elected by the people, to serve the people, with leaders holding on to just that much power which is constitutionally allowed to them by voters. However, if such a people-centered government lacks executive, legislative, judicial, and political gist as well as built-in tools of *checks and balances,* then it breeds the worst forms of injustice, poverty, and oppression. This affirms Winston Churchill's argument that democracy is a terrible way of choosing a government, except that every other known way is worse. No political system of government is perfect.[2] Many people support this Churchillian view, especially since some African democracies have proved to be disastrous right from the beginning of the political campaigns through elections. This raises the question: Why do most young democracies in Africa fail to develop and blossom?

Obstacles to Democracy in Africa

(i)   People's ignorance of democratic principles
For any system of government to become pragmatic and relevant, the people must have a mature civic education.[3] This is lacking in many African countries, especially with regard to principles of *democracy*. The majority of the people at the grassroot can't even differentiate

between a democratic and a dictatorial government. To them *democracy* is a foreign commodity wrapped in a foreign package and presented as a foreign philosophy using foreign methodology. Consequently, legitimately elected governments in Africa are doomed to fail right from the beginning because they neither give civic education to the electorate nor organize free and fair elections. People come to the polls completely ignorant of what is expected of them. They, therefore, vote into office wrong candidates whose interests are power and wealth, but not serving the people who elected them. This group of leaders has no intention of establishing healthy channels of communication between them and the electorate, so they quickly forget the promises they made to the people during political campaigns.

(ii) The unjust social structures

The unjust social structures in Africa breed poverty, dependence, disease, and death. This is what prompted Dr. Bakili Muluzi, the President of the Republic of Malawi, to argue that:

> Democracy without food, clothing, shelter, healthy and educational facilities is void. People do not eat "democracy." A hungry and poor person cannot appreciate democracy. Everybody should take part in the process of eradicating social injustice.

It is the structures of exploitation and domination that cause poverty in Africa. Centuries of colonial rule, poor political leadership, and the international economic system have played a major role in impoverishing the continent. Capitalism (an economic system characterized by freedom of the market with private and corporate ownership of the means of production and distribution operated for profit) has also contributed to the economic woes of the people. It has stimulated the human appetite for wealth, power, and profit, thereby institutionalizing evils like exploitation, corruption, crime, discrimination, privileged classes, poor-rich dichotomy, etc. It has also created an elite class of very wealthy and propertied individuals who, in conjunction with international capitalistic forces around the world, amass wealth at the expense of the majority of the people. The few wealthy and powerful tycoons (state presidents, government ministers, top military and police *officers, judges* and lawyers, businessmen, etc.) exploit the poor, totally blind to the tatter's sufferings, needs, rights, fundamental claims to life, justice, liberty, and pursuit of happiness. They create an environment where bribery, embezzlement of public funds, organized murder sagas, illicit and immoral contracts as well as questionable business deals become the order of the day. This becomes an ideal situation for human misery, social inequalities, and economic woes. There is an urgent need, therefore, that such sinful structures of exploitation, domination, and coercion be condemned by all people of goodwill.

(iii) Nepotism based on tribal affiliations

In his book, *Patterns of Dominance*, Philip Mason describes how tribal groupings acquired dominance, often by accident, but eventually became the motive for a universal process which could earmark the group for dominance throughout the history of civilization. Such a process can be racial, tribal, religious, economic, cultural, moral, or social, but the end product is a group of people justifying their superiority, perpetuating their power by military, social, or judicial instruments while demanding gratitude from all the people whom they rule.[4]

Tribal groupings in Africa have shaped people's philosophy and worldview in such a way that whatever they do or say has tribal bearings. This is detrimental to democracy because tribal loyalties tend to influence presidential and parliamentary elections, job promotions, and appointments to various offices. This creates an atmosphere where tension, indifference, laziness, jealousy, oppression, and all sorts of injustices abound. It also impedes democracy since tribal loyalties naturally overpower democratic ones.

To safeguard democracy, therefore, it is important to separate tribal and national affairs. Where the two have been mixed, there has been democratic disaster, especially when one tribe imposes itself on the nation as the only one with the right and authority to dominate the other tribes. A case in point is the Tutsi and Hutu of Burundi and Rwanda. A scenario where cabinet positions or departmental heads are allocated to a single tribe should be avoided at all costs. No one tribe can have a concentration of personality, talent, training, and experience in any area of government. A situation like this only stagnates democracy, which can contribute greatly to the task of nation-building.

(iv) Government failures mistaken for democracy

Political campaigns in Africa consist of promises like job opportunities, abundant food, low-cost houses, better health facilities, poverty eradication programs, various freedoms, etc., to the people. This raises high hopes, especially among the poor, who are the majority. But, with time, as the new regime shows no signs of fulfilling its *manifesto,* most people become disillusioned. They erroneously associate the government's shortcomings with *democracy.* In such an atmosphere of broken promises, people lose trust in the government. Consequently, young democracies in Africa have not become pragmatic because they have failed to live up to the people's expectations. This, coupled with a poor economy, has hindered democratic growth, thereby blocking *democracy* from being incorporated into the national life. Poverty, ignorance, disease, poor work ethics, and the exploitation of peoples have contributed greatly to this sad state of affairs.

(v) An environment where political intolerance thrives

Democracy encourages multipartyism, a system which creates an atmosphere where people agree to disagree so as to accommodate each other's different political views in a family atmosphere. This, however, -is not the case in most African countries where, once one party has been voted into power, the losing party refuses to accept the results of the elections, accusing the electoral commission of fraud and rigging the elections. This undermines democratic ideals which are based on trust. Therefore, any negative attitude erodes *democracy* and causes a lot of suffering, displacement, and death for the people. But, it needs to be noted that a multi-party system by itself does not guarantee democracy. Some of the worst vote-rigging practices are carried out in countries with more than one political party. Democratic principles must be adhered to.

Although some people argue that democracy can still flourish and hold a nation together under a one-party system, many political philosophers maintain that a one-party system of government does not encourage democratic governance. One of the fundamental principles of democracy is that it must provide an opportunity for a free alternative government. This ensures that leaders relinquish power when they are voted out and that they do not misuse their authority to stay in office. *Democracy* gives the voters the power to change their leaders. Any obstacle to this ideal, therefore, is bound to breed frustration and resentment, and, if ignored, it can be disastrous to a nation. Besides causing anarchy in the country, it may just replace one incompetent regime with another as the case has been in Ethiopia and the Democratic Republic of the Congo.[5]

(vi) An immoral society

The general decline in the moral standards in the African society has resulted in widespread abuse of the freedom of the individual and disregard for human rights. When a government lacks spiritual and moral integrity, it becomes a breeding place for bad politics which cannot promote democratic principles. What Africa needs now is the spiritual maturity necessary for forming a democratic society in which human rights and integral development are guaranteed and safeguarded. It is only spiritual values which will transform the society to become democratic.

In, *Theology of Political Science,* Alexander Kihawayu states that industrialization and urbanization are destroying many African traditional values and religious insights. These are being replaced by a feverish drive for material gain and power-struggle which have not only weakened people's spiritual and moral fiber, but have also seriously damaged the very foundation of the extended family.[6]

In spite of the fact that people go to church, mosque, or shrine to pray regularly, many of them seem to be losing meaning in life. But, faced with the task of nation-building and economic development, Africans need to become God-fearing and respectful to one another because this is what will create an atmosphere that will nurture *democracy.*

Gospel Values: A Firm Basis on Which to Build Democracy

In Luke 4:18–19, Christ presents His mission policy by quoting from the *Prophet Isaiah* as follows:

> The Spirit of the Lord is upon me, because He has chosen me to bring good news to the poor. He has sent me to proclaim liberty to the captives, sight to the blind, freedom to the oppressed and to announce that the time has come when the Lord will save his people.[7]

The *theology of democracy* Christ articulates above has been the basis for the Church's service to the poor, the oppressed, the abandoned, its commitment to the transformation of evil societal structures, and its determination in enforcing genuine democratic principles in the world. Commissioned by Christ to establish God's Kingdom on earth, the Church must work toward justice, freedom, peace, *democracy,* and love for all people. It has a duty, to reflect God's love and concern for humanity. His plan, according to the Scriptures, was that people live peacefully in freedom and justice. *Exodus, Leviticus, Numbers, Judges,* and wings are narrations of God's liberating acts among the people of Israel. God still operates within a similar universal framework in which liberation, democracy, and development of God's people takes place.

It needs to be pointed out, however, that Gospel values cannot be compromised in favor of *democracy* or any other political system. As Buhlmann points out in *Christianity & Philosophy of Western Capitalism,* the fundamental distinction between "the things that are Caesar's, and those that are God's" (Mark 12:13–17) must be maintained.[8] He further argues that no doctrine or human opinion, no matter how true it may be, except for only esoteric things revealed by God, should be imposed upon Christians and a democratic government.[9] But, a Christian is free to choose in favor of any political affiliation so long as it does not trespass against God's commandments and the natural law. A good Christian is essentially a responsible politician (good citizen). This is what St. Paul means when he exhorts all people to be good citizens who have to listen to political leaders and assist them in enforcing democratic principles in the society.[10]

Christian principles which support democratic governance are found in Christ's teaching in *The Sermon on the Mount.* These guidelines can help *democracy* to grow, to mature, and to lead people to genuine liberation and development. Henry Bergson confirms this by writing in *Essence and Nature of Democratic Government,* "Democracy is evangelical in essence, liberating in nature, and its motive power is love."[12] Gospel values like the fellowship of the human race as children of the Heavenly Father, equality of all people before God, importance of socioeconomic coexistence, and sharing what the Father has provided, respect for human rights, inviolability of conscience, and the awareness of God's justice and providence for all His creatures are a firm foundation on which to build *democracy.*

The Church Fathers' Writings: their impact on democracy
The teachings of many Church Fathers which were based on the Scriptures and Apostolic Tradition have helped to define *genuine democracy* and form the basis of many renowned democratic Constitutions, Legislation, and Judiciary of many governments. Those that have left an impact on democratic governance include:

(i)   Clement of Alexandria's Theologiae Sententiarum
Through this document, the Church Father maintained that every Christian has a duty to support a government which has roots in the Biblical principles of liberty, justice, and legitimization. Good govern-

ance is willed by God. Good obedience to legitimate leadership is also willed by God. One can be a good Christian and achieve one's salvation while defending a political philosophy other than the political egalitarianism, just as one was able to be a practicing Christian in the days of the Roman Empire while accepting the regime of slavery, or while holding to the political rule of unquestionable dictatorship.[13]

(ii) Polycarp's De Trinitate Expositio

In this book, the martyr who died in 155 A.D. pointed out that leaders in secular society are God's ministers and stewards. They have, therefore, to look after the people with love, justice, and humility. Most of all, they have to help the people of God attain the eternal life that was won by Christ on Calvary. He further stressed that Christianity is simply living effectively and affectively, building healthy relationships between the Creator and the creatures. In his view, Christianity provides guidelines for the right way of achieving liberty and progress without exploiting others through jealousy, greed, or war. The community which embraces faith, hope, and love, embraces the Trinitarian God and Trinitarian liberty.[14]

(iii) St. Justin's Dialogus cum Tryphone

Here, the Saint advised that every government must honor and advance the welfare of society as well as the dignity and total vocation of the human person. It is important that every human being created in the image of God understands and obeys intelligently God's Law in the community. The voter and the elected should both follow this Law since nobody is above it and nobody is beside it. It is only the person who is guided by the Divine Law that becomes the source, the center and the purpose of societal living toward liberty and salvation.[15] This was confirmed by St. Basil in *Destraum Lorrea Mea,* when he wrote:

> The fundamental purpose of societal governance and living must not be the mere living together without a vision. It must not be a mere multiplication of citizens for a big state. It must not be for personal fame, or profit, or domination. Rather, it must be for the service of God and human beings; and indeed of the whole human beings, viewed in terms of Christian principles and the demands of his intellectual, moral, cultural, spiritual and religious life. Christian life should not be separated from genuine politics, since the two vocations are the servants of the same Trinitarian God.[16]

(iv) St. Augustine's Humanae et Regulae Pastoralis Liber

Here, the Saint stressed that political leaders are duty-bound to care for the weak and poor members of the society by ensuring that justice, where the lowest in the society have a share of the created goods, is adhered to. Under Divine Law, every public officer is obliged to promote the cause of the poor at all costs and not merely out of the former's superfluous goods. Material benefits, where need arise, should be given with love while aiming at helping the recipients to develop themselves toward independence. The Saint observed further that the greatness and prosperity of a government is determined by how its poorest are cared for. When every citizen (rich and poor alike) is empowered with knowledge, energy, and tools for wholistic liberty and progress, then he/she serves best the community for the common good and salvation.[17]

Pre–Vatican II Papal Encyclicals and Address' Effect on Democracy

The *Papal Encyclicals* and *Address* that gave insights on the relationship between the Church and State before the *Second Vatican Council* include the following:

(i) *Rerum Novarum*

This was issued in 1891 by Pope Leo XIII. It stated clearly that the Church is neither a political entity nor can it be dragged into party politics. Although the Holy Father recognized the fact that in any democratic government there should be *the right* to private property, and the workers' right to form associations and to receive just wages, he criticized egoistic desires for political power, exploitation, and unchecked competition. He warned against extreme socialists and other movements hostile to the State and to religion. In so doing, he was laying a foundation for the difference between Church and State. This means that the Church is not committed to any particular form of government as long as the Church is free to function.[18] Later, however, the Holy Father accepted the independence of Catholic political parties which could act on their own. He made it clear that a Catholic political party was *not* the Catholic Church, and Catholic Christians were free to join that party or not. The Pontiff understood the signs of the times, and saw that there was need to face the fact that the new democratic governments were here to stay since the old regimes were either dead or were dying. The Church would, therefore, have to deal with a society which would have many political parties.

(ii) *Quadragesimo Anno*

In this *Encyclical,* Pope Pius XI argued that to solve the many political problems in society, the Church had to teach, to safeguard and facilitate an ongoing interpretation of justice, liberty, and development in democratic governments. According to him, *genuine democracy,* which is an essential part of human existence, is linked to Christianity. Furthermore, the democratic impulse that has risen in human history as a temporal manifestation of the Gospel message and Christianity, rooted in the Scriptures, is the leaven of *genuine* democracy. It teaches responsible citizenship, bears the light of hope for humankind, and guides the State in democratic affairs. It is the secular democratic world and secular integral development that provides a basis for Christianity to work in molding Church and State, faith and *democracy,* without contradiction. [19]

(iii) *Papal Address*

During World War I, Pope Benedict XV (1914–1922) defined the role of the Church amidst the great tragedies of his time. Although the fighting sides accused him of favoritism, he remained *neutral* throughout the war because he knew that there were thousands of Catholic Christians in both camps fighting against each other. His fatherly counsel was that in any political tension, the leaders of governments should end their misunderstanding through prayer and diplomatic means. If the demands of justice and equity are to be satisfied in the world, then vigorous diplomatic efforts must be made without violence to the rights of persons or to the natural characteristics of each government.[20]

He maintained that the Church needs to play an active role in assisting the poor, the suffering, and the dying in times of peace or war. His efforts in alleviating the sufferings of the people and assisting prisoners of wars gave the Church, in general, and the Papacy, in particular, a new prestige. He encouraged military chaplaincy so as to provide spiritual care for the soldiers on the battlefield. He also saw the need for the Church to take up a leading role in diplomatic discussions of ending the war. He was even willing to accept the new governments and have diplomatic relations with most of them because this was the best way the Church would influence the world to foster democratic principles in a free government.

Vatican II's Contribution to Democracy

Numbers 63 to 93 of *Gaudium et Spes* (*The Pastoral Constitution on the Church in the Modern World*) explain the relationship between the Church and the State. It gives the nature and goal of modern politics by specifying the Church's special responsibility to guide governmental politics and to draw attention to the ethical and religious dimensions of democratic politics. In view of the question: How do specific models of politics either help or hinder people's response to liberty, justice and development toward their transcendent vocation? The *Constitution* points out in *Number 64* that the soul of *"democratic politics"* is the human being in the totality of his "interior dimension."[21] The main points raised in the *Constitution* regarding political life include:

i.   The fact that cultural, economic, and social evolution among people has led to changes which have had great impact on the life of the political community, especially on issues concerning universal rights and duties. This is a challenge the Church must address very seriously if it is to help solve modern political problems.[22]

ii. That the Church has a duty to make people aware of their role in politics. They need to be empowered to voice their honest opinions regarding any kind of government, especially where civil, moral, or religious liberty is denied to them, thereby making them victims of ambition and political crimes. It is their right to denounce a regime which fails to pursue the common good, but serves the rulers' selfish interests.[23]

iii. That people must be free to choose government leaders because political authority, whether in the community or in institutions representing the State, should be moral and work for the common good. Since nobody is above the law, it is lawful for citizens to defend their rights against any abuse of authority, provided their defense is within the limits of natural law and the Gospel.[24]

iv. That political leaders must avoid blocking the development of family, social, or cultural groups as well as voluntary bodies and institutions. These groups should exist and implement their lawful constitutional rights without any political hindrance. Citizens, too, should guard against granting the elected government too much power and authority so as to avoid abuse and suppression.[25]

v.   That Christians must be patriotic, generous, and loyal to their country, but be open-minded in their outlook. They ought to be aware of their special and personal vocation to assist the legitimate government to foster liberty, justice, and development.[26]

vi.   That any democratic government should tolerate many political parties since conflicting socioeconomic political views are necessary for building a healthy nation. Christians are, therefore, called upon to respect other people's political parties, provided these are rooted in Gospel values. To achieve this objective requires civic and political education for all citizens.[27]

vii. That both Church and State serve God's people, where the former is the *Conscience of the government's temporal affairs.* Therefore, the role and competence of the Church must never be confused with the political community or bound to any political system. It should always be a sign and a safeguard of the transcendence of the human person. In this way, the political community and the Church remain mutually independent and self-governing.[28]

viii. That Christians must obey legitimate political leaders and participate actively in their government's efforts towards integral development. But, they should not limit themselves to the material welfare, but should strive to promote Gospel values by the way they live out their life's vocation. [29]

ix.   That the Church hierarchy should help political leaders to define *genuine democracy* and implement it. The former should, however, guard against political bribery and flattery. They should be cautious to accept privileges and donations from the civil authority.[30]

x.   That the Church plays its prophetic role effectively. It should boldly denounce all structures of injustice and oppression, the society as well as give constructive criticism and pass moral judgments on matters touching the socioeconomic political order. This can be done through teaching, preaching, and providing guidance to the society by means of *Pastoral Letters.* The Church's mission in the world is to promote liberty, peace, justice, and development among all people, for God's glory.[31]

Pope John Paul II's Social Encyclicals: Sources of Inspiration for Democracy

Pope John Paul II's following *Social Encyclicals* are his reflections on economic, political, and cultural issues insofar as these affect the common welfare of people in society (families, communities and nations):32

(i) *Laborem Exercens* (14 September, 1981)

This is the *Encyclical* in which the Holy Father explains the dignity and role of human work in modern society. His ideas, if taken seriously, can enhance *democracy*, liberty, and development in the society. He urges the Church to teach the importance of work ethics to people so that they can be dedicated to work:

> Through work a person must earn his bread and contribute to the continual advance of science and technology in the society. It is on the eve of new development in technological, economic and political conditions which will influence the world of work and production, and bring true development to democratic govern-ments. Every work should be done for the glorification of God and perfection of creation.[33]

(ii) *Sollicitudo Rei Socialis* (30 December, 1987)

This ethical and theological *Encyclical* analyzes the economic, political, social, and cultural dimensions of world development. The Church is hereby called upon to address itself seriously to (a) lack of effective international solidarity, (b) political rivalry between East and West, and (c) uncontrolled production and selling of deadly arms.

The *Encyclical* also emphasizes that genuine development in a democratic government must be integral (taking into account human beings in the totality of their bodily and spiritual existence). True liberty, justice, and development needs to be based on human dignity which stems from the fact that a human being is created in God's image and likeness (Genesis 1:26–27) and is to exercise *dominion* over creation (Genesis 1:28). This mandate to responsible stewardship and developing the earth is, therefore, everyone's response to the Divine Vocation.[34] Governments have a duty to realize democratic principles which will enable people to respond to their Divine Vocation. This means that each government must reform the unjust structures in its political institutions and replace corrupt and dictatorial forms of government with democratic and participatory ones.[35]

(iii) *Centesimus Annus* (1 May, 1991)

The *Encyclical* looks into such issues as *principles of genuine democracy, human work in politics, new capitalism* and *free market economy.* It reiterates the Church's traditional teaching on the natural right to private property. This is an extension of human freedom, necessary for *the autonomy and development of the person*[36] in view of the following questions: With the failure of communism, should capitalism be regarded as the victorious social system? Should capitalism become the goal for developing countries which are making efforts to rebuild their economies and societies?[37] Regarding the political system of *new capitalism* or *the free market economy,* the *Encyclical* offers the following advice:

> There is the risk of an idolatry of the market in the system of new capitalism. The idolatry of free market economy ignores the existence of goods which by their nature are not and cannot be mere commodities. Many human needs are unable to be satisfied by recourse to market mechanisms. The government, therefore, must provide for the defense and preservation of common goods such as the natural and human environment.[38]

The *Encyclical* also highlights the Church's vision of the dignity of the person revealed in all its fullness in the mystery on the Incarnate Word."[39] The tone of the *Encyclical* clearly favors *authentic democracy* as the political system suitable for fostering human dignity. This is an indication that the Church promotes the democratic system because the latter encourages *subsidiarity* and *solidarity,* which are basic principles of the Catholic Social Doctrine. It is in *democracy* that the structures of *participation* and *shared responsibility*, which are essential for *subsidiarity*, can be nurtured. True *democracy* will also foster *solidarity* within organizations, societies, and between countries as well as international organizations.[40]

Since there are some socioeconomic and political problems which need a faith approach that can only be provided by the Church, governments need to collaborate with the Church on some crucial national issues. The Church is the medium through which God's message of salvation to humanity is interpreted. It, therefore, contributes to the enrichment of human dignity, the anthropomorphic values of liberty, justice, peace, and integral development.[41] To achieve this, it needs the democratic system, since the latter ensures the participation of citizens in making political choices and guarantees that the people elected to office are accountable to the public and can be replaced through peaceful means when their terms expire. *Authentic democracy* has to be nurtured through the advancement of orthodox education and formation in true socio-economic, political, and theological ideals.[42]

The *Encyclical* encourages developing countries to emulate the positive ideas, from the developed West, but avoid scandals like abortion, extreme promiscuity, religious indifference, excessive materialism, moral decadence, blind pursuit of scientific prominence, violence, unnatural gay relationships, etc., because these behaviours demean human dignity. Developing countries should shun financial or material assistance which is attached to these immoral elements of apathy.[43] The *Encyclical* challenges the State to streamline all economic activities in line with democratic, institutional, juridical, and political principles. It should guarantee and protect all forms of freedom, human rights, individual and national property, stable currency, and efficient public services. But, in case of tension, conflict, and misunderstanding in the government (between political parties or organizations), the Church has the responsibility to bring the conflicting parties together and act as a democratic intermediary.[44]

The Church's Role in Establishing Genuine Democracy in Africa

The *Pontifical Encyclicals* and *Vatican II Documents* referred to in this article, present the Church as *servant* and not *lord, liberator* and not *oppressor, development oriented* and not *conventionally static*. To fulfill this role effectively, the Church must be people-centered. It has to take a leading role in defining democratic principles which will ensure freedom, justice, and development for the people by:

(i) Challenging the government to create structures that will liberate people from poverty and injustice

In Africa, the Church must liberate the poor, become the voice for the voiceless, and fight for the human rights of the marginalized. This should be done in an atmosphere of prayer, dialogue, peace, and love. The aim should be to change the social structures which breed poverty, injustice, immorality, conflict, and death. As stated in *Gaudium et Spes*, "The social order requires authentic improvement. It must be founded in truth, built on justice, enlivened by love. It should grow in freedom towards a more humane equilibrium." [45]

The Church in Africa needs to identify itself with the poor and suffering masses in more ways than mere *charity (handouts)*. It has to conduct seminars/workshops in civic education at the grassroot level. These will make people aware of their basic human rights so that they can stand up and demand for them where they are deprived of these God-given rights. People will thus be transformed into self-supporting and responsible citizens. By so doing, the Church will also liberate and transform itself. It is this type of *self-transformation ecclesiology* that Africa needs today. The problems of extreme poverty and social injustice throughout the continent make it imperative for the Church to embark on humanizing and Christianizing Africans, freeing them from poverty and exploitation, and transforming the face of the continent and that of the Church. In liberating Africa, the Church also liberates itself. For it is not only the individual poor persons in the Church but even the

Church itself that should be liberated and transformed through altruistic service like prophetic criticism of social institutions to transform and energize human society by promoting God's Kingdom here on earth.

(ii) Initiating programs of integral development in collaboration with the State so as to bring about genuine democracy

To provide meaningful and relevant development for the people, the Church and the government must collaborate. It is the latter's primary role to direct and coordinate efforts toward achieving social and economic development. The Church and the voluntary agencies must, therefore, integrate their services into the government plan and strategy for development projects. Both Church and State have to educate the people of their responsibility to work for human and socioeconomic development of their country.

Integral development should involve the improvement of the quality of life and *not* just the quantity of goods produced. Consequently, people's use of material goods should reflect God's Plan of Salvation: They have to refrain from possessions and riches as these will not lead them to happiness. In promoting human development, the Church should help people to discern God's will for them here on earth. This means that its developments should be people-centered so as to make them self-reliant. Even in cases where the Church receives financial aid from the government or other foreign donor agencies, it should avoid *ad hoc* projects and reject money or material aid which burns people into perpetual beggars by destroying their self-respect. Any assistance that comes with a bait attached to it jeopardizes true development and blocks the process of genuine democratization.

(iii) Offering constructive criticism to the government where the latter is not open to authentic democracy

The Church has a duty to give people civic education whereby they will be taught principles of *democracy.* This will enable them to appreciate the democratic fruits of liberty, justice, and development. For this to happen, the government has to be open to constructive criticism from the people, since *democracy* is a government of the people. They must be alert to know when a government lacks the mechanism of *checks and balances*, as such a situation can become oppressive, unjust, and ceases to be democratic because it will not tolerate different views from the Church, legitimate opposition parties, professionals, the media, non-partisan *Non-Governmental Organizations*, and the country's legislative and judicial systems.[46]

A democratic system encourages people to have representative discussions with their leaders. The Church must, therefore, create awareness in the people so that they can demand their human rights where these are denied them. It is *democracy* that will ensure that people's God-given rights are not denied them by selfish leaders who usurp rights of the people. By safeguarding human rights, the Church will promote responsible multipartyism, thereby controlling the ruling party from suppressing legitimate opposition parties. All political parties are expected to work together harmoniously for the well-being of their respective countries. People's interests (regardless of party affiliation, creed, tribe, region/province, status quo) should take the first priority: A strong opposition party is, therefore, necessary for creating a conducive atmosphere for an efficacious democratic government where there is a constant exchange of constructive ideas between the rulers and the ruled. This will provide an opportunity for everyone to make his/her political contribution to the best of his/her knowledge and ability. Consequently, there will be a fair distribution of the instruments of power with political responsibility shared by the maximum number of people (*authentic democracy*).

(iv) Helping people to build a spiritual and moral society

The Church has a prophetic role to interpret God's will to people especially in spiritual and moral matters. In this way, it makes each person aware of his/her Divine calling and living up to it. As O'rielly points out in *Government and Christian Principles*, "Without God in the democratic process, there is no hope for freedom, justice, progress and socioeconomic fraternization."[47] Therefore, a good government should respect the principle of *right and wrong* which is taught by almost all religions of the world.

The Church in Africa is especially challenged to instill in people spiritual values which will counterbalance society's obsession with wealth and materialistic gains. It needs to make people aware that a Godless government is a doomed government as is reflected in the following Scripture text: "What does it profit a person to acquire the whole world but lose his/her very soul?"[48] Therefore, building a genuine democratic government calls for a spiritual and moral lifestyle for each person.

(v) Fighting against corruption at all levels

Africa's economic progress has been greatly hampered by corruption which has undermined the leaders' moral fiber and destroyed people's power to fight it. A corrupt system cannot fight itself. It is only the Church which can stand up against *corruption* in line with *Ex 23:8,* which states that, "You shall take no bribe, for a bribe blinds the officials; and subverts the cause of those who are in the right."[49] It is the Church's responsibility, therefore, to eliminate *corruption* from within and from without. As "the light of the world" (Matthew 5:14) it has to show the way in situations where society has been blinded by *corruption.*

If each Christian joins the battle against *corruption* by being actively involved in eliminating it,[50] the Church will have a great impact in this delicate area. Christians in influential positions can use their good offices to influence those around them by refusing to give or accept bribes in the course of discharging their duties. This will, certainly, weaken corrupt systems which will eventually collapse. The Church must, therefore, take a bold stand in its condemnation of corruption in society. It should also be ready to face persecution in this struggle against corrupt social structures. Christians should not only refuse to give or receive bribes, but they should courageously speak out against this evil practice and expose corrupt dealings at all levels. This is no easy task given that *corruption* has become a way of life in many African countries, but it has to be a response to Christ's mandate:

> So if anyone declares himself for me in the presence of human beings,
> I will declare myself for him in the presence of my Father in heaven.
> But the one who disowns me in the presence of human beings, I will
> disown him in the presence of my Father in heaven. (Matthew
> 10:32–33)

(vi) Safeguarding cordial coexistence between Church and State

Church and State are God-given institutions, for glorifying God as well as preparing people for eternal life and for enforcing law, order, justice, liberty, progress, and mutual coexistence in society respectively. The Church appeals to people's hearts and consciences to maintain peace, order, and harmony upon which democratic systems that form a sound government are built. Having been given the mandate from Christ "to teach and make disciples of all nations," (Matthew 28:19) it has the Divine right to guide and direct God's people by criticizing and condemning the unjust and oppressive social structures.

In preaching Christ's message, the Church should never compromise this *Good News of Salvation* to make it palatable to politicians. It should not be lured into some politicians' trap of claiming that since the government has granted *freedom of worship* to the Church, the latter should be submissive to the State as a gesture of appreciation. *Freedom of worship* is a God-given right to people; no government deserves credit for this. The Church need not be used as a platform for polities gains because it is not a government department. However, Church and State must have a healthy relationship. The two institutions should exist in harmony and mutual respect, recognizing each other as independent and distinct entities in their office and function for the same people. This will help people to be loyal to both in the task of establishing *genuine democracy* rooted in God and based on liberty, justice, and respect for human life.

Conclusion

A free and democratic society is the ideal that every nation should be striving for. Human beings are in constant search for free expression of their ideas and integral development. This desire for freedom and development is at the heart of people's struggles throughout their lives. Thus the Church's crucial role of guiding them as they fight against "sins of injustice and exploitation, and the structures produced by these sins." To do this, the Church should put in place pastoral programs which will empower people to take full responsibility in building up the society. This is a task that calls for serious commitment to creating an atmosphere where *genuine democracy and development* can flourish; a slow process which should be undertaken in a spirit of mutual trust. Although many failures and imperfections in this area have been witnessed in Africa, it is encouraging to note that some African governments are seriously moving toward attaining *genuine democracy.* This is the only way Africa will change its image from that of poverty, suffering, and death to that of justice, liberty, and development. In this way, the words of the Prophet Micah, "What Yahweh wants of you is to do justice, to love kindness and liberty, and to walk humbly with her God" will rightly apply to Africa.[51]

Rev. Dr. Clement Majawa holds a Master's Degree in Spirituality (Angelicum— Rome) and a Doctorate in Dogmatic Theology (Urbaniana—Rome). He is the Pastoral Coordinator of Blantyre Archdiocese in Malawi. His address is: Mthawira Catholic Parish, P.O. Box 51291, Limbe, Malawi, Central Africa.

NOTES

[1] Ndlobvu, J., *Democracy in Africa: A Copy of European Political Philosophy* (London: St. Paul's Publication, 1996), pg. 85.

[2] Hoernle, G., "A Theory of Liberty" in *Race & Reason Journal* (Johannesburg: Witmasterstrand University Press, 1989), pg. 72.

[3] Gallagher, J., *Christian Democracy and Rights of Men* (San Francisco: St. Ignatius Press, 1991), pg. 476.

[4] Mason, P., *Patterns of Dominance* (London: Heinemann Press, 1982), pg. 74.

[5] Brown, F., *Models of Christian Liberation* (New York: Paulist Press. 1979), pg. 54.

[6] Kihawayu, A., *Theology of Political Science* (London: Heinemann Press, 1988), pg. 125.

[7] Luke 4:18–19.

[8] Buhlmann, R., *Christianity & Philosophy of Western Capitalism* (Cleveland: The Pilgrims Press, 1992), pg. 78.

[9] *Ibid., pg.* 86.

[10] Romans 13:4–7.

[11] Matthew 5:2–12.

[12.]Henric, B., *Essence and Nature of Democratic Government* (Illinois: Thomas More Press, 1975), pg. 701.

[13] Clement of Alexandria, *Theologiae Sententiarum*, III, q. 5, a. 4.

[14] Polycarp, *De Trinitate Expositio*, V., q. 10. a. 8.

[15] St. Justin, *Dialogus Cum Tryphone*, Pars. VI. q. 17, a. 15.

[16] St. Basil, *Destram Lorrea Mea*, Pars. IX, q. 3, a. 4.

[17] St. Augustine, *Humanae et Regulae Pastorales Liber*, Pans. II, Art. 2.

[18] Leo XIII, *Rerum Novarum*, AAS 23 (1891), pg. 649.

[19] Pius XI, *Quadragesimo Anno'* AAS 23 (1931), pp 200–201.

[20] Benedict XV, *Radio Address to Political Leaders of the World* (1915).

[21] *Gaudium et Spes* (G. S.), no. 64.

[22] *G.S.* no. 73.

[23] *Ibid.*, no. 73.

[24] *G. S.* no. 74.

[25] *G. S.* no. 75.

[26] *Ibid.*

[27] *Ibid.*

[28] *Ibid.*, pg.76

[29] *Ibid.*

[30] *Ibid.*

[31] *Ibid.*

[32] Skok, C., "Social Encyclicals" in *The Modern Catholic Encyclopedia,* M. Glazier & H. Hellwig eds. (Collegeville: Liturgical Press, 1994), pg. 281.

[33] Miller, M., ed., *The Encyclicals of John Paul II* (Indiana: Our Sunday Visitor Publications), pg. 152.

[34] John Paul II, *Solicitudo Rei Socialis*, (December 30, 1987), no. 30.

[35] *Ibid.*

[36] John Paul II, *Centesimus Annus*, (May 1, 1991), no. 30.

[37] *Ibid.*, no. 42.

[38] *Ibid.*, no. 40.

[39] *Ibid.*, no. 47.

[40] *Ibid.*, no. 46.

[41] *Ibid.*, no. 47.

[42] *Ibid.*

[43] *Ibid.*

[44] *Ibid.*, no. 48.

[45] G S., no. 26.
[46] O'reilly P., *Government and Christian Principles* (London: Macmillan Press, 1993), pg. 348.
[47] *Ibid.*, pg. 353.
[48] Luke 9:25.
[49] Exodus 23:8.
[50] Cunningham, B., *Theology & Church in Modern Politics* (London: Oxford University Press, 1996), pg. 774.
[51] Micah 6:8.

SELECTED BIBLIOGRAPHY

Abbott, W., ed., *The Documents of Vatican II,* New York: Herder & Herder Press, 1966.

Baum, G., Capitalism–Ex Cathedra in *Health Progress,* 73 (April, 1972), pp. 44–48.

Bayer, R., Christian Personalism & Democratic Capitalism in *Horizon,* 21 (1994), pp. 313–331.

Bergson, H., *Essence and Nature of Democratic Government,* Illinois: Thomas More Press, 1975.

Brown, F., *Models of Christian Liberation,* New York: Paulist Press, 1979.

Buhlmann, R., *Christianity & Philosophy of Western Capitalism,* Cleveland: The Pilgrims Press, 1992.

Byron, W., Solidarity: Path to Development and Peace in *America,* 158 (1988), pp. 445–446.

Cunningham, B., *Theology & Church in Modern Politics,* London: Oxford University Press, 1996.

Fortin E., Free Markets Have Their Limits in *Crisis Magazine,* 10 (November 1992), pp. 20–25.

Gallagher, J., *Christian Democracy and Rights of Man,* San Francisco: St. Ignatius Press, 1991.

Hoernle, G, A Theory of Liberty in *Race & Reason Journal,* Johannesburg: Witmasterstrand University Press, 1989.

John Paul II, *Solicitudo Rei Socialis,* Vatican Press: December 34, 1987.

John Paul II, *Centesimus Annus,* Vatican Press: May 1, 1991.

Kihawayu, A., *Theology of Political Science,* London: Heinemann Press, 1988.

Mason, P., *Patterns of Dominance,* London: Heinemann Press, 1982.

Miller, M., ed., *The Encyclicals of John Paul II,* Indiana: Our Sunday Visitor Publications, pp. 152–155.

Myers, K., ed., *Aspiring to Freedom: Commentaries on John Paul II's Encyclical "Sollicitudo Rei Socialis."* Grand Rapids: Eerdmans, 1988.

Ndlobvu, J., *Democracy in Africa: A Copy of European Political Philosophy,* London: St. Paul's Publication, 1996.

Neuhaus, R., John Paul II's Thoughts on Capitalism in *The First Things,* 41 (1994), pp. 65–67.

O'reilly, P., *Government and Christian Principles,* London: Macmillan Press, 1993.

Weigel, G, ed., *A New World Order. John Paul II & Human Freedom,* Washington: Ethics & Public Policy Press, 1992.

CHAPTER 7

Mission and Social Formation:
Searching for an Alternative to
King Leopold's Ghost

Emmanuel M. Katongole

I n this essay I argue that the greatest challenge facing mission as a force for human socialization is one of social imagination. I define the nature of the sort of social imagination I have in mind as well as the direction it needs to take in Africa in the fourth and last section of the paper. The first three sections of the paper show why the task of social imagination is not only required, it is urgent given the challenges facing Christianity in the 21st century, particularly in Africa. Accordingly, in the first section, which serves as an extended introduction, I outline the key social challenges confronting the church in Africa. In Section II, I briefly examine the alternatives through which the church has tended to view and attempted to meet these challenges. In Section III, I show how these attempts are rendered insufficient in view of the specific story embodied within the nation-state in Africa, thus pointing to the need for social imagination.

The missionaries had come to the Congo eager to evangelize, to fight polygamy, and to impart to Africans a Victorian sense of sin. Before long, however, the rubber terror meant that missionaries had trouble finding bodies to clothe or souls to save. Frightened villagers would disappear into the jungle for weeks when they saw the smoke of an approaching steamboat on the horizon. One British missionary was asked repeatedly by Africans, "Has the Savior you tell us of any power to save us from rubber trouble?"(Hochschild 1998:172)

On July 13th the four bishops comprising the investigating committee published their report. In this they listed all the reasons advanced for or against removing the bishop, and tried to arrange them in some sort of order. This report seemed to support the bishop, but its recommendations seemed to acknowledge the basic justice in the rebel's cause. The first of these recommended that the diocese be split into three new dioceses, and the second that Bawoze remain as a diocesan bishop if requested to do so by any of the three new dioceses, or take early retirement within one year of the acceptance of the report. This report, however, solved nothing, because when Archbishop Okoth on August 10th visited the diocese to communicate the recommendations of the committee, the anti-Bamwoze faction refused to meet him in a hotel and assembled at the cathedral instead. The archbishop refused to speak to the crowd assembled inside on the technicality that he could not enter a cathedral in his province without the consent of the local bishop, and offered to address the crowd outside the cathedral. The "mammoth gathering which had now turned into a mob" insisted that he address them inside the cathedral, and began dragging him there. It was only with considerable difficulty that the archbishop reached his car, and managed to drive off, the "rear window smashed by stones thrown by the wild crowd." On August 27th [bishop] Bamwoze himself was subjected to similar physical violence at Batambogwe (Gifford 1998: 126–127).

I. Introduction: Mission and Social Formation in Africa

(a) Facing "King Leopold's Ghost"

Sometime in the summer of last year, I got a chance to read Adam Hochschild's *King Leopold's Ghost*—a very moving but extremely disturbing book. It recounts the crazy and unstoppable ambitions of King Leopold II of Belgium and his domination and brutal plundering of the Congo Free State. It is the story of untold death, wanton destruction, and civilizing barbarism as Leopold used his mercenary army of *Force Publique* to drive the Congolese natives into mines and rubber plantations, to burn villages and mete out sadistic punishments, including the severing of hands and other forms of dismemberment. In numerous descriptions and personal narratives of survivors, we catch horrifying glimpses of how the natives viewed, endured, and suffered the throngs of what was later to be mythologized as the "wonderful benefits of civilization." This is how, for instance, one Tswambe remembers the state official Léon Fiévez:

> All blacks saw this man as the devil of the Equator . . . From all the bodies killed in the field, you had to cut off the hands. He wanted to see the number of hands cut off by each soldier, who had to bring them in baskets . . . A village which refused to provide rubber would be completely swept clean. As a young man, I saw [Fievez's] soldier Molili, then guarding the village of Boyeka, take a net, put ten

arrested natives in it, attach big stones to the net, and make it tumble
into the river . . . Rubber causes these torments; that's why we no
longer want to hear its name spoken. Soldiers made young men kill
or rape their own mothers and sisters. (Hochschild 1998:166)

In one story after another, the tales of senseless violence are
recounted. What perhaps is even more disheartening than these particular accounts is the realization that these may not be isolated instances
of a particular form of terror (rubber, and limited to King Leopold's
Congo). Rather, as extreme and bizarre as these stories are, they reflect
the sort of memories that will forever remain ingrained about the
colonial presence in Africa. As Hochschild remarks: "What happened
in the Congo could be reasonably be called the most murderous part of
the European scramble for Africa" (Hochschild 1998:280). But is it just
that—"the most murderous part." For "the sad truth is that the men who
carried it out for Leopold were no more murderous than the many
Europeans then at work or at war elsewhere in Africa. Conrad said it
best: "All Europe contributed to the making of Kurtz" (Hochschild
1998:283).

Our intention in drawing attention to Hochschild's book in a
discussion of mission and social formation, however, is not to rehearse
this somewhat familiar and tired argument in which mission would just
be conceived as an extension of this colonial domination. I would
instead wish to see if and what sort of resources mission can offer to
deal with such vicious violence and dispossession. Accordingly, I was
particularly struck by a paragraph in Hochschild's account. Getting
away from the accounts of torture, plundering, and violence, Hochschild
remarks:

> The missionaries had come to the Congo eager to evangelize, to fight
> polygamy, and to impart to Africans a Victorian sense of sin. Before
> long however, the rubber terror meant that missionaries had trouble
> finding bodies to clothe or souls to save. Frightened villagers would
> disappear into the jungle for weeks when they saw the smoke of an
> approaching steamboat on the horizon. One British missionary was
> asked repeatedly by Africans, "Has the Savior you tell us of any
> power to save us from rubber trouble?" (Hochschild 1998:172)

That, I think, is a significant question, today as well, even though
we seem to be living in a completely different set of circumstances.
Even within the Congo, much has changed since the 1890s of King
Leopold. For instance, the Belgian government would soon take over

the administration of the Congo Free State, renaming the territory Belgian Congo; King Leopold died in 1909, Congo became independent (and Congo Kinshasa) in 1960; became Zaire under Mobutu; and has since been renamed (by Kabila) the Republic Democratique du Congo (RDC). The most significant development of all: 70% of Congo's 50.5 million people are now Christians. A lot has changed.

Yet, from another point of view, a very disappointing point of view I must admit, it looks as though not much has changed. Even though Congo remains one of the richest countries in the world in terms of natural, mineral, and cultural resources, the Congolese people, whether under Mobutu's Zaire, or under the RDC of the Kabilas, have continued to live under the grip of massive poverty, military violence, and regimes as disempowering as King Leopold's rubber terror. This is not just true of the Congo, but of a great many African countries. Nigeria, Liberia, Sierra Leone, Rwanda, Angola, to name but a few, all tell the same story of dictatorship, state inspired corruption, the breakdown of social services, etc. Even within the more "promising" African countries by World Bank and IMF statistics, Uganda and Ghana, for instance, their much celebrated recovery or "economic turn around" has still to trickle down to the majority of citizens in terms of a better way of life and of stable structures of peace and progress.

If the name of King Leopold evokes a history of violence and dispossession in the Congo, then there is indeed something like King Leopold's ghost hanging over a great part of Africa. Accordingly, I will use the metaphor of King Leopold's ghost to refer to the economy of violence, dispossession, frustration, and exploitation which greatly characterizes the life of millions on the African continent. Neither Africa's Independence nor what has been dubbed the "second revolution" of the 1980s brought any significant gains for the majority of African peoples, but increasing marginalization and dispossession. Like the frightened villagers in King Leopold's Congo many in Africa today are wondering whether Christianity has any power to save them from this nightmare.

This question (whether Christianity can save Africa) lies at the heart of Christian social ethics in Africa and, in fact, of any discussion on mission and social formation. For, as I understand it, the topic of mission and social formation tries to underscore the role of church in creating conditions for social life in all its forms. I do not think that the assumption that mission creates or at least ought to create conditions for human social life in its richest and fullest sense needs any justification.

After all, mission, as Bediako (Bediako 1995:121) notes following Sanneh, is *Missio Dei*, the same God who in Jesus Christ comes so that "they may have life, and have it to the full" [John 10:9]. What is at stake here is the fact that if such mission has to be relevant for Africa, then the question of whether Christianity can indeed save Africans from King Leopold's ghost is a relevant one. For, the way the church will be able to provide resources to rightly name, confront, and conceive alternatives to this ghostly nightmare will be the litmus test of the church's mission in the 21st century. But this is a challenge not just for the African church, but for all Christian churches. For the way we meet or fail to meet this challenge will reflect on the sort of resources available to us within Christianity, and on the sort of people we have become or at least ought to become if we are to embody the mission of the Church truthfully.

The question is not only significant and relevant. Within the context of Africa, it is urgent for at least two related reasons: First, given the fact that for some inexplicable reason the same continent that seems to be haunted by King Leopold's ghost is a massively Christian continent, and secondly, given the growing skepticism concerning Christianity's ability to "save" Africa. I will briefly tease out the implications of each of these factors.

(b) The two faces of Africa: Probing the connections

The poverty, violence, and distressing social and political conditions in Africa must be seen against the background of Africa as a Christian continent. Recently, Tinyiko Maluleke has drawn our attention to the two valid but often perceived to be disconnected, faces of Africa (Maluleke 1998). On the one hand, there is the picture of a distressed and distressing Africa: widespread poverty, political instability, the civic unrest and ethnic tensions/clashes in many countries. Add to these the tremendous health and infrastructure problems, recently complicated by the HIV–AIDS epidemic (and Ebola), then one sees how dire the situation is. In a slightly earlier article which assesses Africa's situation in the global economic situation, Maluleke depicted Africa as a modern-day Job sitting on the global rubbish dump (Maluleke 1997). A very distressed and distressing picture of Africa which, perhaps not surprisingly, tends to generate an increasing mood of "Afro-pessimism".

There is, however, another face of Africa, of a massively Christian continent, and still growing. A look at recent statistics confirms this picture¹which is not just due to the projected but often misleading accounts of population growth, but to a "momentous outpouring of Christian conversion throughout the continent." In fact, as number of theologians have noted, in Africa, the church is one of the most widely spread and "most sustainable social institutions, especially in the rural areas." (Mugambi 1995:225; Cochrane 1995:90). Such indications of a massive Christian presence on the continent seem to ground a certain optimism not only from the fact that "the Christian way of life is here to stay" (Bediako 1986:229), but also from the sense that the future of the church might perhaps be in Africa.²

But how are these two faces—of a distressed and distressing Africa on the one hand, and, on the other, of a massively Christian continent —to be accounted for, Maluleke (1998:332) asks? Are these two faces of Africa just accidentally or somehow also logically connected to one another? If so, how? Is Africa a distressed continent in spite of its being Christian, or perhaps because of this? What is the relevance of African religiosity for Africans problems? "Is this religiosity authentic, or is it superstition arising from despair?" (Maluleke 1998:330). These are indeed tough questions, which invite (and this is Maluleke's point) an honest and hard introspection as a first step toward a constructive way forward in African theology.

One lesson I have personally drawn from Maluleke's probing questions is the sobering realization that our theological investigations cannot proceed as "usual" by simply suggesting strategies to shoulder, repair, or to make less distressing the distressed Africa, as if we ourselves (the church, Christianity) are external to (outside) the distressed Africa. For as Maluleke notes, Africa's troubles and problems are not just "events, processes and ideologies that take shape outside of the church and of Christianity" (Maluleke 1998:325). Accordingly, our constructive suggestions for a way forward will involve a critical look at the history of the continent which Christianity has either simply assumed or/and unwittingly underwritten, thereby limiting her own resources for naming, let alone confronting and providing an alternative to the story of violence and dispossession on the continent.

(c) A growing skepticism: Can African Christianity be "saved"?

Any discussion of the mission and social formation in Africa must also take place against the backdrop of what seems to be an increasing skepticism, overt or implicit, regarding Christianity's potential role in the positive transformation of Africa. *The Economist* (May 13, 2000) painted a very bleak picture of Africa as a continent slipping further into chaos and despair. The front cover of the issue said it all. Set within a map of Africa against a dark background was the picture of a young man carrying a heavy RPG on his right shoulder and wearing a murderous grin on his face. And above it, the title in big and clear yellow letters: "The Hopeless Continent."[3] Both the level of analysis (shallow) as well as the prognosis of Africa's problems left much to be desired, but I guess one should not expect much of either from this particular publication.[4] What, however, was striking was the eloquent absence of Christianity from the picture. The Christian churches received no mention at all either as part of the landscape of the "Hopeless Continent" or, as I hoped would be the case, as part of the hope. How could the "most sustainable social institution in Africa" be simply and easily written out of the picture, even by a publication like *The Economist*? Was this another confirmation, if one ever needed one, of defective and misleading social analysis on Africa typical of many publications in the West? Or could this be a pointer to a very disturbing realization that, in spite of Christianity's massive presence in Africa, few are willing to take it seriously as a formidable social force?[5] It is not clear how widespread such skepticism is within Africa itself, but given the ambiguous role Christianity has had in Africa, and in more recent cases like Rwanda,[6] skepticism regarding the future role of Christianity in Africa may as well be on the rise. Maluleke himself, in the article referred to above, seems to harbor such doubts regarding the assumption that African Christianity can be shaped into a formidable weapon in the hands of distressed Africans. He notes:

> A question which is not entirely irrelevant for the purposes of our essay is whether the objective of shaping the Christian faith into a formidable weapon in the hands of the oppressed is either feasible or attainable. Can Christianity become a "formidable" weapon? Has it become a formidable weapon? If so, why and how? And again, if not, why and how not? (Maluleke 1998:330)[7]

Coming from one of Africa's leading theologians, such doubts and hesitations need to be taken seriously, especially as they reflect a sense in which the question about Christianity's potential role in the social transformation of Africa is, in a great measure, also a question about Christianity's future in Africa. But we should also be careful not to allow the current shortcomings of the church in Africa to dull our imagination and blind us to the resources which Christianity can provide for social reconstruction. I personally remain a stubborn and hopeless optimist (the result of being both a Christian and an African?) regarding the church's potential for social transformation in Africa. Even then, I realize that for such potential to be realized, we must be willing to move beyond the present conceptions of church as well as present formulations of her social role. In other words, the first and primary challenge before any potential can become available is one of social imagination.

Constructively, the task of social imagination will require nothing less than a recovery of the social *telos* the church or, which is the same thing, a willingness to engage a conversation of what it means for us Christians to be socially formed, thereby offering alternatives to the current narratives and forms of social formations in Africa (I will come back to this in the last section of the paper).What must be noted now is that for such constructive social imagination to become a possibility, it must involve, and, in fact, begin with, a critical and thorough evaluation of some of the assumptions which have greatly shaped the church's social mission generally, in Africa in particular. One such key assumption is the conception of the "social" and "religious" as two distinct spheres. When left unexamined, the distinction works to invest the presumably "neutral" state with the power to define, manage, and determine the particular form the social sphere takes. That this has certainly been the case for Christian social ethics in Africa is obvious from the way the different paradigms of conceiving the church's social role have not questioned the story of the nation-state.

II. Mission and Social Formation: The current paradigms

As a distinct and coherent disciple, Christian social ethics is relatively undeveloped in Africa. This does not mean that contributions within African theology have shown little or no concern for social issues. On the contrary, given the often distressing sociopolitical conditions in Africa, theological contributions have generally felt the need to be relevant to the demands of the time. At the risk of oversimplification, there seem to be three dominant paradigms from which the social concerns affecting Africa have been approached within African theology: a spiritual, a pastoral, and a more explicitly political paradigm. Since these paradigms are not mutually exclusive, the scheme here may just reflect an emphasis adopted in response to a particular need, or just different faces within the mission of the church, generally understood.

(a) A Spiritual Paradigm: Theologians working from this paradigm exhibit the least engagement with social concerns, a trend often associated with evangelical theology but also with the dominant theologies of inculturation. According to this paradigm, the goal of mission is the formation of Christian *spiritual* identity. Among theologians, it is perhaps Kwame Bediako who provides the most articulate expression of this paradigm. Bediako understands his theological task in the "quest and demonstration of the true character of African Christian identity" (Bediako 1992). It is an identity, however, which Bediako understands or characterizes in primarily spiritual terms as the "history of *religious* consciousness"(Bediako 1989:49, emphasis added), and as the process through which "Jesus Christ . . . has become a reality in the universe of their [African's] *religious* ideas, forces, powers and *spiritual* agency" (Bediako 1995:85, emphasis added). Of course it is not the case that Bediako thinks that there is no relationship between this spiritual process and the social/material conditions of the Africans in the world. This spiritual process can have and has had far-reaching consequences.

One such effect, Bediako notes following Sanneh, has been, way in which it has "imbued local culture with eternal significance and endowed African languages with a transcendental range" (Bediako 1995:120). Also, Bediako notes how this "spiritual" process can have significant consequences for African politics where a key problem, which has its roots in the ancestral world, is a tendency to sacralize power and authority. In contrast to this view of authority, one is confronted within Christian theology with Jesus Christ, who desacralizes all earthly powers and politics, thereby checking its inherent tendency to absolutize itself. Accordingly, "the recognition that power truly belongs to God, which is rooted in the Christian theology of power as non-dominating, liberates politicians and rulers to be humans among fellow humans, and ennobles politics" (Bediako 1995: 247). These, however, are not benefits which can be directly pursued by Christians. Rather, they are benefits that kind of "flow over" from the primary challenge of the formation of a true spiritual vocation or identity.[8]

(b) A Pastoral Paradigm: A more recent statement of the commitment to this paradigm can be found in Pope John Paul II's post-synodal extortion, *Ecclesia in Africa*. Coinciding with the 1994 Rwanda genocide, the synodal meeting of bishops expressed great concern about

this event, and about the worsening social, economic, and political conditions of Africa in general. "What has become of Africa?" the pope and bishops wondered (John Paul 1995: #39–40). The synodal bishops were nevertheless convinced that the Church can still make a difference and indeed be "Good News" "in a continent of bad news." What sort of difference?

> For many synodal fathers contemporary Africa can be compared to the man who went down from Jerusalem to Jericho. . . . Africa is a continent where countless human beings . . . are lying as it were, on the edge of the road, sick, injured, disabled, marginalized and abandoned. They are in dire need of Good Samaritans who will come to their aid. For my part, I express the hope that the Church will continue patiently to tirelessly do its work as a Good Samaritan. (John Paul 1995: #41)

To be sure, Catholic social ethics in Africa have been far more complex that this statement from the post-synodal exhortation seems to suggest (Katongole 2001). The statement is, however, consistent with the church's historical role in the provision of education, health, and, more recently, development services generally. Such "outreach" has been sustained not just by a humanitarian concern but by the conviction that the Gospel is a liberating social force which can help the poor to "rediscover their humanity" and regain a sense of dignity. What is particularly noteworthy is the way in which this paradigm is often couched in terms of "intervention"—a response to a crisis (poverty, suffering, instability etc.)—situations which are either the direct result of government policies, or the cumulative effect of the breakdown of government services. Given the dismal failure of the nation-states in Africa, it is not surprising that the Church in Africa has increasingly found herself engaged in programs and services meant to assist marginalized Africans to "recoup their energies so as to put them at the service of the common good" (John Paul 1995: #41).[9] It is in fact against this background that the Christian churches in Africa have increasingly come to understand themselves as "partners in develop-ment"—partners, that is, with the state.

   (c) A Political Paradigm: This paradigm reflects a call for the Church to play a more explicit role of challenging oppressive political structures and urging political reform. The urgency as well as increasing prominence of this paradigm in Africa can be gleaned from a recent

statement by José Chipenda, the Secretary General of the AACC. Responding to, 1994 Rwanda tragedy, Chipenda noted:

> The concern for justice must permeate every action by churches; and justice involves looking at the murky political issues which cause massacres and refugee exoduses and denouncing injustice without taking partisan positions. It seems in the case of Rwanda that de-politicized emergency aid is easier than long range initiatives for justice, peace and reconciliation. (McCullum 44)

In the recent past such "initiatives for justice, peace and reconciliation" have been many, and have taken various forms. The 1993 Leeds Conference on "The Christian Churches and Africa's Democratization" took account of many of these initiatives especially in connection with Africa's second revolution (Gifford 1995; Gifford 1998). They [initiatives] range from pastoral letters issued by bishops and religious leaders (individually and collegially) to denounce injustice, dictatorship and violence to bishops taking a more explicit involvement in the public affairs of society, by chairing national conferences, or commissions of inquiry and/or reconciliation, as the case of the TRC in South Africa clearly indicates. The results of many of these initiatives have been significant, even granting the ambiguous political role of some of the churches (Gifford 1995, 5). Perhaps what we need to note here is how theological discussions within this paradigm often appeal to the justice, democracy, and human rights in a manner that assumes that these notions name (or at least are intrinsic to) the social order which is at once human and Christian. We thus get such calls for the churches to be "midwives of a democratic transition and reconstruction" and to provide an ethos for a culture of justice and human rights (De Gruchy 1995). In what he has called a "theology of reconstruction", Villa-Vicencio has in fact argued that the church not only has a stake in "responsible nation-building," at a deeper level the task of nation–building, democracy, constitutionalism, the promotion and defense of human rights on the one hand and Christian theology on the other converge. Both are about the "affirmation of a God who calls people ever forward to a new, better and transformed society" (Vicencio 1992).

Even though the three paradigms seem to be markedly different in their theological self-understanding, and provide different strategies for engaging the social order, they are sustained by the common assumption of the nation-state as the primary social/political actor. While the focus on a spiritual identity assumes a clear separation of church and state, the pastoral paradigm responds to the crises arising out of the nation-state's failure or breakdown, by positioning the church as a "partner in development." The political paradigm seeks to make the nation-state more just or, which it is assumed will have the same effect, more democratic. None of the paradigms, in other words, have been able to challenge, let alone provide an alternative to, the basic story embodied within the nation-state in Africa. In fact, even within more recent studies which underscore the role of the Christian churches in developing forms of civil society, the need for democracy (and by extension) the nation-state seems to be foregrounded (Gifford 1998; Nelson 1998). Not even within black theology in South Africa, radical as it was (is?),[10] was the nation-state ideology called into question. The moral and political legitimacy of an apartheid state was challenged, but not, it seems to me, the nation-state project *qua* nation-state.

This inability to question the nation-state is perhaps not surprising given the dominant tradition which has shaped Christian social ethics since the Enlightenment. The tradition—a version of what Milbank has characterized as the liberal protestant metanarrative (Milbank 1990: 92)—has tended to move in a Weberian fashion, by assuming that the social and religious constitute two distinct fields each with its own relative autonomy.[11] The effect of this distinction is to underwrite a specific conception of the state–church relationship, in which the state becomes the primary social actor, with power to define, manage, and control the social realm, even as it is acknowledged that the religious field (managed by the church) can have far-reaching social implications.[12]

Once such assumption has been accepted, however; it means that the Church's social mission will always be externally driven, that is, conceived as an "extra" or a contribution to a neutral space which is already "given" (self-defining or defined by some other agency). As long as this is the case, then the need for a critical introspection which may reveal the church's *telos* to be an essentially social *telos* will never arise. Instead the church's relevance or significance as well as her primary challenge becomes one of devising "adequate" strategies or drawing relevant implications from its otherwise "religious" message to make both the state and the social sphere as a whole more nearly just.

Suppose it is the way in which the nation-state defines, narrates, and frames the social sphere which is the problem. Then the church is left with very little resources to challenge that narrative let alone provide an alternative definition, naming, or conception of what it means to be socially formed. This seems to be the case in Africa, where the Christian churches find themselves caught up in an irony of importance and impotence: their massive presence notwithstanding, they have not become a formidable social force. The reason they have not, I suggest, has to do with their inability or failure to both challenge and provide an alternative to the story of the "social" realm which the nation-state in Africa embodies. The latter is a false story based on all sorts of lies and contradictions, particularly the violent suppression and exploitation of local aspirations and differences. It is in this connection that I see the African nation-states as an embodiment, and a tragic perpetuation, of the same story of dispossession, violence, and greed as the one depicted in Adam Hochschild's *King Leopold's Ghost*.

This is a very serious indictment of the nation-state which needs to be substantiated. I therefore need to look closely at the story embodied within the nation-state in Africa with a view of showing how and in what sense this story is false, and how, given its false contradictions, it has tended to inscribe the social order in Africa within an economy of violence and powerlessness. I do so by drawing attention to Davidson's work (Davidson 1992) on the nation-state in Africa.[13]

III. The Nation–State in Africa: On the politics of dispossession

The central thrust of Davidson's argument in *The Black Man's Burden* can easily be stated: Africa's crises of society derive from many upsets and conflicts. But the root problem seems to arise from "the social and political institutions within which decolonized Africans have lived and tried to survive. Primarily, this is a crisis of institutions" (10). More specifically, the crisis relates to the nation-state, "Europe's last gift to Africa"(188) whose introduction to Africa would be shrouded in myriads of ironic contradictions, none perhaps as frustrating to Africa's efforts toward peace and stability as the victory of the national struggle over the social struggle (138).

One way in which Davidson develops this argument is by assembling, at various places in the text, helpful stories and discussions which provide a very interesting comparison of the process of nation-state formation in Europe with the African version of the same. One clear difference between the two is the role which local history— understood as the history of local struggles and aspirations—plays in each process. For example, Davidson recounts how the rise of nation-states in 15–16th century Europe would emerge out of the competing struggle of interests and ambitions, set within a shared history of customs, loyalties, and traditions. The "middle strata" as Davidson calls them (135–8) would play a key role in this process, particularly in aligning their interests with the needs of the "laboring poor" and their hopes for a "better life" and fueling these into a sense of "nationalism" or "national consciousness" that would eventually find embodiment within the nation-state. As Davidson says,

> the rise of nationalism it its nineteenth century context was the outcome of a combination of effort between the rising "middle classes". . . and the multitudinous masses of the "lower orders." . . . Indispensable to nation-states success in all the many upheavals of the nineteenth century . . . were the agitations and uprisings of peasants and urban workers. (134)

Whatever else one can say about the complexity and particular directions these agitations would take in the various European contexts—and Davidson provides helpful asides in this direction—the role of the *social* struggle is foregrounded in the process that would eventually result in the nation–state as some kind of "supreme problem-solving formula" (137) within European history of social existence. In any case, European nation-states are inconceivable except in terms of a *process* of transformation and adjustments within a local history, in which the social struggles would become the crucial factor, exerting, from below as it were, a force (nationalism) that would eventually shape and give legitimacy to the nation-state ideology.

It is precisely this bottom–top process—the valorization of local history and the social struggles it embodies as a force for nation-state formation—which is completely missing and has been, from the very start, subverted within the story of the nation-state in Africa. One notices in the first place that whereas nation-state formation in Europe was a *process*, in Africa it became a *project* which both the departing colonialists and their nationalist bourgeois successors would come to assume as inevitable for Africa's modernization and/or independence. But what is even more noteworthy is the fact that within this "peculiar chemistry of nation-state formation" as Davidson calls it, "the dynamic element which so decisively transformed the social struggle of the masses into the national struggle" was, on the whole, smuggled out of hearing (159). In fact, the social struggle was not just smuggled out of hearing, but intentionally suppressed under the colonial lie of an "Africa without history" (21–51)—without, that is, any experience in social existence, customs, traditions which could serve as a helping starting point in what was seen as an inevitable project of modernizing nation-statism.[14] Already under the colonial dispensation, and within the political and social anthropology that sustained it, but one that would remain greatly unchallenged much into the present time, all such local history would be devalued into "folklore" while the rich wealth of cultures, traditions, and social struggles would come to be branded as "tribalism", and "as such retrogressive."[15] As Davidson notes: "The diversity, it seemed, had to be just another hangover from an unregenerate past" (Davidson 99) which would have to be superseded and overcome by the modernizing project of the nation-state.

Even though one may disagree with some of the assumptions that sustain Davidson's work,[16] his analysis of the factors that came into play in nation-state formation in Africa is highly instructive for locating the contradictions as well a source of many of the problems that would become endemic to African nation–states, thus frustrating Africa's social existence and stability. Five key ones stand out.

First, the fact that the nation-state was accepted as the "only available escape from colonial domination" helps somehow to explain, the superficial character of African nation-states. Not founded on any enduring sense of historical adjustments within the local aspirations and struggles, the nation-state as well as other institutions of Africa's "independence" would evolve out of a void. They were accordingly bound to become "shell states" (12), having juridical statehood, but not empirical statehood. This greatly explains why even today, as Gifford notes, "not a few countries in Africa are countries in a cartological sense only; they are presented in a distinctive color on the map; . . . though they are recognized legal entities, they are not, in a functional sense, states" (Gifford 1998:9).

Secondly, Davidson's analysis also helps to show how a peculiar feature of Africa's politics is the way in which the national struggle remains alienated from the social struggle of the masses. Davidson traces this alienation back to the inherited colonial attitude towards Africa's pre-colonial past. By accepting the story which viewed Africa's pre-colonial history in terms of "tribalism" and stagnation, and committing themselves to modernization and civilization, the "new nationalists" who would become Africa's future leaders, accepted their own self-alienation as a necessary process of liberation (50). But this would also mean that the "national" power which they sought and over which they would come to preside would stand in a constant tension with the local history and social struggle of the masses, from which they had not only become alienated, but set out to overcome in the name of modernity and civilization. In other words, (and the comparison with the European case is obvious), it would not be the struggle for the social improvement of the masses–Africa's 'laboring poor', which would be at the center of, or which would come to characterize, nationalist politics. On the contrary, the "the competing interests of the 'elites' as they began to be called by sociologists and others, took primacy over the combined interests of the 'masses. The 'social conflict'. . . was subordinated to the 'national conflict'" (112).

Thirdly, and what would become a significant aspect of African politics, is the new exploitative relationship that would develop between nationalist politics on the one hand, and the masses and their social struggles on the other. For, as Davidson shows, lacking any social struggle in which it would be grounded, the nationalist rhetoric began to sound vacuous and self-serving.

Once the nationalists realized this, they "discovered" that they needed the masses, and they took steps to recruit them:

> Having formed their parties of national liberation, the educated elite had to chase their (masses') votes. And so they did, penetrating places never before seen, crossing rivers never before encountered, confronting languages never before learned, and all this with the help of local enthusiasts *somehow recruited*. They thus made contact with these "masses" quite often with only the assistance of aged Land Rovers able, with their four-wheeled drive, to go where no other vehicles had ever been, but only just able, and not seldom abandoned by the way. (108) (emphasis added)

We need to dwell a little longer on the phrase "somehow recruited" for its significance for African politics even today. Instead of being a force which shapes and determines the national debates, the masses and their aspirations are only belatedly "discovered" and only "somehow" recruited within the nationalist politics in an occasional, token, and exploitative manner. The various "tribalisms" (in the sense of all local and particular social struggles)—once rejected and dismissed—would now be "discovered" to be potent political capital, to be exploited by the nationalists seeking political power. This factor alone explains the ambiguous role "tribalism" plays within African politics. Leaders openly declare "tribalism" to be the key enemy to national unity, and therefore vow to fight it. Ironically, however, without appealing to some kind of "tribal" loyalty, they would lack even the slight support they have. The "recruitment" also greatly explains how what develops out of this "discovery" of the masses is really not "the politics of tribalism, but something different and more divisive. This was the politics of clientelism" (206).[17] However, except for these occasional "contact with the masses" in search of votes, the aspirations and social struggle of the masses are simply smuggled out of hearing, or censored out of sight. As Davidson notes in relation to the pre-independence nationalists: "Having won their national struggle as they thought, they completely forgot about all the social struggle"(145).

Fourthly, the "somehow recruited" is important from another angle as well, a lesson that Africa would learn soon after independence, when the competing interests of the nationalist elites would increasingly take a violent turn. This outcome should perhaps not be surprising since a political order founded on a violence—in this case, the denial, suppression, and exploitation of local aspirations—would increasingly appeal to violence to affirm its legitimacy. In this sense, the colonial dispensation itself was sustained largely by its coercive sophistication. What, however, would become a distinct feature of post-independence violence of military coups, civil and/or ethnic clashes, was the fact that these were struggles between competing interests of the nationalist elites, in which once again, the masses would get "somehow recruited." Once again, the various "tribalisms" would become "useful" for providing the stronghold or bases of the violent schemes of the competing nationalist politicians. Again what develops here is really not a politics of tribalism, but an exploitation and recruitment of local differences at the service of the nationalists' struggles, turned violent. This is not to suggest that there was no violence in pre-colonial Africa, but one needs to see that the form of "pathological violence" prevalent in Africa today is incomprehensible without the particular history we have outlined above. Any attempt to abstract it from this particular story will transform it into a bizarre cultural or natural trait of Africans, or, as it is often put, "one of the many things we don't understand about Africans."

The result of this endless cycle of violence in terms of destruction of life and property, as well as the psychological impact and frustrations of local ideals, cannot be overstated. A far more serious and long-term consequence, however, lies in the gradual naturalization of violence within the social order and within individual lives. For as the social order gets increasingly mired in violence, violence becomes an ingrained aspect of practical wisdom, namely, that the only way to deal with difference or to advance one's ideals is through violence. With the naturalization of violence, the menacing grip of King Leopold's ghost has come full circle with the line between the ghost and its victims becoming increasingly blurred, and eventually lost.

The fifth and final point. The combined effect of this top–bottom trajectory within Africa's politics is to make obvious the sense in which the story embodied within the nation-state underwrites a sense of helplessness, disempowerment, devaluation, indeed frustration of the everyday local struggles of the masses. I think it is quite true that the most damaging impact of colonialism in Africa was psychological: the freezing of Africa's history and the erosion of her self-confidence. But to the extent that this same story is embodied and perpetuated within the nation-state, the latter has indeed become a burden,"the black man's burden" and even an "enemy" (9), whose constraining grip and violence the masses would constantly have to survive in an attempt to advance their social struggles. In the final analysis, the critical issue arising out of this discussion is really not about the failures of the nation-state in Africa. The question is not what the nation-state has failed to do *for* Africans, but what it is doing *to* Africans—how it is narrating, defining and structuring their lives in terms of helplessness, disempowerment, and violence.

In terms of *telos*, this means that everyday practices cease to have any meaningful *telos* to energize them into forms of commitment, precisely because they are defined or narrated by the overriding story in such a way that denies them of being capable of any *telos*. This is indeed disempowering, and points to the need for alternative narratives which can radically challenge and even provide an alternative definition of everyday social struggles in view of energizing those activities within a hopeful *telos*. Without any such alternative, the majority of Africans will feel condemned to a wobbly existence where survival becomes their chief and perhaps only project.[18]

If this has been a long discussion, it has been worthwhile. For the story of the nation-state is rarely told, least of all from a theological point of view. As I noted earlier, Christian social ethics in Africa has simply accepted the nation-state, without ever looking at the story which informs the nation-state. The result has been that her greatest engagement with the social order has been limited to a challenge of offering suggestions aimed at making the nation-state more just or democratic. What these standard approaches may not realize is that by assuming the story of the nation-state, they unwittingly allow the church's own *telos* to be narrated and defined by this story. In this way, the church herself gets reduced to the space of the social—the "merely" social, to become part of the local/everyday history which history, as per the nation-state story, does not really matter or has no *telos*. Perhaps this "placement" explains the irony of importance and impotence in which the church is caught up in Africa. For, even as the "most influential and most sustainable social institution," the church has not become a "formidable weapon" of social transformation. It *cannot*, given the story above. For, now reduced to the social space, the church, just like all the other tribalisms that make up this space, is regarded by the dominant story at once as "temporary nuisance" to be tolerated and as potential capital, to be "somehow recruited" its ever expanding web of clientele politics. Accordingly, within these politics, the church is awarded all sorts of favors from the "right to worship", tax exemptions, and all sorts of "facilitations" to ensure their "non-partisanship" publicly, and their support privately. The most unfortunate consequence of this placement, however, is that once it has assumed the dominant story, the church's own existence and practices come to be increasingly marked by the same economy of hopelessness, despair, and violence as the rest of the other struggles within the everyday space. Nowhere is this disturbing reality more dramatically portrayed than in the story of Bishop Bamwoze (cf. the second epigram at the start of this essay).[19]

IV. Toward A Constructive Social Imagination

We need to return to the question which started off this inquiry in the first place. Can Christianity save Africans from King Leopold's ghost, that is, from the politics of dispossession, violence, and powerlessness? If our analysis concerning the sort of practices and characters which the African nation-state engenders is correct, then any hope for salvation cannot assume the nation-state. Rather, it must come in terms of an alternative story capable of engendering new practices set within a *telos* of hopeful peace. No doubt, to many the claim of Christianity providing an alternative will sound like a dangerous form of theocracy—an attempt to establish some kind of Imperial Christendom of the European Middle Ages. To view it in this way, however, is to still suppose something like a neutral social sphere out there (as a given) to which either the state or the church can externally *impose* its narrative agenda or frames or reference.[20] The effect of our analysis has been to call into question this assumption of the social realm as a given, and to show how it is constantly being narrated, framed, and constructed in a particular way by the politics of the nation-state. While this conclusion allows us to see the limitations and effects of the story embodied by the nation-state in Africa, an even more determinate effect is to challenge the church to rethink her own *telos* and the place of social formation within that *telos*. For once the social is not a given but rather in great part dependent on how different politics narrate or define it, then the most determinate task and challenge of theology becomes one of social imagination, i.e., one of imagining new and better ways of conceiving those everyday struggles and aspirations which lie at the basis of a people's social existence. In the remaining part of the essay, I will outline—a full fleshing out of this outline would be the task for another occasion—the direction which the theological task of social imagination needs to take.

a. Church as social mission
   The first and primary task of social imagination must be to rethink the church's own telos in such a way that the social formation is seen to be integral, in fact, the core of that *telos*. Those familiar with the work of Stanley Hauerwas will, I am sure, recognize how much the above claim draws upon his sustained argument to the effect that a social ethic lies at the heart of the church's existence and mission in the world.[21] To put it in this way might in fact still be misleading. For Hauerwas does not simply suggest that the church ought to contribute to social formation or transformation, but rather that the church itself is social formation. This is to say, that the church is not simply called upon to develop a relevant and effective social ethic; but to be a social ethic, which in effect provides an *alternative* to the story embodied within the nation-state politics. As Hauerwas notes:

> The church does not exist to provide an ethos for democracy or any other form of social organization, but stands as a political alternative to every nation, witnessing to the kind of social life possible for those that have been formed by the story of Christ. (Hauerwas 1981:12)

Whereas such claim might sound extreme and even dangerous, it represents an attempt to shift the locus of the church's social mission from being the state or the world (outside there) to the church herself. This shift is made possible by a recognition that the church's own story involves—or rather is—a politics (a distinctive way of naming, narrating, and framing what it means to be socially formed). In other words, the call to discipleship is not just a call to believe certain things about God, Christ, and the World, which beliefs might have social implications. It is a call for Christians to be socially formed in a distinctive way. But this formation is not an "extra" to what it means to be Christians. It is at the core of the call to discipleship. For without being so socially formed, Christians would not even know what it means to have the convictions they have, let alone to claim those convictions as true. In any event, once one has accepted that the Christian story is a politics, then the call for imagination is a call for the church to see that the story of the nation-state is not "inevitable." Instead, the church can (ought to) embody a different (better) narrative of social existence than the one embodied by the nation-state in Africa. Another way to underscore this alternative is to point to the embodied nature of social imagination.

b. Embodied imagination

While the recommendation for an alternative *narrative* or *definition* may easily suggest an intellectual exercise, what actually is at stake is not just the framing of new doctrines or formulations, but the availability of an alternative set of practices. This is not to suggest a misleading dichotomy between doctrine and practice, but to insist on the embodied existence of the church as itself being the narrative. In other words, the alternative "story" the church provides cannot be separated from the social existence concretely and historically embodied by the church. Social imagination, as Hauerwas notes, is "not something we have in our minds. Rather, the imagination is a pattern of possibilities fostered within a community by the stories and correlative commitments that make it what it is" (Hauerwas 1994:179; Hauerwas 1985:12; 51–60). The church is, or at least ought to be, such a community. This is what makes the question of mission and social formation essentially an ecclesiological question—an inquiry into what it means to be a church, i.e., a people formed by the story of Christ's life, ministry, death, and resurrection as contained in the scriptures and witnessed within various historical communities across time. It would, in this connection, be interesting to survey this ecclesiological dimension in relation to the classical claim of *ex ecclesia nulla salus*. For our purposes here it simply means that for people living under the story of the nation-state in Africa there is no way for them to even know that there is another (hopeful) way of narrating their social struggles apart from the existence of communities who live by a different story of what it means to be socially formed. Accordingly, the most urgent task for the church in Africa is the building or realization of such local communities of hope, precisely because they have come to locate their social struggles and aspirations within a hopeful *telos*.[22]

c. Valorization of the everyday

But what does this Christian telos concretely look like? At the risk of underwriting a misleading spiritual-material dichotomy, the embodiment referred to above sits very uneasily with the highly spiritualized or pietistic accounts of salvation characteristic of a great deal of African Christianity today. Instead, the social imagination envisioned will have to draw on those biblical narratives and early church tradition which portray salvation in terms of concrete and material expectations. Different from the banal sense in which the gospel serves to secure material rewards, the biblical narratives portray Jesus' life, cross and resurrection as the inauguration of the Kingdom of God—as a Kingdom of hope, peacefulness, and forgiveness. In any event, it is a Kingdom whose site is "on this mountain"—i.e., within the space of everyday social struggles and aspirations (Luke 4:16–21).

Accordingly, what the discussion in the previous chapter showed as lacking in Africa, and what the task of social imagination seeks to recover, is a valorization of the daily struggles and the ability to re-energize these everyday struggles within the hopeful *telos* of the Christian story. For as J.M. Ela notes in a critical essay aimed at overly spiritualized accounts of salvation within African Catholicism:

> We must rediscover the gospel as a decisive force in history's march to the fore . . . the Kingdom of God (manifests itself) wherever the new universe is under construction—not a new world in the sense of a world–beyond, but in the sense of a different world right here, a world being gestated in the deeds of the everyday. (Ela 1986:53)

If we must take this call seriously, especially in Africa where, as our analysis in Section III shows, the everyday is increasingly marked by an economy of hopelessness and violence, then the task of social imagination cannot be separated from a concern for the material production within those communities. There can be no blueprints for the form which such local communities can and will eventually take. But the call to social imagination seeks to realize communities in which the daily tasks of ploughing, harvesting, or pasturing; in which the cultivation of vegetables and the digging of wells; the immunization against malaria and the construction of pit latrines is as much as a matter of Christian salvation as the celebration of baptism, the Eucharist, and the reading of the scriptures.

If this sounds like a utopian vision, it is because Christian imagination is always a call to realize and embody an utopian dream of the Kingdom of God. At any rate, the church is not without resources from which it can realize this imagination. Certainly not for Africa where "the church is one of the most sustainable social institutions, especially in the rural areas." Unfortunately, it is here in the rural areas that the worst effects in terms of exploitation, dispossession, and violence of the nation-state's story are felt. For the church so located, the realization of such local communities of energized social existence is at once an urgent but viable necessity. Whereas such communities cannot be a panacea to all Africa's problems, which are connected to many other global processes as well, they will at least provide African Christians not just with resources to name the violence and despair that is part of their daily lives, but also an alternative way to conceive and narrate their lives and ordinary struggles in a purposive manner. What an exciting possibility this will be. Not just for Africa, but for the church as a whole such communities will be an instructive experiment toward a novel understanding and exemplification of mission and social formation.

Emmanuel Katongole
Duke Divinity School

NOTES

[1] On the statistical strength of Christianity in sub-Saharan Africa, see e.g. Gifford (1995), where a quick sample indicates that Christians make up 78% of Uganda's population; 60% of Ghana's; 65% of Cameroon's; and 75% of Zambia's (P. 61, 119, 183, 251 respectively). The overall statistics for the continent indicate that over 41% of Africa's 550 million people were Christians (Gibelleni, 1994).

[2] Catholics especially note this optimism through such questions as to whether the next pope will be from Africa. For my more extended reflections on this optimism, see Katongole, 2001

[3] The more recent issue of *The Economist* (Feb 24–March 2, 2001) paints a similar picture of gloom with its cover story of "Africa's Elusive Hope."

[4] I, for instance, find both inadequate and misleading *The Economist's* attempt to blame Africa's current problems on its bad leaders, its traditions and culture, its environment, colonialism—on everything else, except the current institutions, national and multinational.

[5] Even Kwame Bediako, his positive, and almost triumphalistic assessment of African Christianity notwithstanding, seems, even though reluctantly and only hypothetically, to allow this possibility (Bediako 1995, 263).

[6] The chilling story of the 16-year-old Josephine Uwamahoro (a name which literary means the "peaceful one") is as instructive as it is unnerving. Josephine lost all her family and all her friends in the massacre in the church at Nyamata, the same church in which she and her family had celebrated the Eucharist every Sunday together with some of the would-be murderous militias. That she herself survived was a miracle. She was left for dead in a heap of festering bodies of her family and friends after her neck and legs were hacked. After the war was over, she tearfully whispered to one of the missionaries: "We will never come back to this church. The angels have left us." See Hugh McCullum 1995: xix

[7] To be sure, this is an issue that has bothered Maluleke for a while, but one to which he has not provided a definite answer even though on at least one occasion he has tentatively suggested that it might perhaps be time "to drink from our own wells" —thereby encouraging Black and African theologies to take more seriously African culture and African traditional religions, not just as "preparations for the Christian gospel", but in their own right as offering resources and "alternative strategies for survival" (Maluleke 1996).

[8] There might in fact be something like a Weberian scenario here where the less explicitly socially active forms of Christianity might ironically provide the far more enduring social benefits (Weber 1992).

[9] Mugambi's suggestion for a theology of "reconstruction" also seems to boil down to this: The Gospel, Mugambi notes, ought to be Good News, which "rehabilitates individuals and groups that are marginalized by various natural and social circumstances. In contemporary Africa the Good News is understood in this way, ought to rehabilitate the afflicted individuals in every region, country and locality. The Gospel ought to help Africans regain their confidence and hope" (Mugambi 1995: 176).

[10] The future of black theology following the end of apartheid has been a matter of debate. Whereas many have been quick to write eulogies of black theology, Maluleke still sees a future for it (Maluleke 1995).

[11] For a more extended treatment of this assumption, see Katongole, *Beyond Universal Reason* (Notre Dame, 2000), especially pp. 180–212.

[12] Ernst Troeltsch's *The Social Teaching of the Christian Churches* (New York. Macmillan, 1931) has been the classical text on understanding the social role of the Church. This tradition has been particularly dominant in America in the Social Gospel Movement of Raushenbuch, and following him the Niebuhr brothers. See Walter Raushenbusch, *A Theology for the Social Gospel* (Nashville. Abingdon Press, 1945).

[13] Unless otherwise suggested all the page references in this section refer to Davidson (1992). Basil Davidson, *The Black Man's Burden. Africa and the Curse of the Nation-State* (Oxford. James Currey Press, 1992).

[14] Much of Davidson's work has been to show what a lie this is. See also Davidson 1994. *The Search for Africa. A History in the Making* (London. James Currey, 1994).

[15] Chapter Four is particularly telling on the invention of tribalism and the decisive role this invented notion would play in the purported and highly misleading debate between the Modernizers and the Traditionalists (or tribalists).

[16] For instance, there seems to be an underlying positivism in Davidson's work, which seems to assume class structure, capitalism, the nation-state as the natural flow and final destiny of all social formations. His argument seems to suppose that left within their history, African forms of social existence would eventually have turned into nation-states similar to the ones in Europe (the case of Asante: which is "not peculiar" but only drawn on given its "dramatic clarity" (52–73). Another problematic assumption by

Davidson is the way in which he projects Enlightenment sociological views of religion upon African colonial history (religion as a sacred canopy to provide coercive force to independently originating social norms [81ff]).

[17] Gifford (1998: 1–20) too has noted this aspect of Africa's politics in reference to the authoritative work of Bayart (1993).

[18] As William Sissane remarks in relation to Guinea, a remark that could be made in reference to much of post-independence politics. "Sekoure Toure's revolution has created there types of mutants: the flatters, the floaters, and the deflated" (Diawara 1998: 50).

[19] The story is set in 1993 in the Anglican diocese of Busoga (Uganda) where the diocesan bishop Bamwoze was the center of controversy and leadership struggle (Gifford 1995: 126–127). If one thought that the church had more (or better) resources to conceive and deal with power and differences, that belief is shattered by the way in which Bamwoze's church-based power struggle perfectly mirrors the same story of violence and intrigue as any nationalist power struggle. The biggest irony of course is that the onus would fall on the nation-state agencies, the police in particular, to pacify the competing church struggles!

[20] For my more extended discussion on the category of story within politics and theology as an alternative story of "in the beginning," see Katongole, 2000: 214–251.

[21] This has been the central thrust of Hauerwas' constructive re-visioning of Christian social ethics. It is therefore difficult to give it a localized reference. Whereas his later work assumes this argument, it is in his earlier work that Hauerwas more explicitly states or argues this thesis. See particularly Hauerwas 1981and Hauerwas 1983.

[22] It is in this respect that one can say that "the church does not have a social strategy; the church is a social strategy" (Hauerwas 1994: 43).

SELECTED BIBLIOGRAPHY

Bayart J, F., 1993: *African Politics. The Politics of the Belly* (London. Longman).
Bediako Kwame, 1989: "The Roots of African Theology," *International Bulletin of Missionary Research* 13: 58–65.
———. 1992: *Theology and Identity. The Impact of Culture upon Christian Thought in the Second Century and in Modern Africa* (Oxford. Regnum Books).
———. 1995: *Christianity in Africa. The Renewal of a Non-Western Religion* (Maryknoll. Orbis Books).
Cochrane J.R., 1995: *Circles of Dignity. Community Wisdom and Theological Reflection* (Minneapolis, Fortress Press).
Davidson Basil, 1992. *The Black Man's Burden. Africa and the Curse of the Nation-State* (Oxford. James Currey Press).
———. 1994: *The Search for Africa. A History in the Making* (Oxford. James Currey Press).
De Gruchy John, 1995: *Christianity and Democracy* (Cambridge. Cambridge University Press).
Diawara Manthia, 1998: *In Search of Africa* (Cambridge. Harvard University Press).
Economist, The, 2000: "The Hopeless Continent." May 13–19.
———. 2000: "Africa's Elusive Hope." Feb 24–March 2.
Ela Jean Marc, 1986: *African Cry* (Maryknoll, Orbis).
Gibellini Rosino, ed., 1994: *Paths of African Theology* (Maryknoll. Orbis).

Gifford Paul, 1998. *African Christianity. Its Public Role* (Bloomington. Indiana University Press).

Gifford Paul, ed., 1995: *The Christian Churches and the Democratization of Africa* (Leiden. E.J. Brill).

Hauerwas Stanley, 1981: *A Community of Character: Toward a Constructive Christian Social Ethic* (Notre Dame. Notre Dame University Press).

————. *1985: Against the Nations. War and Survival in a Liberal State* (Minneapolis. Winston–Seabury Press).

————. 1993: *The Peaceable Kingdom. A Primer in Ethics* (Notre Dame. University of Notre Dame Press, 1983).

————. 1993: *Dispatches from the Front. Theological Engagements with the Secular* (Duke University Press).

Hochschild Adam. 1998: *King Leopold's Ghost* (New York. Mariner Books).

John Paul II, 1995: *Post-Synodal Exhortation "Ecclesia in Africa"* (Vatican).

Katongole Emmanuel, 2000: *Beyond Universal Reason. Questioning the Relation Between Ethics and Religion in the Work of Stanley Hauerwas* (Notre Dame: University Press).

————. 2001: "Prospects of Ecclesia in Africa in the 21st Century," *Logos* 4/1: 179–196.

Maluleke Tinyiko S. 1995: "Black Theology Lives! On a Permanent Crisis," *Journal of Theology for Southern Africa* 9/1: 1–30.

————. 1995: "Black and African Theologies in the New World Order. A Time to Drink from Our Own Wells," *Journal of Theology for Southern Africa* 96:3–19.

————. 1995: "A Letter to Job from Africa," *Tam Tam*, Sept/Oct 1997: 5.

————. 1995: "Christianity in a Distressed Africa. A Time to Own and Own Up," *Missionalia* 26/3: 324–340.

McCullum Hugh, 1995: *The Angels Have Left Us: The Rwanda Tragedy and the Churches* (Geneva. WCC Publications).

Milbank John, 1990: *Theology and Social Theory. Beyond Secular Reason* (New York. Blackwell).

Mugambi Jesse K.N., 1995: *From Liberation to Reconstruction: African Christian Theology After the Cold War* (Nairobi. East African Education Publishers).

Nelson Kasfir (ed)., 1998: *Civil Society and Democracy in Africa. Critical Perspectives* (Ilford, Frank Cass, 1998).

Raushenbusch Walter, 1945: *A Theology for the Social Gospel* (Nashville. Abingdon Press).

Troeltsch Ernst, 1931: *The Social Teaching of the Christian Churches* (New York. Macmillan).

Villa-Vicencio Charles, 1992: *A Theology of Reconstruction. Nation-Building and Human Rights* (Cambridge. Cambridge University Press).

Weber Max, 1992: *The Protestant Ethic and the Spirit of Capitalism* (London. Routledge).

CHAPTER 8

The Rediscovery of the Agency of Africans

An emerging paradigm of post–cold war and post-apartheid black and African theology[1]

Tinyiko Sam Maluleke

ABSTRACT

I dentifying the most creative edges in an emerging post–cold war and post-apartheid paradigm of African theology, this article proposes that theology retains a unique role in acknowledging, valorizing, interpreting, and enhancing the agency of African Christians in their daily struggles against the cultural, religious, and economic forces. Around the central rediscovery of the agency of Africans, African theologians are attempting to construct a less embittered and less schizophrenic relationship between Africa and Christianity on the one hand, and between Africans and their painful Christian past on the other. Although many of the basic assumptions of the past continue to be influential, there is a search for theoretical tools and perspectives that will enable us to understand and account for the mythical, the sociocultural, and the popular in religion and society, highlighting the sociopolitical importance of popular religious movements and the need to develop adequate and relevant theoretical tools for understanding them. This search is related to the criticism of the fraudulent project of the postcolonial nationalist bourgeoisie and the grand narratives of Africa, African culture, and the political liberation projects with its worn-out metaphors. While African women's theology has been by far the most prolific and challenging in the past decade and a half, Mosala's and Petersen's work is discussed in more detail.

Introduction

The twenty-year period (1980–2000) during which I have learned, practiced, and taught theology has been one of change and transition. It is an era in which the demise of apartheid was accelerated, culminating

in the installation of Nelson Mandela as South Africa's first democratically elected president to head the first democratically elected
government in the country's history. But we cannot forget that one of
the most repressive and most gruesome eras in the history of South
Africa can also be located in the same twenty-year period. Therefore, I
bear in my soul and psyche the scars of the repression that swept South
Africa from 1976 (when I was a secondary school student in Soweto)
through to the violent darkness of the mid-1980s and early 1990s. For
this reason, while I have been unable to avoid South African white
contextual or liberation theology—what student of theology in South
Africa during the past twenty years could avoid David Bosch and John
de Gruchy?—the deeper influence on me has been from the passionate
and critical South African black theology. But I am also informed by
and respectful of the scholarship and the Christian "Africanism" of the
likes of John Mbiti, Fasholé Luke, Harry Sawyerr, Bolaji Idowu,
Gabriel Setiloane, and others. The sharp and satirical tongue of Ugandas
Okot p'Bitek in his "songs" and essays touches my very gut as does the
articulation of African identity, its crisis, its tragedy, its incompleteness,
and its dreams encapsulated in the works of the likes of Achebe,
Soyinka, N'gugi wa Thiongo, Ayi Kwei Armah, Eskia Mphahlele, Can
Themba, Alex Laguma, and others.[2]

I write as an Anglophone Protestant from a largely Anglophone
Protestant country. I write from the new South Africa—one of the
world's youngest democracies. I speak as a theologian who is keen to
understand and possibly help fashion out a role for Christian theology
in the new South Africa and the "new" Africa. I am specifically
interested in the possible role of theology in interpreting and enhancing
the agency of Africans in the light of cultural, religious, and economic
marginalization. After the euphoria of the end of apartheid, it would be
accurate to say that South African theology and South African
ecumenism are in some kind of recess if not a kind of disarray. Without
being too presumptuous, it is fair to say that up until the early 1990s
South Africa had been one of the most theologically prolific places in
the world, producing some of the best, as well as the worst, packages of
Christian theology this side of the Second World War, outside of
Germany. Perhaps the apex of this creativity was the publication of *The
Kairos Document* in 1985. But even *The Kairos Document* dismally
fails to capture all of the theological creativity that emanated out of this
country. It is therefore not difficult to observe the fatigue in ecumenical
South African theology. The silence has been sudden and deafening.

How have the cries of the poor majority been suddenly silenced by the shouts of the joyful minority?

As a young theologian in post-apartheid South Africa and post–cold war Africa, I suddenly experience intense and acute spiritual and intellectual loneliness. This is both bad and good. Bad because I miss the defiant, passionate, and humourous "image of God" *ubuntu* theology of Desmond Tutu. There is a huge gaping hole that has been left by my esteemed mentors and colleagues, Itumeleng Mosala, Takatso Mofokeng, Simon Maimela, Smangaliso Mkhatswa, Frank Chikane, and others—all of whom have "gone secular" by becoming all manner of administrators and state functionaries. But my "loneliness" may yet be a cause for joy. Perhaps my esteemed colleagues have responded to a "higher" calling. Those who criticize the abuse of power must be prepared to take and reshape it. Those who call for "liberation" must take the liberation project to what they see to be its logical conclusion. Perhaps. Perhaps the South African Christian community must wake up from its dependency on the Tutus and Mosalas of this world and take up its prophetic calling with or without them.

Fortunately, my "loneliness" as a theologian and committed academic is not total. I hear encouraging voices from other parts of Africa and other parts of the world. I am speaking here of the voices of the likes of Jesse Mugambi of Kenya,[3] Kwame Bediako of Ghana,[4] Kä Mana of the Democratic republic of Congo, Mercy Amba Oduyoye of Ghana,[5] Lamin Sanneh of the Gambia,[6] Dwight Hopkins[7] and others. I am encouraged by these voices. Within South Africa itself, such bold, innovative post-apartheid studies as those by Villa-Vicencio,[8] Landman,[9] Naudé,[10] Petersen,[11] West,[12] Cochrane,[13] and Tutu[14] have kept me hopeful. But more than these particular works, it is the continued relevance of much of what has been done in cold–war era African theology that inspires me.

The Task of This Article
My aim in this article is to advance a proposal that a post–cold war and post-apartheid paradigm of African theology is emerging. It is a paradigm whose shape has yet to take a complete form, yet I will suggest that we can already see some of its contours. I wish to further explore the possible role of theology in interpreting and hopefully enhancing the agency of African Christians in particular and Africans in general in the face of cultural, racial, gender, religious, and economic marginalization. My reading of some recent developments in African

theology has persuaded me that theology retains a unique role to play in (a) acknowledging, (b) valorizing, (c) interpreting, and (d) enhancing the agency of African Christians in their daily struggles against the cultural, religious, and economic forces of death which seek to marginalize them. However, it is a task in which African theology cannot partake unless it undertakes serious methodological changes. In other words, it is a task which cannot be undertaken by African Christian theology alone. What are the theoretical and methodological tools necessary for African theology to make constructive contributions in the task that I have outlined above? I believe that the basic clues and the fiduciary indicators as to how we might answer this question are already provided in several new proposed directions for African theology.

In this article, I attempt to identify what I consider to be the most creative edges in some of these theological proposals. It is a constellation of these creative impulses in each proposal which present us with a glimpse of what I have chosen to call an emerging paradigm in African theology. Let me hasten to add that a paradigm, as used in this article, does not imply a homogeneous theological project in which African theologians are in harmonious agreement. The theologies being proposed are diverse and not necessarily in agreement with or even aware of each other. Therefore, if there is "a paradigm" emerging, it is myself who is deliberately constructing it out of my reading of new developments in African theology. It is therefore also important to note that I call this "an" emerging paradigm rather than "the" emerging paradigm.

Also, we need to note my contextual limitations. It is impossible for one single theologian to be completely up to date with all developments in all African theology. Africa is a vast and diverse continent—diverse in religions, Christian confessions, language, cultures, and so forth. My suggestion that there is an emerging paradigm in African theology is therefore built upon a largely Anglophone, mainly Protestant reading of recent developments in ecumenical African theology. Furthermore, this article assumes a familiarity with many of the essays I have myself written on diverse issues relating to recent developments in African theology and developments within post-apartheid South Africa. Similarly, familiarity with such recent publications in African theology as I refer to in this article will help the reader in understanding the contents of this article. My task is to paint a rough picture of what I see as an emerging paradigm rather than to present detailed analyses of new developments in African theology. I suggest below ten "lines" in the rough pictures of the emerging paradigm. Let me hasten to say that there is nothing final or magical about the ten factors I highlight—it is merely a manner I have found most useful in presenting the emerging paradigm for now. But first, I make reference to the old in African theology.

Old and New Paradigms

The old

A few years ago, I wrote a popular article in the form of a letter addressed to Job of the Bible, under the fictitious name of a woman called Africa.[15] In this letter, Africa likens her circumstances and her fate to that of Job. Having lost everything she once had, Africa now sits on a rubbish dump outside the city gates. Africa has been victimized and raped by explorers, slave traders, colonialists, and dictators born out of her own womb. Like Job, Africa is religious—"notoriously religious," as Mbiti once put it. In many African countries one is struck by the extent and public display of religious symbolism. Yet in her letter to Job, Africa wonders aloud whether her religiosity is not in fact part of the problem rather than part of the solution. Where is the hand of God in the story of Africa, she wonders? What are the fruits of her religiosity? Poverty? Underdevelopment and exploitation? "How can we explain that (one of) the most religious continents in the world is also the poorest?" asks one of Africas sons, Jesse Mugambi.[16] Therefore Africa wonders how Job can praise God for taking everything away and how Job can "explain it all away" by declaring "naked I was when I was born and naked I will be when I return to dust." Although Africa's letter to Job takes the post–cold war situation of Africa into account, it is still framed in terms of old and established frameworks of African theologizing. The overwhelming picture is one of Africa as a victim, hard done by one and all. Cold–war era African theology, whether it be "inculturational" or "liberational," proceeded out of the recognition of Africa's massive victimization and exploitation.

The metaphor of liberation

From the point of view of southern Africa there is widespread agreement that *The Kairos Document*[17]—its shortcomings notwith-standing—represented a notable high point in local theologies of liberation—if not in its theological content, definitely in its timing, prophetic edge, and the process out of which it was born. What were the basic presuppositions of such cold war African theologizing? Quoting from the final statement of one EATWOT meeting, Per Frostin[18] suggests five factors as representative of the liberation theology paradigm in African theology: (a) the poor as the primary epistemological interlocutors for African theology; (b) the pursuit not of the question "Does God exist?" but rather of the question "Why does God allow idolatry, blatant blasphemy, and oppression?"; (c) the understanding of human reality as conflictual; (d) commitment to an analysis of "what is going on, on the ground" by "reading the signs of the times" and the consequent reliance on social sciences rather than on philosophy as has been traditionally the case for theology; and (e) the insistence that theology begins at sunset and that commitment is the first act in theology—a notion clearly borrowed from Latin American theology. Two other cross currents of African theology closely related to the foregoing are South African black theology and African women's theology. In these two theologies the notion of "the poor" is broken down to mean "women," "African women," "blacks," and or "the black working class," so that there is a deliberate emphasis on gender, race, and class issues. Yet perhaps the most enduring contribution of black theology to African theology is not in its privileging of race as a sociotheological tool, but its biblical hermeneutics.

The inculturation metaphor

The so-called African theology of liberation was only one current in African theology. There were others. There was the so-called "inculturation" current, whose precursors and inspirations were the likes of Placide Tempels' *La Philosophie Bantoe* (first published in 1945),[9] Griaule's *Dieu d'eau: Entretiens avec Ogotemmêli*[20] as well as the kinds of early socio-anthropological studies of African religions done by Evans-Pritchard and others. Indeed the first generation of self-conscious and written African theology during the twentieth century was deeply influenced by these works. For this generation of theologians nothing was more important than the quest for a coherent African religious identity which would account for the African past as well as the African present. Adrian Hastings noted during this period that "the African theologian finds that the chief non-biblical reality with which he must struggle is the non-Christian religious tradition of his own people, and African theology in its present stage is shaping as something of a dialogue between the African Christian scholar and the perennial religions and spiritualities of Africa."[21] Fasholé-Luke explained the task of this generation of theologians in this way:

[T]he quest for African Christian theologies which has been vigorously pursued in the last decade, amounts to attempting to make clear the fact that conversion to Christianity must be coupled with cultural continuity. Furthermore, if Christianity is to change its status from that of resident alien to that of citizen, then it must become incarnate in the life and thought of Africa and its theologies must bear the distinctive stamp of mature African thinking and reflection. What African theologians have been endeavouring to do is to draw together the various and disparate sources which make up the total religious experience of Christians in Africa into a coherent and meaningful pattern.[22]

At its most radical—and consequently its most ambiguous—this current was represented in the utterances and writings of the likes of John Gatu (who inaugurated the moratorium debate), Kibicho, Gabba, and Setiloane—who argue, in various ways, that the God of Africa is as good as the God of Christendom if not better.

Bits of the new
In the fictitious letter of Africa to Job referred to above, Africa notes with a touch of ironic nostalgia that she was once needed even though she was needed only for what could be taken from her. There was once a scramble for Africa! Africa was once "valued" however warped the motivations and values of those who wished to have her. Now Africa wonders if she is still of much use even to her erstwhile exploiters and admirers, as she sits on the world's rubbish dump. Those who were scrambling for Africa, such as the states of Europe, are now organizing themselves into such powerful economic blocs as the European Community. The end of the cold war has created new priorities for Europe and America, and Africa does not appear to be one of them. The internal decay within Africa itself has led to what some have termed "Afropessimism." Indeed Africa's letter to Job is desperate and pessimistic.

Even the Africans in the diaspora who once invested their hopes and energies in "Mother Africa"—dating back to Crummell, du Bois, Blyden, and others—appear to now have a weakened resolve. An African American journalist for the influential *New York Times*, based in Nairobi in order to report on, amongst other things, the Rwandan genocide, was so horrified by the barbarities committed there that he wrote a book in which he thanked God that his ancestors were made slaves and taken out of Africa.[23]

We cannot forget that the same week when South Africa and the world joyfully inaugurated Mandela as the first president of a democratic country, genocide was taking place in Rwanda. Thus, it can be said that while the old is dying in Africa, the new has not yet been born. Clearly, the demise of the cold war and the emergence of the new world order, signified as it is by accelerated globalization, brings no automatic blessings for African countries. It will take more than the "African renaissance"[24] rhetoric (in South Africa and Uganda) to get out of the rut of centuries of exploitation and the more recent ravages of neocolonialism, dictatorship, and internal decay. Even the end of apartheid is not automatically positive for the poorest of the poor.

It also appears that our inherited frameworks, theological methods, and metaphors are increasingly being seen as inadequate if not expired. Africa finds herself in a "new place" and its thinkers and leaders are desperately looking for new language and new frameworks. The African poor are pouring scorn at "liberation-rhetoric" regardless of the quarters from where it emanates because long after independence they remain poor if not poorer—if they have not been killed off by disease or the guns of the more powerful. African women are mobilising without and despite African men (in fact they are seeking alliances with other women from all over the world and from all walks of life). Note the simmering anger and the implied call for decisive sisterly action in the following quote:

> [T]he women of Africa, are expected simply to look on, to keep the peace; they are not to seek heroic actions and/or learn self-defense, for the lions and the wild hogs and the hyenas that threaten the communal life are their own brothers. [They] . . . are expected to be supportive and to hide from outsiders, the festering wounds. They are supposed to be the custodians of all the ancient arts and keepers of the secret that numbs pain inflicted by internal aggressors. They are to pray and sing and carry. They are to tend the wounds from battles in which they are not allowed to fight. They are only permitted to look on from afar, "for their own good." So they stand by, shaking loosened wrists in desperation, powerlessly watching their brothers flounder.[25]

In a sense, Africa-both the geographical entity "Africa" and the "idea" in its Pan Africanist sense—as well as the "idea" of an African nation-state are all daily imploded before our puzzled faces. The Ghanaian philosopher, Kwame Appiah,[26] scoffs at all notions of a united, homogeneous Africa, African identity, and what he calls racialist Pan Africanism, declaring that Africa is like "my father's house in which there are many mansions," meaning that there are and should be many and various ways of being African!

Rediscovery of the agency of Africans

I want to suggest however that while the view of Africa painted in the fictitious letter I recount above is real, current, and valid, this reality does not exhaust all the faces of Africa. In the midst of all this tragedy, ordinary Africans are surviving. In countless African villages in remote areas unreached and ignored by government, people find ways and means to survive. In countries without infrastructure, without effective government, and with the lowest GDP imaginable, Africans are surviving. Despite the heavy assault of certain destructive versions of American culture, urbanized Africans are fashioning out their own ways of being. By diverse means ordinary Africans are finding ways to neutralize the stifling "hands" of globalization and IMF policies. This view of Africa is informed by a slightly different gaze at Africa—it is a gaze from within and a gaze that zooms in on Africa's creative, innovative, and agentic spirit. Such a gaze must not however be seen to replace and disprove other gazes on Africa—a fatal mistake committed by so many optimistic Africanists (as opposed to so-called Afro-pessimists). Africans are, have, and continue to be victimized from within and from without. There is no denying that.

The gaze I propose is therefore not based on some simplistic, positive-thinking philosophy such as is often promoted by conservative behaviorists who glibly suggest that Africans would succeed if they tried harder, believed more fervently, and thought more positively. The reality of the African situation is far more complex and far more grinding than the diagnosis implied in simplistic positive-thinking philosophy. In the view of Cornel West, it is such "conservative behaviourists" who flippantly

> [T]ell black people to see themselves as agents, not victims. And on the surface, this is comforting advice, a nice cliche for downtrodden people. But inspirational slogans cannot substitute for substantive historical and social analysis. While Black people have never been simply victims, wallowing in self-pity and begging for white giveaways, they have been—and are—victimized. Therefore to call on Black people to be agents makes sense only if we also examine the

dynamics of the victimization against which their agency *will,* in part, be exercised.[27]

It is therefore important that my call for a slightly different gaze on Africa be understood in terms that differ radically from those stemming from conservative behaviorism. Indeed my call is not a call for an artificial reorientation of attitudes toward and about Africa, Africans, and Africanness. I invite my readers to join me in observing, analyzing, and interpreting some of the tactics and strategies of Africa's indomitable spirit.[28] I am not calling for an artificial conjuring up of a positive attitude toward Africa in the facile hope that such a positive attitude will magically produce a triumphant Africa.

My reading of the situation takes its cue from some of the recent developments in African theology. On the basis of these I suggest that we are being called to a humble but careful observance of the struggles of Africans to be agents against great odds, not by ignoring or discounting the odds, but by confronting them. Africans have always been agents, never "simply victims, wallowing in self–pity"; they have always exercised their agency in struggles for survival and integrity. However, their agency has not always been recognized, let alone nurtured. Speaking from a South African perspective, my sense is that there is a new wave of awareness of the agency of ordinary marginalized Africans. In fact, at their best and most creative, African theologies have always proceeded on some gut-feeling and almost stubborn insistence that Africans were agents and not mere doormats trampled upon by civilizers, missionaries, and colonialists.

An Outline of an Emerging Paradigm

How would we characterize the emerging paradigm of post–cold war African theology? Here are the ten "lines" that reveal some basic contours of the emerging paradigm. Firstly, many of the basic assumptions of cold war African theology continue to be basic to the overwhelming majority of the new proposals for African theologizing —admittedly to various degrees. It is important that we recognise that post–cold war African theologies are continuous with previous African theologies even if and when their proponents espouse and proclaim a radical discontinuity. African theology cannot and will not abdicate the gains made—and ambiguities inherited—during the past fifty odd years. A careful reading of Villa-Vicencio reveals that although he genuinely seeks to propose a new metaphor for theology and a slightly different orientation,[29] he is methodologically still beholden to the liberation paradigm. Ironically, Mugambi's "take" on reconstruction is methodologically also still largely beholden to the inculturation paradigm.[30] Robin Petersen's otherwise groundbreaking and "different" study of AICs turns out to be largely a pursuit of such familiar categories of classical ecumenical theology as oppression/domination, protest/ resistance, and *kairos*.[31] In fact, Petersen himself admits that his study is merely a "reconstruction within the prophetic theology paradigm itself."[32] In many ways the works of Kwame Bediako and Lamin Sanneh offer a sophisticated continuation of certain discourses within West— (and East—?) African inculturation theology. In both of them we are still confronted with inculturation theology's unease with the agenda of political liberation. Thus we see Sanneh doing his best not only to distance his project from alleged generalizations on missionaries, mission, and imperialism, but also to relegate these kinds of issues to a lower level than those of translation and inculturation.[33] With Bediako we observe an astonishing disinterest in the kinds of "political" issues raised by such African women theologians as his own compatriot Mercy Oduyoye. But this is largely in keeping with inculturation theology.

Secondly, in post–cold war African theology, we have seen attempts at constructing a less embittered and less schizophrenic relationship between Africa and Christianity on the one hand, and between Africans and their painful Christian past on the other. Two examples of theological approaches that pursue one or the other (or both) of these twin tasks spring to mind. The first example is represented in the works of Bediako and Sanneh—the "translation theology" school. Bediako's proposal, built on the works of Walls and Sanneh, is that Christianity is not intrinsically and irredeemably foreign to Africa, anymore than it is intrinsically and irredeemably Western. The clue to understanding the "true nature" of the Christian faith is in its translatability—a notion expounded over a decade by Sanneh. Therefore, it is not what the missionaries or colonialists did or did not do, wished or did not wish, that accounts for the massive presence of Christianity on the continent, but the logic of its translatability which necessarily enlists the agency of local (read African) Christians enabling them to truly own the faith. In similar fashion, Andrew Walls boldly suggests that African Christianity is legitimately "an African religion" which represents simultaneously a new chapter in the histories of both Christianity and African religion.[34] Therefore being African is not in opposition to being Christian and vice versa. This assumption must be abandoned as a fundamental starting point for African theology, the likes of Bediako and Walls suggest.

The second example of an attempt to construct a less embittered and less schizophrenic relationship with the painful "Christian" past is represented by what I will tentatively call "Desmond Tutu's theology of humanity and forgiveness," most eloquently articulated in his *No future without forgiveness*. Here, Christian forgiveness and the African spirit of *ubuntu* are put forward as theological resources for dealing with and overcoming the painful past of dehumanization and oppression in the name of (Christian) religion. In this way black Christians can and need not only remain Christian, but they may, for their own sakes and for the sakes of others, forgive and embrace those who oppressed, dehumanized, and "killed" them.[35] But there is a striking difference between Tutu's quest for a less embittered basis for doing African theology and that which is advanced by Bediako, Sanneh, and Walls. Tutu confronts the pain of "Christian" complicity in oppression head-on while the others do not. Yet even with Tutu we cannot fail to observe some ambiguities. He too does not always recognize the "impossibility" of forgiveness. This is especially true in cases where the very people best qualified to forgive have been "killed" both literally and meta-phorically by the very people needing their forgiveness. It may be instructive to recall that, as he hung on the cross, Jesus chose to defer the question of the forgiveness of his tormentors to his Father. In many other situations Jesus offered forgiveness quite easily, so he became notorious with the religious authorities for precisely this practice. One sometimes gains the impression of a rushed even forced and superficial notion of forgiveness in the work of the South African Truth and Reconciliation Commission.

Third, there is a conscious and deliberate attempt to supplement and even substitute worn-out metaphors and starting points fashioned out of the cold-war era. The past decade has seen the introduction of such metaphors as reconstruction and translation. There is a palpable hunger and search for a new paradigm that will enable African theology to "speak" to the local situation. For example, the notion of reconstruction as a new metaphor around which African theology could be done has been taken up by the likes of Jesse Mugambi,[36] Charles Villa-Vicencio of South Africa,[37] and Ka Mana of the Democratic Republic of Congo in Francophone Africa. Mugambi proposes an end to the well-rehearsed debate between "inculturation" and "liberation" by suggesting that both have expired. He substitutes the notion of "reconstruction" for both.

Similarly, Villa-Vicencio suggests that liberation theology's commitment to solidarity with the poor may be supplemented by what he calls a "critical solidarity" with a democratic state where and insofar as such a state seeks to address the concerns of the poor. Another area of such a search for new frameworks and metaphors is in African women's theology. It is interesting that both the terms "feminist" and "womanist" have not received automatic and unqualified reception among all African women theologians.[38]

Fourth, post–cold war African theology intends to be critical of the "fraudulent project of the post colonial nationalist bourgeoisie"[39]— something that the likes of Jean-Marc Éla and the late Engelbert Mveng of Cameroon had already been bringing to the fore in the 1980s. Let me quickly add that this is proving quite difficult in many African states, South Africa included, perhaps because it is extremely dangerous to criticize post-colonial African governments. Engelbert Mveng died in mysterious circumstances. In South Africa, it is simply very difficult to be critical of anything that has the support of Mandela and Tutu. So, while Tutu and Mandela have been tremendous assets in the struggle against apartheid, I doubt they can be assets in a continued critique of abuse of power after apartheid. But the task of being prophetic in post-independent Africa is one that has been acknowledged as a necessary one.

Fifth, there is a growing criticism of the grand narratives of Africa, African culture, and the political liberation projects. Not only is African culture being found to be extremely various, but African women theologians are, for example, mounting a fundamental critique of it. As indicated above, the notion of Africa or African states as homogeneous and liberative "ideas" is now being imploded in various disciplines.

Sixth, whereas cold war African theology granted epistemological privilege to the poor (blacks or women) in ways that portrayed the poor as conned and helpless victims needing to be roused from their slumber, post–cold war African theology is cautious about portraying the African poor as helpless and successfully brainwashed victims of the powers that be. There is a new realization that the African poor, African Christians, and Africans in general are not without resources, intellectual, material, and spiritual resources for survival and resistance —even if such resistance may be covert and coded rather than overt and public. In other words, the agency of African Christians and the African poor is being rediscovered, explored, and respectfully interpreted.

Seventh, I wish to suggest that African women are arguably the one section of most African societies which is engaging in the most passionate, the most vibrant, and the most prophetic forms of praxis (theory and practice). African women's theology has been by far the most prolific and challenging in the past decade and a half—at least in Anglophone Protestant Africa.

Eighth, as evidenced by the works of the likes of Mosala and Petersen, one new direction in the emerging paradigm of African theology is the search for theoretical tools and perspectives that will enable black and prophetic African theology to understand and account for the mythical, the sociocultural, and the popular in religion and society. In order to achieve this task, Mosala invokes theoretical resources from a carefully chosen group of unconventional and even dissident Marxian scholars whom he uses in his own specific ways, and fuses these with a specific reading of black experience. For his part, Petersen adds to the modernist theoretical kitty of "prophetic theology" insights from "neo-modernist," post-modernist scholars and theologians such as Michel de Certeau, James Scott, Jean and John Comaroff, Rebecca Chopp, Moishe Postone, and David Tracy. Regardless of whether and how successful Mosala and Petersen are in their attempts, it is important to recognize the significance of the alert they raise in highlighting (a) the sociopolitical importance of popular religious movements and (b) the need to develop adequate and relevant theoretical tools for understanding them.

Ninth, post-apartheid African theology is increasingly confronting issues around biblical hermeneutics—the most enduring legacy of South African black theology. Black theology's declaration of intent "to use the Bible to get the land back and to get the land back without losing the Bible" is also a declaration of a most difficult enterprise. Which biblical hermeneutics are the most appropriate and liberating for African Christians? Various African theologies have answered this question variously and the search for the most useful paths is still on. What has become very clear is that it is no longer possible for African theologians to pretend that the Bible, the gospel, or the "Christian faith" interprets itself and that things only go wrong when people misrepresent a "faith" or the Bible which is itself essentially "pure" and "good." The question of hermeneutics has been thrust to the fore and many African theological approaches have bidden farewell to hermeneutical innocence and have begun to take conscious responsibility for this important and complex task of hermeneutics, not only in relation to the

Bible but also in relation to the social reality in which African Christians find themselves.

Lastly, the one factor that cuts across all of the factors highlighted above is the rediscovery of the agency of Africans. All of the new proposals in African theology, each in its own way, foreground the notion of Africans as agents. Admittedly, the protagonists are not always consciously and deliberately doing this. Nor are they all aware of the fact that they may be advancing similar and mutually supportive projects, so some even operate in ignorance of others. Yet a careful analysis of the newest offerings in African theology—from the work of Lamin Sanneh and Kwame Bediako, through that of Oduyoye and her sisters in the Circle of Concerned African Women Theologians, Mugambi and Villa-Vicencio's reconstruction theology, Mosala and Mofokeng's quest to understand how black Christians may and do intend to "use the Bible to get the land back and get the land back without losing the Bible," Tutu's theology of forgiveness, Gerald West's quest for creating dialogue between Africa's trained and Africa's ordinary readers, to Robin Petersen's riveting attempt to understand "what really goes on" in African independent churches (AICs)—reveal a rediscovery of the agency of African Christians in the face of great odds.

One of the salient moves that Lamin Sanneh makes in his work is to wrest the creative initiative from missionaries to "the Gospel" and consequently to its African translators and assimilators. It was and could only be Africans who translated the gospel into vernacular idiom and not the missionaries, he argues. Furthermore, Sanneh argues that Africans conducted and discharged the translation process in such a way as to strengthen their own identity and position in the world. For several years now, the renowned Zimbabwean scholar of AICs, Marthinus Dance, has argued not only that the AICs represented the most contextualized and inculturated form of African Christianity, but that the total life, witness, and praxis of these churches was so *agentic* that it constituted a form of theology. Therefore, as Daneel has argued, these churches constituted not merely the "raw material" and the "sources of theology," as some had claimed, but that they themselves were a form of African theology and a face of African Christianity in their own right. In his work, Robin Petersen presents a complex argument for viewing AIC members as agents and resistors. In similar ways, the work of the Circle of Concerned Women Theologians highlights that women are not passive, brainwashed, and duped members of African societies. They are resisting agents who are taking the initiative. In his work, Gerald West shows that poor, uneducated, illiterate, and/or untrained African readers of the Bible are not destitute. They provide their own intelligent, coherent, not only different but better, readings of the Bible.

A Glimpse of the Methodological "Wires" of the Emerging Paradigm

Methodologically, the most instructive have been the works of Robin Petersen, a South African prophetic theologian, on the relationship between what he calls prophetic African theology and AICs, and those of Itumeleng Mosala (and Takatso Mofokeng), operating from within South African black theology, in their quest for black theological and biblical hermeneutics as a means of understanding and constructively influencing the paradoxical—if not tragic—nature of black Christianity.[40]

Mosala and His Legacy

More than any other South African theologian, Itumeleng Mosala has labored hardest to seek a liberative and truly independent hermeneutical framework. For Mosala, liberative theology must be situated within and grow out of "the social, cultural, political and economic world of the black working class and peasantry." [41] It is this slant that has made his brief and frugal research on AICs unique and extremely valuable. For him, AICs are made up of "the poorest of the poor" and they constitute "an autonomous cultural discourse under conditions of a monopoly capitalist system which is over–determined by a racist political and social structure."[42] But Mosala also recognizes that while AICs may provide "liberation from the brutalities of late capitalism" through their subversive hermeneutics of distortion and mystification, this is achieved at the cost of "ideological enslavement to the authoritarian structures of a feudal leadership with undoubted capitalist aspirations and activities."[43]

For Mosala, therefore, it is important that the domination of working-class blacks be understood comprehensively—as cultural, political and economic—and that the struggle against such domination be pitched consciously and deliberately at all these levels. To articulate his notions of culture, race, and class, Mosala creatively invokes certain types of Marxian historical materialism, referring to the likes of Cabral, Cornel West, and Terry Eagleton. He also suggests that while commitment to the liberation struggle is necessary, it is not enough as a basis of liberative theology. This is in my opinion a momentous suggestion. What is *crucial* is that theology must go beyond mere commitment to effecting an "ideological and theoretical break" with dominant ideologies, practices, and discourses.[44] Indeed the sharpest edge of Mosala's tongue is reserved for those types of liberation theologies, who despite their genuinely good intentions, nevertheless remain trapped in the ideological and theoretical frameworks of the very oppressors whom they seek to undermine and ultimately dethrone. He singles out several types of contextual theology for this kind of critique. Thus for Mosala, a thoroughgoing class analysis of society, the church, and theologians is necessary.

The other side of Mosala's push for a hermeneutically and theoretically "liberated" theology is found in his biblical hermeneutics. He rejects the equation of the Bible with the Word of God as ultimately only a ruling-class ploy to present themselves through the Bible as a self-interpreting single-message "voice of God." He calls for a critical regard for the Bible and a commitment to exposing and exploring the ambiguities in its messages—in the service of the struggles of the poor working-class blacks. Mosala (and Mofokeng) suggests that not all of the Bible is liberative. In fact, he argues that most of it is not liberative —at least not automatically so. If "left to its devices" the Bible will manufacture and reinforce oppression—thus the need for a break with oppressive hermeneutics. In similar manner, Mosala was not satisfied to bless everything about the "black experience," black culture, or the praxis of AICs. In this way he refuses to romanticize either African culture or the African poor such as those who are members of African independent churches in the way that Daneel, Petersen, and Gerald West are disposed to doing.

Reconceptualization of Dominance and Resistance

Next to the work of Mosala, Petersen's PhD work on the relationship between South African prophetic theology and AICs—*Time resistance and reconstruction: rethinking Kairos theology*—is one of the most important theological works to come out of post-apartheid South Africa. I have suggested above that one of the most creative currents common to all theological orientations in the emerging paradigm of post–cold war African theology is the rediscovery of African agency. In this important work, Petersen seeks to (a) explain why and how prophetic liberation theology has never been able to "make its mind up" about AICs, (b) propose some methodological and theoretical strategies which can help prophetic theology evaluate AICs more creatively and more coherently, and thereby (c) assist prophetic theology to achieve an integration of its "ethical-political norm"[45] with an ability to analyze, understand, and articulate the "sociocultural" and the popular as represented in such groups as AICs—in other words, to understand the *kairos* not merely and narrowly in overt political terms, but also in terms of disrupted *chronos* and the disrupting of *chronos* such as what happens in ritual praxis.

But Petersen goes further and explores what might be necessary for prophetic/liberation theology to achieve this integration. There is a need to reconceptualize *kairotic time,* the political, domination, and resistance. Petersen charges that the largely Enlightenment-beholden tools—various forms and appropriations of Marxist analyses, for example—of conventional liberation or prophetic theology are not adequate to achieve this task. He invokes "other theoretical resources that open up new possibilities for a thicker description and analysis of the social, and for different conceptualizations of what counts as political, as resistance, as religious and as ethical."[46] To achieve these tasks, Petersen refers to the works of four scholars, Michel de Certeau (historian of religion and theorist of culture), James Scott (a sociologist), and Jean and John Comaroff (historical anthropologists). Other South African theologians have followed Petersen down this path, notably Gerald West[47] and Jim Cochrane.[48] But these do not, in my opinion, achieve the kind of theoretical depth, criticality, and command of issues that Petersen achieves.

Conclusion

Positive implications for theology

If I am correct in suggesting that the most creative dimension of the merging paradigm for African theology lies in the rediscovery and emphasis on the agency of Africans, then the scholars cited above offer us the most fruitful tools for articulating this agency. The tools they put forward have the potential to help both liberation and inculturation theology account for the mythical, popular religious groups—through the manner in which the ethico-political is combined with the sociocultural. However, Mosala's refusal to accord total agentic power to AICs, de Certeau's suggestion that the anti-disciplinary action of consumer networks are not self-conscious, combined with the Comaroffs' talk of a realm and moment in which "individuals or groups know that something is happening to them" without knowing what it is exactly, is a necessary caution against a total romanticization of the consciousness and activities of the dominated.

Some reservations

The emerging discussions around agency are both promising and problematic. The first problem is that these discussions tend to be led and propagated mostly by people whose ancestors and themselves were not directly at the receiving end of the colonial and civilizing Christian project which victimized African Christians. The danger of glorification and romanticization of the mystical and the popular is a very real one. One catches worrying glimpses of it even in the work of the likes of Petersen[49] and West.[50] Although Petersen is very aware of the short-comings of James Scott's rather blanket suggestion that the dominated are always fully conscious of their domination and of their own potential for agency, he nevertheless refuses to countenance any dark and/or unconscious side of AIC praxis. Similarly, West offers little critique with regard to Scott and very little critique of the consciousness of marginalized "ordinary readers."[51]

The closest we come to a critique of the consciousness of West's marginalized "ordinary readers" is in his insistence that they need "trained readers"—which is why he defines his intellectual project as being one that explores the relationship between "ordinary" and what he calls "socially engaged trained readers." Yet since he does not help-fully elaborate or evaluate either the ordinarization of his "ordinary readers" or the training of his "trained readers," we really do not know why ordinary readers of the Bible should need trained readers of the Bible and vice versa.[52] So with him we come face-to-face with the possible dangers of (a) a noble but further marginalization of whom-soever he defines as "ordinary readers"—marginalization by romanti-cizing, romanticizing by the imposition of an uninterrupted self-conscious agency on them, at least, and (b) the romanticization of "trained readers" by assuming that their training, social location, race, gender (etc.) is of no real consequence as long as they are "socially engaged" and aware of being "partially constituted"[53] by their poor and marginalized interlocutors.

The romanticization of the popular and the mystical religious movements is as serious a danger as their outright dismissal. Equally dangerous is the romanticizing of the academy and its actors. In this case, Mosala presents the most balanced regard for both such popular religious movements as AICs, as well as their academic interlocutors. It is precisely here that Mosala's critique of the ideological location and commitment of fellow theologians[54] must at its best be reckoned as an exercise in self-criticism.

Furthermore, could there be grounds for suspecting that the newfound valorization of popular and new religious movements might degenerate into a belated cleansing of the consciences of the missionaries and the colonizers and oppressors, by suggesting that since marginalized blacks and women were always resisting in covert ways, their oppression was not in fact all that crushing and their oppressors not at all that powerful? What does it mean when males suggest that the females whom they oppress are not completely crushed by oppression? It is one thing when the women say it themselves but quite another when males say it. Secondly, much discourse about African agency runs the risk of glorifying survival and equating it too quickly with strategic and purposeful resistance. Survival tactics must be recognized, but to read too much into them may be counter-productive. Thirdly, not all proposals purporting to highlight African agency actually do that. It is, for example, debatable whether Sanneh's (and by extension, Bediako's) translation metaphor really highlights the agency and initiative of Africans in their encounter with missionary Christianity and colonialism. Apart from attributing almost everything creative done by Africans to the genius and logic of the gospel, rather than Africans, the proposal seems more concerned with the activities of missionaries and colonialists than those of Africans.[55]

Tinyiko S. Maluleke is Professor of Black and African Theologies at the University of South Africa, Pretoria, South Africa. <danisa@yebo.co.za>

NOTES

[1] The financial assistance of the Centre for Science Development (South Africa) toward this research is hereby acknowledged. The opinions and conclusions which are expressed in this essay are those of the author and are not necessarily to be attributed to the Centre for Science Development.

[2] I am also curious about the self-definition and "success" of "white African" writers, such as J.M. Coetzee (two times winner of the prestigious Booker Prize for English literature), Nadine Gordimer (the Nobel Prize literature laureate), and others. When I read some of their works, I cannot help thinking that they are writing *about* and even *for* me also.

[3] J. N. K. Mugambi, *From liberation to reconstruction: African Christian theology after the Cold War* (Nairobi: East African Educational Publishers, 1995).

[4] Kwame Bediako, *Theology and identity: the impact of culture upon Christian thought in the second century and modern Africa* (Oxford: Regnum Books, 1992) and *Christianity in Africa: the renewal of a nonwestern religion* (Edinburgh: University Press; Maryknoll: Orbis Books, 1995).

[5] Mercy Amba Oduyoye, *Daughters of Anowa: African women and patriarchy* (Maryknoll: Orbis Books, 1995).

[6] Lamin Sanneh, *Translating the message: the missionary impact on culture* (Maryknoll: Orbis Books, 1988).

[7] Dwight N. Hopkins, *Black faith and public talk* (Maryknoll: Orbis Books, 1999); *Black theology of liberation* (Maryknoll: Orbis Books, 1999) and *Down, up and over: slave religion and black theology* (Minneapolis: Fortress, 2000).

[8] Charles Villa-Vicencio, *A theology of reconstruction* (Cambridge: Cambridge University Press, 1992).

[9] C. Landman, *The piety of Afrikaan women: diaries of guilt* (Pretoria: University of South Africa, 1994).

[10] Piet Naudé, *The Zionist Christian Church in South Africa: a case study in oral theology* (Queenston: Edwin Mellen, 1995).

[11] Robin M. Petersen, "Time, resistance and reconstruction: re-thinking Kairos theology," PhD thesis, Chicago, University of Chicago, 1995.

[12] Gerald O. West, *The academy of the poor: towards a dialogical reading of the Bible,* Interventions 2 (Sheffield: Sheffield Academic Press, 1999).

[13] James R. Cochrane, *Circles of dignity: community wisdom and theological reflection* (Minneapolis: Fortress, 1999).

[14] Desmond Mpilo Tutu, *No future without forgiveness* (Johannesburg, London, Sidney, Auckland: Rider, 1999).

[15] Tinyiko S. Maluleke, "A letter to Job—from Africa," *Challenge,* no 43 (August/September 1997) 14–15 (also published in *Tam Tam* [September/October 1997], 5).

[16] Mugambi, *From liberation to reconstruction,* 33.

[17] Institute for Contextual Theology, *The Kairos document* (Braamfontein: Institute for Contextual Theology, 1985).

[18] Per Frostin, *Liberation theology in South Africa and Tanzania* (Lund: University Press, 1988).

[19] Placide Tempels, *La philosophie Bantoe* (Paris: Présence Africain, 1959). This work is fruit of research among the Luba people.

[20] Marcel Griaule, *Dieu d'eau: Entretiens avec Ogotemmêli* (Paris: Fayard, 1966). It is important to note that the research—the thirty-day-long series of interviews—on which this work is based was conducted among the Dogon people in 1946.

[21] Adrian Hastings, *African Christianity: an essay in interpretation* (London: G. Chapman, 1976) 52–53.

[22] E. W. Fasholé-Luke, "The quest for an African Christian theology," *The ecumenical review* 27:3 (1975) 267–268.

[23] Keith B. Richburg, *Out of America: a black man confronts Africa* (New York: Basic Books, 1997). Unfortunately (or fortunately) Richburg's arguments on what is wrong with Africa are poorly substantiated and his comments on the Africans he met and interacted with are generally so contemptuous and patronizing that the discerning reader must conclude that Richburg has not only misunderstood but abused the hospitality of Africans.

[24] See Emmanuel Katongole's incisive critique of the African renaissance project. Emmanuel Katongole, "African Renaissance and the challenge of narrative theology in

Africa: whose story/whose renaissance?" *Journal of theology for southern Africa,* no. 102 (1998), 29–39. See also Thabo Mbeki, *Africa: the time has come* (Tafelberg: Mafube, 1998).

[25] Oduyoye, *Daughters of Anowa,* 10.

[26] Kwame Anthony Appiah, *In my father's house: Africa in the philosophy of culture* (Oxford: Oxford University Press, 1992).

[27] Cornel West, *Race matters* (Boston: Beacon Press, 1993), 14.

[28] See Achille Mbembe, *L'Afriques indociles: Christianisme, pouvoir et etat en societé postcoloniale* (Paris: Karthala, 1988).

[29] Villa-Vicencio, A *theology of reconstruction.*

[30] At least in his 1995 work.

[31] Petersen, "Time, resistance and reconstruction."

[32] Petersen, "Time, resistance and reconstruction," 14.

[33] Sanneh, Translating the message.

[34] A. Walls, "Africa in Christian history—retrospect and prospect," paper given at the Conference on the Church in the African State in the Twenty-First Century, Akropong, Ghana, September 1997.

[35] An African American theologian—Michael Battle—who recently did a PhD on Tutu's *ubuntu* theology, remarks in the preface that "Tutu is not a theologian, he is better." In saying this, Battle was pointing out the lack of a clear and rigid system in Tutu's theology. However, there are other ways in which Tutu was not a typical theologian; i.e. his theology is also his personal life and witness and perhaps this is what commends his "theology" more than anything else.

[36] Mugambi, *From liberation to reconstruction.*

[37] Villa-Vicencio, *A theology of reconstruction.*

[38] See *Bulletin for contextual theology in southern Africa & Africa* 4, no. 2 (July 1997)—an entire issue devoted to Women's Theology.

[39] Mosala in Katongole, "African Renaissance."

[40] Mosala has also written no less than three incisive essays on African Independent Churches.

[41] Itumeleng J. Mosala, *Biblical hermeneutics and black theology in South Africa* (Grand Rapids: Eerdmans, 1989), 21.

[42] Itumeleng J. Mosala, 1996. "Race, class, and gender as hermeneutical factors in the African Independent Churches' appropriation of the Bible," *Semeia,* no. 73 (1996), 53.

[43] Mosala, "Race, class, and gender," 52

[44] Mosala, *Biblical hermeneutics and black theology in South Africa,* 4.

[45] According to Petersen, "Time, resistance and reconstruction," 34, the ethico-political assumes that "all theologies and religious practices need to be evaluated in terms of their ethical consequences and their political horizon; i.e., the valuation of these theories anti-practices in terms of their engagement in and enhancement of the struggle for liberation."

[46] Petersen, "Time, resistance and reconstruction," 12.

[47] West, *The academy of the poor.*

[48] Cochrane, *Circles of dignity.*

[49] Robin M. Petersen, "The AICs and the TRC," *Facing the truth: South African faith communities and the Truth and Reconciliation Commission,* eds. James R. Cochrane, John W. de Gruchy, Stephen W. Martin (Cape Town: David Philip, 1999), 114–125.

[50] West, *The academy of the poor.*

[51] West, *The academy of the poor.*

[52] See Tinyiko S. Maluleke, "The Bible among African Christians: a missiological perspective," *To cast fire upon the earth: Bible and mission collaborating in today's multi-cultural global context*, ed. Teresa Okure (Pietermaritzburg: Cluster Publications, 2000).

[53] West, *The academy of the poor*, 120–123.

[54] Mosala, *Biblical hermeneutics and black theology in South Africa.*

[55] The Comaroffs also run this risk.

CHAPTER 9

Acting as Women

Amba Mercy Oduyoye

Hey, Maria, be stationary!
No! My sister, keep moving.

Apopular cartoon strip in a Nigerian newspaper once featured the following episode between Big Joe and Maria, two characters created by Cliff Ogiugo.

Big Joe (coming behind Maria): Hey, Maria, be stationary! (Maria stops and turns to face Joe and he continues.) There is an eclipse! If you've any reflective pieces of metal like coins in your pockets, better drop them or you're dead.

(Maria stands and looks on as Joe empties her pockets of all her money and lines up the coins in two rows of five on the ground. He then turns Maria to face the direction she was originally going and with what looks like a "loving" push from the back, Big Joe explains to her):

Big Joe: OK. You're all right. (Meanwhile as an aside): Thanks to the eclipse.

This particular cartoon strip is typical of the relations between Joe and Maria. Good-natured but slow, Maria always loses out in her encounters with Big Joe. In this episode, Big Joe, no taller or bigger than Maria, robs her of all her pocket money by showing fake loving concern. As I stand in solidarity with Maria, as a woman with other women, I can do no other than to warn her: Next time Big Joe asks you to stand still, give the matter serious thought. Watch to see that he also drops his "reflective pieces."

The Church Is Us

The African church is a human community in which women are commanded to be stationary. The baptismal creed of the church at Corinth and the Tridentine decision to grant women souls demand that women assert and put into practice their intrinsic worth before God as

171

being equally human with men.[1] We women must take our lives into our own hands, as men have always done. To be able to give an account of ourselves, we must respond to God with our own voice. It will not do for us to say to God (or ourselves), "The men you gave me dictated what my talents ought to be or what I did for your church." As the first Jews who followed Christ's way declared, their obedience was to God instead of to humankind. We women must insist on having the opportunity to participate in the church according to our God-given talents rather than according to the dictates of men. We must offer the church what we feel able to, so that we will conscientiously work out our own salvation without any gender-based constraints imposed on us by a particular culture. Theocracy should be salvific and liberating. Any theocracy, however, can be distorted by a patriarchal lens to oppress or dehumanize women. When this happens, men are also debased and sexism rears its head even among men otherwise committed to freeing the oppressed and searching out the humanness of "the other."

Reading the Bible

Our lifestyle as Christian women is shaped not only by traditional imagery of religion, culture, and society but also by the incorporation of Western colonial norms in the teaching of the church. In Africa, Pauline language has been used to set the tone for a theology of order and of gender. Because of its widespread treatment of the Bible as an infallible oracle, the church in Africa is slow to change its attitudes, and this is particularly true of its attitudes toward women.

Africans, so adept in our culture of orality, have a prodigious memory for what "the Bible says" just as we do for our myths, tales, and proverbs. With our finely tuned ears and memory, prooftexting can be an easy but nonetheless lethal tool as we pull passages from our memory and recite them at will. This lack of *contextual* reading of the Bible has meant, for example, that we misinterpret passages from Genesis 3 or that we are able to ignore studies that show that Paul's language about women is not part of an exclusive revelation to Paul, nor is it exclusively or especially "Christian": It follows that if most learned writers of Paul's time used the same language, Paul's words on women are not necessarily a direct message from God to the church. Similarly, problems of same-sex love, which made Paul clamp down on women's freedom in Christ, were also discussed by his contemporary Jews, Greeks, and Romans.[2]

Another factor that African women should not overlook is that, generally speaking, those who advocate ideas that are initially liberative often revert to more conservative positions. This is shown in the way in which Paul contradicts his original message of freedom in Christ Jesus (Galatians 3:28) and reverts to a language of subordination of women, which conformed with that of his contemporaries. Similarly, after the death of Muhammad, Islam turned away from his visions for women's humanity and personhood.[3]

It is crucial that Christian women be aware that what men claim the Bible and other sources of religious teaching, for that matter, say is not necessarily definitive. Wide variations in translations and the facile manipulations of those translations are sufficient reasons for us to listen very carefully and to continually raise questions.[4] Women cannot leave Bible translation, study, or interpretation to an all-male clergy. We have Bible scholars who are women and they are increasing in number. We must support them and listen to them.[5] But most important of all, we must begin to question and to do our own thinking. Each of us has a duty to contribute to theological thinking. Leaving theology in the hands of an all-male caste whose pronouncements on the Bible are hardly ever questioned—not by men, and certainly not by us women—is to be content to respond to God through others.

We have to study the Bible ourselves with our own life experiences as the starting point. That is what the authors of the Bible did. Indeed, the Bible gathers together theologies made up of experiences of individuals and whole communities over hundreds of years to answer the questions: What is God doing? or, What is God saying to us? Even though biblical times are removed from us by nearly two millennia, we believe that God continues to work and to talk to us through the Bible, a human story with events, scenes, and beliefs, some of which we feel very close to as Africans. As we review and record our own experiences of God, we begin to write a "new book" of how God deals with today's world and its peoples. Nothing lies beyond the scope of this "African Testament."

We women must reread the Bible to seek guidance on how to listen to God and to recognize where God is at work in our world today. Although today's issues may at times appear different, they are none-theless the same fundamental human dilemmas, such as the meaning of marriage, the value of human relations, the nature of sin, the functioning of grace. As women, we need to engage in a continuing synthesis of our past experiences and present possibilities instead of simply accepting the dogmas and lifestyles imposed upon us by religion or culture. So we read the Bible, remaining always open to the voice of God and knowing that what works in one situation or time period does not necessarily or always work in another.

Take, for instance, the women we meet in the Bible. Study them as individual women who lived in a particular place at a particular time. There is no one image of woman, just as we found no single image of woman in the Akan-Yoruba folk talk. Some we will admire; some we will not. And, if we study in a group, then we must honor the choices and interpretations of other women. Dialogue informs any vision of society. If we conclude that we women have little in common except that we are all female and thus the center of new life—the potential of being the "mother of all life"—we still share a biological gift that makes women life-affirming and life-loving.[6]

We do not, of course, always find women in the Bible who provide answers for the problems of today. But we do find women who inspire us to devise the answers. Although Hebrew women could not be priests, they could be prophets. African Christian women today can be both prophets and priests. In the past and today, our presence as mediums with therapeutic powers and our powers of dreams, visions, and prophesies have been interpreted as attempts to exercise power over others. Such an interpretation is detrimental to the work of priest-healers of Africa, a number of whom are women.[7] This could lead to our religious roles, such as they are, becoming further demeaned, suspect, marginalized, or even outlawed by future legislation. But if women appropriate both our Christian and African heritages, we can be social commentators on behalf of justice and true religion as well as cultic functionaries. We can be prophets in our churches, like Anna, who saw in the baby Jesus the vision of a New World (Luke 2:36–38), as well as prophets like the *Ahemaa* and the *Iyalode* who stood for social justice and women's participation in political decisions.

Women and Religious Ritual

When women seek to participate at the Christian communion table, a fundamental problem surfaces that seems to go back to the sacrificial rituals of primal religions, including those of Africa. The Holy Table was reserved in the early church for an exclusively male priesthood, a community that obviously excluded women. Yet, the Holy Table attempts to become a communion table of the entire Christian community by the generous invitation made by priests at the altar, which enables women to come forward to share the meal. In some churches in Africa, the synthesis of Hebrew Bible teachings with the traditions of African religion prevents women who are life-giving —those who are menstruating or those who have just given birth—from participating in this life-giving table. Why do women need a rite of purification after birth? Why does Christianity not celebrate this life-givingness? Should not African women in the church question this ritual and seek to demystify the patriarchal ideologies that tend to marginalize women?

Akan myths of *ntorɔ* incorporate some of this same identification of what is spiritual with what is male. Two different myths of origins tell of how an animal (a python or a crocodile) teaches human couples how to copulate and then the myths associate that animal with the engendering of life and with semen. In this way, a patriarchal psycho-spiritual power is established. Both the child and the mother must submit to the father's spiritual power and oversight in order to have a stable life.[8] So although we can quibble about whether or not the Supreme God has a genderless imagery, the immediate spirit that guides one's life is male, what I am prone to call a literal case of "phallocracy."

As Christian women we do have a precedent. Jesus once asked his followers, "Who do you say that I am?" Asked such a question, we have no need to echo anyone else's findings about God: we can raise our own voice. For me, Jesus Christ as Lord does not permit *any* priest, man or woman, to lord it over the church. Jesus specifically excluded oppressive hierarchies that were operated by a self-serving leadership. In the same way, the phrase "God is Father" means that God is like the male spirit that "made my head" and guards it. But the source of my being is *abadae* (womb compassion), and no man or woman can represent God to me who does not exhibit what I see of God. It is the man or woman who acts to set things right, who fills the poor with good things and sends the rich away empty-handed who is God-filled; such people create "good" from chaos and ugliness. People who respect my person enough to call me to the responsibility of being about "good" are the people who are godly.

For me, therefore, the grammar of the gender of God is not the heart of the matter. It becomes so only when the male imagery of God is used as a tool of patriarchal oppression to dampen the spirits of the sisterhood or to draw boundaries around women's participation in the church's ministry. If our imagery of God continues to be that of a male and father, then we must remember that God safeguards our autonomy as persons and our freedom to live as responsible human persons.

African society is organized in such a way that all able-bodied persons work almost as soon as they can walk; when they can no longer walk, they still function as a source of wisdom and as the storehouse of the collective memory of the family. Because of this, it was not easy to marginalize (and thus control) any group of people. While women were obviously neither physically nor intellectually weak, their one distinctive physical characteristic was the biological factor of menstruation and parturition. Historically in Africa, as communities became more and more centralized and gravitated to increasingly larger units, women were left behind in the homes, and control through the "government" moved into centralized administrative facilities. It is interesting to observe the same process in church development: the earliest churches were in homes with women presiding; eventually, they gathered together under an all-male curia in Rome.[9] This is true of other patriarchies as well.

In the history of our Akan communities, menstruation became a focus of mystification and played a negative role in women's participation. It continues to function this way in African Christianity. If the church dares to label God's chosen creative process as unclean, should not women work to strip menstruation of this mystification? The church has set up an idolatrous system around a god of "purity" who does not seem to have anything to do with justice and right-doing and who lacks respect for baptism and all that it means in the Good News of Jesus Christ.

When we examined African Traditional Religion, we questioned why women must wait until their creating fountain dries up before they can participate in life-seeking and life-affirming rituals. Perhaps what I have called the god of "purity" is instead the god of male being, establishing norms of being human. Traditional Akan thinking matched and balanced the bloodless semen power of *ntorɔ* with the female blood power. Does the church have a female counterpart to provide balance for its all-male clergy? Instead of being oriented toward what is love and all that we think of as godly and god-ward, we women await men to tell us just what limits to observe. We have allowed patriarchy to breed and thrive unchallenged in the church. At this point, I begin to understand why some women have argued that using male language to talk about God has in fact made God male and as a result excluded women from full humanity. We should ask why widows and celibate women were accepted in the ministry of the early church. Do men claim the most active years of women's lives for *their* service and leave the residue for

God? Should women accept this scheme for our service in the church? We need to do a thorough job of filtering Christianity to determine what really liberates us to be the church.

On Loving Others

Women have begun to see women's complicity in the situation. They have surrendered not only to a man-made world but also to a man-made God who has decreed the isolation of women from public life and sentenced them to serve in obscurity and silence.[10] If, indeed, we are accomplices to our own marginalization, we have to find out why. We African women have been brought up, and folktalk has been part of our education, to be devoted daughters, sisters, wives, and mothers, to always love others more than self. It seems to me that in this process we have also learned to vote against the self, always preferring others and loving them more than we love ourselves, doing for them what we decline to do for ourselves because we consider ourselves unworthy of such attention. We have been content to work for, rather than with, children, spouse, and other relatives. We have declined to exercise power over others; this in itself is just as well, but in the process we have also given up power over our own lives. The result is that we are in the process of losing our voices, even though, as the proverb says, our tongues are stronger than other muscles.[11] We have reduced ourselves at times to moving to the streets in protest or to employing "power" in other ways; it is disturbing that we seem to glory in these situations. In my opinion, such ploys are demeaning. Instead we should seek to accrue dignity and respect for our persons and personalities. I often ask myself why women should be placed in positions where we have to feign submission to men. Where are dignity and respect for oneself and for others?[12]

This abdication of autonomy is exalted in many cultures as a hallmark of "the virtuous woman." Even if our divestiture of self or power and our acceptance of the need to have a male as the head have been voluntary, we should still question why gender is the ultimate distinction between human beings. Other qualities—those that determine how we interact with other human beings and with our environment—seem far more significant. Instead of congratulating ourselves for knowing how to "get our way," we should seek ways of achieving our common goals while being true to ourselves and to others; if we cannot achieve our goals without pretense, then perhaps we should take another look at our goals.

We desecrate our life-giving function if our kitchens with their pots and pans or our sexuality become arenas for exercising control over others, rather than ways of sharing and participating in life. Instead of prostituting our kitchens or profaning our bodies, church women would do well to loosen our tongues and raise our voices, telling aloud our real hurts and seeking redress. Using the kitchen or the bedroom is simply playing the man's game. When market women have been really pushed by unrealistic taxation or price control, they have taken to the streets in protest. We must ask, though, why women were not present in the first place when these decisions were being made.

African women have always been sensitive to the coherence of the communities to which we belong; we have hidden the violence the system does to us even from ourselves. Our *afis ɛn* (domestic affairs) are never washed and hung outside. Our preoccupation has been with the integrity of family life. We have been content to spoil our children, our husbands, and anyone else who has come our way. The result is that our services are now taken for granted and even demanded.[13] Yet, when we have carried on even under extreme hurt, we have often been rewarded with more sexist exploitation, a situation in which we are made to believe that it is even more blessed to love others more than ourselves. We forget then that being human is having and exercising a choice. Judged by traditional reciprocity, we are being most "*un*african" by loving people more than they are prepared to love us.

The existential situation of women in Ghana is one of gradually crumbling traditional social support systems that make it difficult if not impossible for women by themselves to be the custodians of tradition. While women, in their bondage to culture, have been working at the task of replenishing the communal bowl, men have often preferred to seek individual advancement. As custodians of communal land, men continue to move women off farmlands to sell the land to monied investors—hence, the continuing disintegration of the system.

As culture's bondswomen, we have tried to follow traditional principles within a world that is fast changing and among people who themselves show unwillingness to keep their side of tradition. Reflecting on a radio program urging women to stay at home, I said to myself that it is the professional women and salary earners who can afford modern institutions like childcare who go on the radio telling all women that their first duty is to their home, husband, and children. We create a situation of conflict if we do not see that the woman with one child on her back and perhaps another in tow as she peddles tomatoes and peppers throughout the day is also doing her duty. We Christian women, and particularly those of us who are part of the educated urban elite, might be creating a new African woman who will end up carrying the burdens of the Western woman on top of her traditional ones. As we re-image our womanness, we must remember that women need to stand by women, and that, contrary to our proverbial sayings, all women are not the same. Celebrating both unity and diversity, women can stand together.

Women Supporting Women

"If we do not know where we are going to, at least we know where we are coming from," says the Yoruba proverb. Our past, where we are coming from, did have ways of supporting women. Traditional society worked for women through networks of kindred, friends, wives of an affinal home, women selling the same commodity, or women passing on skills of pottery, weaving, or beadwork. Whether it was a birth, marriage, or funeral, Yoruba women got together and worked. Women supported women, standing in solidarity as women. How can we adapt this traditional experience to help us in these changing times, knowing that its bifocal system (one male and one female) of community organization was partly responsible for the resilience and strength of women in traditional society? Its bifocal nature may help us discover or evolve aspects that will enable our effectiveness as women in modern structures and give us access to decision making. With our collective strength—numerical, financial, and cerebral—we can draw on this bifocal system to gain entry into political structures to help formulate laws under which we all can live as free and responsible human beings.

As church women, perhaps we should transform Mothers' Unions into Women's Unions to gain inclusiveness and a better representational voice in the assemblies of the church. We must remember that the ecclesiology that marginalizes us as women is built upon theories of exclusion. We cannot heal breaches within the Christian community if we ourselves operate exclusive structures. The African Instituted churches[14] have shown us a direction to follow as, for example, Captain Abiodun and others who have claimed the early and medieval Christian tradition of women leaders founding religious houses. By enabling and empowering women, women as a whole will achieve a stronger presence and a voice that will be heard. Standing as individuals our oppression readily weighs us down, one by one. But when we Christian women stand by other women, we are not only following traditional

African structures and women in church history, we are also following Elizabeth, the cousin of Mary, the older woman who believed the pregnant virgin's fantastic tale. The bonding of Mary and Elizabeth was so liberative that it enabled a virgin with child to put away fear and shame to declare that God had done great things to her. Their bond of solidarity becomes ours.

This growing solidarity of sisterhoods around the world enjoins us to not allow a precious heritage to atrophy and die. West African women need to listen to their sisters from other parts of the African continent. We need to take on our share in enabling others to recover their own worth as women and to empower other women to survive and struggle against injustice. Asian peasant women and factory workers, the landless women of Latin America, and the lace makers of Switzerland all endure oppression peculiar to our gender. Their stories and ours are one. That women are an underclass is a global reality, for what is crucial is for us to be clear on the point that being universal does not make sexism a manifestation of the will of God.

Gender binds us together in many ways. The taboos of sexuality among Westernized Christian women in Africa continue to show up in our encounters in society. So intimidated have we been that we have not even asked the church to reevaluate menstruation and pregnancy in relation to Eucharistic ministry. Yet our participation is crucial. During informal conversations we women have sometimes shown as much unease about pregnant women at the Holy Table. If we ourselves regard pregnancy as an unholy state, we can contribute nothing to the discussion of the ordination of women priests or pastors. If we continue to associate coitus with defilement or to accept the supposed double defilement that comes with bearing a girl, we hold on to traditional religious beliefs of pollution and see ourselves as the major pollutants. It is the women who must initiate rational discussion of these subjects in the church and the academy. Our responsibilities for community education are clear.

Another area in which our voices are silent is the treatment of single and childless women whose grim fate undermines the solidarity of all women and serves to uphold patriarchal norms. The easy labeling of women as prostitutes evades the whole issue of the defiling mate. If we open up these issues we shall unmask the patriarchalization of the economy, the political structure, and the absence of effective educational structures for girls that collude to throw girls into the streets. Studies in other countries, especially in Asia, have uncovered the close link between prostitution and the burdens of young girls and women who have to support members of their family, often their parents. These are women who, like Rahab, are concerned not so much with their own survival and finery—as we very smugly judge them—but for the survival of others whom we do not see in the streets.[15]

Our sisterhood of concern must keep these issues of the unequal burdens of women in the public sphere in order to tackle the roots of the problem. These marks of patriarchal oppression are evident even in the transfer of northern Euro-American industries to southern third world countries where profits are multiplied as factory hands—the majority of whom are women—receive paltry wages. The problems, religious, social, and economic, are complex, but this is no excuse to do nothing. We must be able to recognize and name patriarchal oppression.

Because we are human and participate in structures of class and race, there are oppressors and oppressed among us as well. Women in high positions, having strength of character and being loyal to tradition, can be either negative or positive assets in our liberation struggle. Similar to the Ohemaa or the Iyalode, they are close to the centers of power. Yet, if they become isolated from other women, or, like Jezebel, are uncritical of the prevailing roles of women, then they are bound to hurt the women's cause. It was Jezebel's uncritical appropriation of her own culture, coupled with insensitive universalizing of that culture's demands, that prompted her actions (2 Kings 21:1–29). Sarah was also a culture-bound woman in an authority role. Oppressed by a culture that put no value on childless women, she in turn became oppressor to Hagar, whom both she and Abraham exploited under the patriarchal provisions of their times (Genesis 16:1–16; 21:8–21). Cruelty between and among women is often cited to dismiss our just demands or to muffle our voices. We must continually struggle to transcend the structures of race or class and any forms of oppression when we relate to other women. The "suicide" of both race and class is necessary for effective solidarity among women.

An analysis of the patriarchal hierarchy shows that we have survived at the bottom of the pyramid by building our own pyramids of hurt within that sub-structure. Imagine patriarchy as a big conical structure within which several other conical structures of oppressive hierarchies fit. At the bottom of each cone will be women. In Africa we have a special cone, the "Ideal Woman," at the bottom of which is the childless prostitute and, sitting comfortably at the top, the wife who is the mother of sons and daughters. Church women's groups can begin here to break the silence around this women's patriarchally controlled valuation of themselves. Polygynous marriage seems to provide an obvious starting point as such a marriage visibly groups women together in a hierarchical order. Serious studies by women of polygyny as a system will uncover its strengths and weaknesses as a human organization. If we cannot find ways to work out conditions under which it can be life-promoting, then we should find ways of ending it in order to eliminate the psychological burdens it imposes on women, children, and men. Simply to acquiesce because men want this system in which women must marry and have children shows the extent of our domestication and alienation from our own humanity. Acquiescence to this form of patriarchy does not seem to me to work toward building a just and loving community.

As we search for solidarity, we should examine how solidarity among women in Egypt was God's instrument to bring about the Exodus as Hebrew mothers and Egyptian midwives collaborated to save baby boys. One specifically privileged woman (an Egyptian princess) collaborated with a slave woman (mother of Moses) to save and nurture one of the baby boys who grew up to become a leader of the people. The sister of Moses, perhaps the youngest of the women of that drama, showed a resourcefulness and intelligence that made her the catalyst in that unplanned but cooperative venture that had its source in women's love of life. It is essential that we Christian women celebrate such collaboration as we struggle for liberation from patriarchal structures, political, ecclesiastical, and economic. Without these foresisters, those of Exodus and those of our own African tradition, we have no history; if we have forgotten where we are coming from and we do not know where we are going, we become easy prey. So we turn to our history of struggle, collaboration, and solidarity. We seek knowledge and we seek to free ourselves from the preeminence of men to work out new and life-giving ways of relating to others.

The image of the African Christian woman as wife and mother is modeled on Proverbs 31:10–31, which has close affinity with our culture. Womanhood in Africa is almost synonymous with motherhood. Woman's experience of being human is that of making space for others to grow, mothering, assisting at the "making of the human in others" and being simultaneously affected by that effort. Instead of Eve, the source of all sin,[16] we should bring to the fore Eve, the mother of life who is an intelligent educator and counselor. She is not a superhuman, but only a person who is very human and life-loving. We must study texts such as Proverbs 31 against their own background as well as ours, for biblical models also can grow obsolete.[17]

The Role of Self-Affirming Language

We must refuse to cooperate in the devaluation of our persons or humanity. We were not born with any of the behavioral patterns called feminine and masculine and, as such, we owe them no honor; rather, we have a duty to nourish our humanity. If our bondage to culture means that we have accepted myths of womanhood, knowing full well ourselves that there is no such thing as *the* woman, it is incumbent upon us to review these myths and test all the language that says "It is not good for you." What is not positive imagery of women should die from disuse, or it will continue to hamper our desire to live as human beings who are female. I do not think it helps to be swallowed up in androgynous imagery that may end up as male as "man" or "men" always have been, in spite of their legal inclusiveness.[18]

The delicate task of evolving a new language, positive myths, and dynamic icons that will project the humanity of women as partners in creation and in community is gigantic and exciting. Perhaps it even intimidates us African women. But we have the responsibility to begin, to do our part in our generation. We seem hesitant and apprehensive because we are aware of the delicacy with which the process must be undertaken. It is a task that must engage all our thoughtfulness, because it involves breaking the very chains we have been wearing and examining them one by one, link by link, gold and lead alike.

I was still in school when a friend, then in a coeducational teacher training college, told me the following incident. A tutor, frustrated at the seemingly nonchalant attitude of his students toward submitting assignments, was doing his best to impress on them the implications of this for their future careers. He knew what to say to men. At a loss as to what might motivate women, he gave up with a statement to the effect that the women did not need to worry about doing well in college: while men have to struggle for greatness, women become great by association. Living somebody else's life—even if that person is a husband, son, father, or even a daughter—is a fragile existence. Can such a frail image of self endure throughout life? That story greatly worried me.[19] How does one account for one's self using someone else's life? If we do not live our own lives, we shall continue to sing other people's songs.

We must also demand the opportunity to live as independent persons capable of participating in all areas of life, and to develop this model of woman's being in home, church, and country. Our quest for identity and recognition demands acknowledgment that our work and earnings constitute an indispensable part of what goes into the family's well-being and, beyond that, what makes us feel autonomous. We must be cautious with language that refers to us adult women as "dependents," even while we contribute to family budgets. Such language renders our participation invisible and makes us into perpetual minors. We need to develop and use inclusive language for domestic matters. It is our family, our children, not his children; we had them with him and not for him, and it is our home if we live there, not his house. This may sound trite, but such language creates an entirely different set of images about women. We are not employees of the men we marry; we are partners. If a human being may be described as belonging to another human being, we both belong to each other. We ought to be able to say, "We had children for us."

The most difficult part of re-imaging ourselves and affirming our experience is to articulate our oppression. Our inhibitions are valid because we have been brought up to smile—even when suffering. Any collective hurts we identify are immediately personalized and particularized.[20] We must, therefore, find ways of acting not just as individuals but collectively.

Sources of protest are many. A woman may simply ask herself, "Why do I have to do this?" Another woman who is looking for the divine image in humanity may ask, "What does it mean for both men and women to be in the image of God?" The latter woman may protest against the church orders that seek to subordinate her humanity. Other women simply act in affirmation of their humanity and by their very style of life protest against the patriarchal ordering of the world. The life carrier, according to Eve's name and Akan beliefs, cannot sit by and watch that life demeaned, oppressed, or marginalized, least of all her own life. For such a woman, feminism is the positive application of human culture.

The next time you might hear an African man rise quickly as a spokesperson for the African woman and say she has no need of liberation, do some reinterpretation. He has spoken so spontaneously because he expects her to be unable to speak for herself. If he says the women's liberation movement is an imported commodity, he is admitting that it has found a market (as do other Euro-American exports) in Africa. If he tells you that feminism is promoted by "unfulfilled" women, understand that he means those women whom society has been unable to "socialize" and who therefore are not accomplished at being "docile doves." And if he tells you that feminism is middle class, listen most skeptically. Women who speak against polygyny, those whose sweat fertilizes the rural farms, those who petition for water near their kitchens without success, those who leave their wares in the market to march against arbitrary taxation, price control, and marital and inheritance laws—all are of one class, the female underclass.

Making the World Our Home

To make where she lives a home, an African woman is ready and -willing to adopt the style of "putting up with," for her style of life is directed by working things out and smoothing over domestic conflict. If need be, she becomes the sacrifice.[21] In a crisis, she is the one who risks being thrown out to be replaced by another woman. This domestic picture is reflected in employment, in politics, and in the church. A woman's most creative role is to be a facilitator. Whatever will provide space for others to expand, she gladly provides, whether it is by her silence or her word, her presence or her absence. We daughters of Anowa put up with injustice to ensure peace and harmony and growth for others. We are the first to excuse those who walk over us or to take the blame for the failures of others.

Our desire to make a home is positive. The problem with our home-making is the unilateral way in which we women appropriate the process, shielding men and male children from learning self-giving. Should we not examine this? If politicians cared for the needs of nations the way women run homes—putting the nation before their individual need to be "great"—and if the armed forces protected the people—as a hen gathers her chicks and guards her eggs with her life—rather than warred with them, we might see a new day in Africa. The spectre of armies raised and paid by nations to war against their own people militates against the homemaking efforts of African women. We should not keep quiet in our opposition of death-dealing regimes. Militarism has got to be the most insane manifestation of patriarchy.

Several biblical models of homemaking can aid us. Eve explored her environment looking for what might be useful; a lover of knowl-edge, she was generous at giving. The princess who nurtured Moses nursed his sense of justice and holy anger at exploitation. Hilda the prophetess was a political and military consultant to kings anxious for the nation to remain a home to its people. Mary of Nazareth and her program for God's jubilee year show the reign of God revealed to her, an ordinary person visited by God. We women must stay sensitive to social injustice. We must listen to the voices too weak to be heard on political platforms, in parliaments, boardrooms, or military tribunals.

Women need to take stock of available resources. We need to place our oppression in the larger context of our country, church, and world. We have to recognize what demons are at work and name them. Whatever subjugates also dominates; whatever exhibits superiority divides and manipulates. Systems that are so well-ordered as to intimidate us are not for our good. Religious structures that leave us with little other than "the man says that God says" have to be suspected, even if the man is a priest.

Women's demand for fuller participation is therefore not a self-serving call. Our accumulated wisdom of mothering can serve the nation by community building. What African woman, having a chance to run from disaster, would leave children and relatives behind? If forced to do so, what African woman would not look back on the disaster? For women the figure of Lot's wife is a portrait of the cost of compassion, not the punishment for disobedience of a patriarchal injunction.

At Home with the Future

One empowering strand in the church's teaching enables us to live as if all the good we hope for is in fact already in our hands, giving us the courage to be what we hope to be. Writing the Book of Revelation in a period of extreme suffering and uncertainty, St. John the Divine had a vision of the New Jerusalem coming on earth and called attention to it. Look! The New is already here. We do not have to go up to heaven; heaven has come down to meet us. If only we have eyes to see, we can observe God walking among us. This dramatization of Christian hope in a new myth enables us women of Africa to live our future today. Our future as women is in living our true humanity in a world that we have helped to shape, and in which even now we have begun to live and to enjoy, conscious of our situation and seeking conscientiously to change structures and attitudes. Even the prospect of being a part of this calls for celebrating.

In this transformed world, our new home, life is not structured on a "me or you" mentality. With transformed relationships, we begin to see the whole earth as a home where hostility, hunger, and oppression are no longer our companions. With such a vision the world is our home. Even though the hurt of all our sisters has to be healed if we are to be whole ourselves, we praise God that we have sisters. Global solidarity on life issues like abortion, same-sex love, female prostitution, male prostitution, child abuse, and child care bind us together. We are open to share our experiences, to learn to deal with them, and to teach our strategies to others. In the understanding company of the global sisterhood, a home is created for women to be themselves, to assess and critically appropriate our various cultures.

With a frank turning to face the old world with its tangled web of oppression, we set about unraveling it. Each may pick a different thread. While doing this we learn to live in close proximity, interacting with people on the same project. While working together, we already live in the future as we sing new songs to one another and, together, promote our new imagery. New myths, tales, and proverbs evolve from our real lives, true stories that are stranger than fiction. As we unravel our oppression, we weave new patterns of living from our boundless human creativity.

NOTES

[1] It is significant to point out that men admitted this fundamental principle not so that women might have as much human value as men, but so that women might equally stand before God's judgment and answer as persons.

[2] See Bernadette Brooten, "Paul's Views on the Nature of Women and Female Homoeroticism," in Clarissa W. Atkinson, Constance H. Buchanan, and Margaret R. Miles, eds., *Immaculate and Powerful* (Boston: Beacon Press, 1985), pp. 61–87.

[3] Azizah al-Hibri, ed., *Women in Islam* (Oxford: Pergamon Press, 1982), pp. vii–x.

[4] Compare, for example, translations of Jeremiah 31:22 in the Jerusalem Bible, the Revised Standard Version, or the New English Bible; or study men's manipulations of the Eve story in the Qur'an and Hadith. An example in African tradition may be found in the story of Anowa. Anowa's childlessness was due to her "restlessness" rather than to Ako's impotence, which remained a secret between him and the Diviner.

[5] See the work, for example, of Teresa Okure (Nigeria), a New Testament scholar specializing in the Gospel of John, or of Musimbi Kanyoro (Kenya), Joyce Tzabede (Swaziland), or Bette Ekeya (Kenya).

[6] I always think of the women in Exodus, the Egyptian midwives, the mother and sister of Moses, the princess of Egypt. These typically nameless women were God's chosen ministers in bringing about the Exodus liberation. And so many other women made decisions that affected Hebrew history: Tamar, Rahab, Deborah, Ruth, Esther, Elizabeth, Mary of Nazareth, to name a few.

[7] Kofi Appiah-Kubi, *Man Cures, God Heals: Religion and Medical Practice among the Akan of Ghana* (Totowa, NJ: Allanheld Osum Publishers, 1981), pp. 35–71, 81–125.

[8] Rattray quotes an Asante proverb, *Die wahye wo ti sene ono na obo no* (The person who puts a pot over your head is the one who breaks it). The proverb is interpreted to mean that the father makes the child's personality and protects or even molds the child's head; if a child gets on the father's wrong side, the father can also destroy the child. (*Religion and Art in Ashanti* [1927; reprint, New York: AMS Press, 19791, p. 51.)

[9] Elisabeth Schüssler Fiorenza, *In Memory of Her: A Feminist Theological Reconstruction of Christian Origins* (New York: Crossroads, 1983), pp. 288–294 (on the patriarchalization of church and ministry) and pp. 309–315 (on the genderization of ecclesial offices).

[10] Walter Davis, *Orita, Ibadan Journal of Religious Studies* 10:2 (1976), pp.122–46.

[11] The Akan proverb, *Tɛkerɛma bediɛ ɛfa adiɛ sen ahoɔdenfo* (The female tongue achieves more than brawn can accomplish), recognizes the diversity of approaches to solutions (Robert S. Rattray, *Ashanti Law and Constitution* [1911; reprint, New York: Negro Universities Press, 1969], p. 16).

[12] For a discussion of women's "ploys for power," see Christine Obbo, *African Women: Their Struggle for Economic Independence* (London: Zed Press, 1981), pp.144–151.

[13] I do grow concerned from time to time with one issue: Why, in the midst of this, do we seem to enjoy a perverse kind of power? Has our monopoly of caring turned it into a tool for seeking power?

[14] These churches established and led by Africans have been variously labeled as Separatist, Prophetic, Indigenous, Independent, Charismatic, and so forth. Many of them have come together in an all-Africa body with the name "Organization of African Instituted Churches."

[15] For a brief but comprehensive discussion of the causes of prostitution in Zaire, see "Human Sexuality, Marriage, and Prostitution" by Bernadette Mbuy-Beya in *The Will to Arise: Women, Tradition, and the Church in Africa* (Maryknoll, N.Y.: Orbis Books, 1992), pp. 155–179.

[16] The image of Eve does not correspond with the Qur'anic image. See Rabiatu Ammah, "Paradise Lies at the Feet of Muslim Women," in Oduyoye and Kanyoro, eds., *The Will to Arise*, pp. 179–188.

[17] The images of mothering and motherhood I have raised up here are not intended to exclude other forms of being woman. But I believe that mothering is the closest that human beings come to the Compassionate God who makes us free.

[18] N. Ogundipe–Leslie, "Sisters Are Not Brothers in Christ: Global Women in Church and Society" (Geneva: World Council of Churches,1995), pp.179–188. A report of a meeting of the WCC held in Japan in December 1988 to help focus the WCC's "Ecumenical Decade, Churches in Solidarity with Women."

[19] This story made a great impression on me, shaping my life and my relations to men. Before I had heard that story I had been made to stand on a desk during a mathematics class while the teacher told the class, "Look at her, she is not pretty, she is not going to find a husband, and she will not pay attention in math class." That year I won a prize in mathematics, the only one I won in school. Since I had nothing to do with how I looked, I was determined to show this teacher that I could stand on my own feet.

[20] This becomes a serious problem for if a woman calls attention to the tensions of childlessness, it is immediately seen as *her* problem; if a woman seeks to talk about the abuses of prostitution, she is personally involved through her husband, son, or daughter; if she talks of domestic violence, *she* is being battered at home. ("*Poo mmɔbɔ*"—Sorry, that's sad, that husband is a beast.) Yet these are public issues that involve all women.

[21] A woman from Sierra Leone told of a couple who were desperate for a child. Told by the doctor that having a child might mean the death of the woman, the husband, a clergyman, is reported to have said, "If that is what it takes, let it be so." The wife went along with the decision. She died in childbirth, having had a son. The husband said, "Thank God it is a boy."

CHAPTER 10

From Liberation to Reconstruction

J.N.K. Mugambi

Introduction

Christian theological reflection is essential for the healthy development of any church. A church which is incapable of producing its own theologians cannot be said to be mature. In the New Testament we find St. Paul addressing the doctrinal, pastoral, and organizational problems which faced the churches he had helped to stall. It is clear in the epistles that the congregations to which St. Paul writes looked up to him for theological guidance, because they did not have their own theologians to discern conclusive solutions to the problems pertinent to each local church.

Thus, St. Paul articulates general theological principles derived from the Gospel as he understood it, then makes specific recommendations applicable to the particular problems raised by the congregations to whom he addresses his respective epistles. Sometimes it became necessary to write a follow-up letter, if the first one did not adequately resolve the issue at stake. Some epistles are addressed to individuals, such as Timothy and Titus, who are being counseled on matters concerning proper churchmanship. The epistles also provide indications of the existence of factions in the apostolic church. Some Christians tended to identify themselves with Paul, others with Peter, others with James, yet others with Apollos. St. Paul criticized this factionalism, and appealed for unity among all Christians, emphasizing that all should regard themselves and treat one another as members of the one body of Christ.

African churches have for a long time depended on theological mentors from the parent denominations in Europe and North America, just like those churches of the Mediterranean region during the apostolic period depended on St. Paul for theological leadership and guidance. One important question that African Christian theologians must ask themselves at the end of the twentieth century and at the beginning of the twenty-first is whether African churches should continue to rely on theological packages designed for other cultures and historical contexts.

If the answer is positive, then African Christian theologians must further ask themselves what their role is, and why they should have been trained as theologians in the first place. On the other hand, if the answer is negative, then African Christian theologians must provide theological guidance and leadership for their churches. Such guidance and leadership does not necessarily have to negate the insights from theologians of the "parent" denominations; however, it must show clearly the contextual relevance of the Christian message to the specific needs of particular African churches within the African cultural and historical settings.

The purpose of this book is to offer some suggestions on new directions for Christian theological reflection in Africa. In the recent past, *liberation* and *inculturation* have been taken as the most basic concepts for innovative African Christian theology. The former concept has been closely associated with anglophone Protestant theologians, having been first popularized by Latin American and African-American theologians. The latter concept has been associated with some African Catholic theologians, having been first popularized by Catholic missionary scholars, notably Aylward Shorter.

This book introduces *reconstruction* as a new paradigm for African Christian theology in the New World Order. The concept should be of interest to African theologians of all doctrinal persuasions, considering that the task of social reconstruction after the Cold War cannot be restricted to any religious or denominational confines. At the same time, reconstruction is a concept within the social sciences, which should be of interest to sociologists, economists, and political scientists. The multi-disciplinary appeal of reconstruction makes the concept functionally useful as a new thematic focus for reflection in Africa during the coming decades.

Historical Background

Liberation as a theme for Christian theological reflection has been derived from the Exodus narrative in the Old Testament. The people of Israel are portrayed as having been delivered from bondage in Egypt through the divinely inspired leadership of Moses. This narrative greatly appeals to peoples who have suffered colonial and other forms of domination. As victims of oppression, they identify themselves with the Israelites. They also identify their leaders with Moses, the inspired hero who confronts the oppressor and victoriously urges: "Let my people go!" (Exodus 10:1–6).

In Latin America, the dictatorial regimes of the 1960s and 1970s motivated Catholic theologians and social scientists to mobilize Christians for liberation, and the Exodus motif was found to be very potent as a clarion call. Gustavo Gutierrez became the leading theologian to articulate this approach to social change in Latin America. The United Nations' Development Decade beginning in 1955 led to disillusionment rather than hope among Latin Americans. The Marshall Plan had helped Japan and West Germany to reconstruct their respective economies from the rubble of World War II. In the same way, it had been hoped that the first 'Development Decade' (1955–65) would help Latin American countries to take off economically and industrially.

However, by 1965, most of those countries were much poorer, in absolute terms, than they had been ten years previously. They were heavily indebted, and their economies were in shambles. This frustration led Latin American social scientists and church leaders to review the promises of developmentalist programs. The consensus emerging from that review was that developmentalism could not bring about human dignity in Latin America. The people themselves must become masters of their own destiny. *Liberation* became the slogan for progressive thinking. Ironically, much of this "progressive" thought was conducted under the leadership of secular priests amongst the laity of the Catholic Church, despite the traditional view of Roman Catholicism as a conservative force in society. By 1968, Theology of Liberation had become associated with progressive church leadership in Latin America. Throughout the 1970s, leading Latin American theologians were very articulate in shifting international campaigns for social transformation from developmentalism to liberationism.[1]

In North America, the fact that a century after the American Civil War African-Americans still did not enjoy social equality led civil rights activists in the 1950s and 1960s to discern theological motifs that would help them to mobilize the community for change. Again, the Exodus motif proved very potent. Leaders such as Martin Luther King were popularly likened to Moses, whose task was to lead the people to the promised land. It was James H. Cone, perhaps more than any other African-American theologian, who gave theological rationalization to the civil rights movement in the USA. In his book, *Black Theology and Black Power*, Cone lucidly showed that there was a logical and historical connection between the civil rights movement and the religious consciousness of black communities throughout the history of the USA.[2] Cone's recent book on Martin Luther King and Malcom X emphasizes this link between the campaigns of civil rights activists and the sermons and marches of African-American preachers in the 1960s.[3] Gayraud Wilmore further elaborated on this link in his book, *Black Religion and Black Radicalism,* which was written from a phenomenological perspective.[4]

In their two-volume book *Black Theology: A Documentary History*, Cone and Wilmore have shown that the link between the civil rights movement and the African-American churches is not a matter of coincidence, but a natural development of interrelated factors.[5] When the World Council of Churches held its Fifth Assembly at Nairobi, Kenya, in 1975, the theme of *liberation* had become commonplace in Africa. Portugal had abandoned her colonies of Angola and Mozambique, and the struggle for majority rule in Zimbabwe had accelerated. In September 1975, the World Council of Churches had sponsored a consultation in Geneva on Racism in Theology and Theology Against Racism.[6] The following year, the Ecumenical Association of Third World Theologians (EATWOT) was launched at Dar es Salaam, in August 1976. The launching conference was attended by theologians from Africa, Asia and Latin America. Representation of African-American theologians was minimal.[7]

At the conference in Dar es Salaam it became increasingly clear that there was a difference of emphases and perspectives between African, Asian, and Latin American theologians. African theologians wanted to highlight cultural and racial domination, and liberation was viewed particularly in these terms. At the same time, Asian theologians emphasized the burden of castes and vedic traditions, and interpreted liberation in terms of the quest to be free from the bondage of the oriental heritage. Latin American theologians, on the other hand, were emphatic on liberation as the process of social transformation through class struggle, with the oppressed as the "subjects" rather than "objects" of history. Race and culture were peripheral to their concerns. These differences in perspective and emphasis were evident in the Communique issued by the conference.

During the 1980s, the economic situation in Africa deteriorated greatly. The balance of trade increased against Africa, and the debt burden weighed very heavily upon African nations and peoples. As the ideological pressure of the Western Bloc against the Eastern Bloc intensified, the marginalization of Africa became more evident. The theme of liberation called for review. If most of Africa had been liberated in the 1950s and 1960s, what happened to that 'liberation'? As early as 1945, during the Fifth Pan African Congress, African leaders had issued the commitment that no African country would consider itself liberated until the entire continent was free from colonial domination.[8] South Africa was considered the last bastion of colonialism, and the OAU was unanimous in its condemnation of *apartheid.* The Exodus motif continued to be presupposed in most of African theological imagery until the late 1980s. As the Soviet Union began to crumble, there were signs that South Africa would also be free, at last. What theological imagery would be appropriate for Africa thereafter?

In March 1990, the Executive Committee of the All Africa Conference of Churches met in Nairobi to ponder these questions in addition to the normal business on its usual agenda. I was invited to reflect on the Future of the Church and the Church of the Future in Africa. [9] The theme of reconstruction appeared most appropriate in the New World Order. My presentation proposed that we need to shift paradigms from the Post-Exodus to Post-Exile imagery, with *reconstruction* as the resultant theological axiom. It turns out that the 1990s were a decade of reconstruction in many ways, with calls for national conventions, constitutional reforms, and economic revitalization. The 21st century should be a century of reconstruction in Africa, building on old foundations which, though strong, may have to be renovated. During the 15th and 16th centuries, Europe went through such a process, in reaction to a long period of cultural stagnation and Islamic onslaught. In secular circles, this awakening was called the Renaissance, and in ecclesial circles it was called the Reformation. The 1990s were the beginning of Africa's Renaissance and Reformation. They commenced the process of Africa's reconstruction.

Liberation and Salvation
There has been a tendency among Christian theologians to polarize themselves—in support of *either* Liberation *or* Salvation. This polarization arises from differences over their appreciation of the role of the Gospel in social transformation. On the one extreme, some theologians prefer the concept of salvation, suggesting that the Gospel is primarily focused on spiritual conversion (John 3:1–3). Only after such conversion, according to this view, can social action follow. The Church, such theologians continue, should concentrate on preparing its

converts for life after death—for God's kingdom in heaven, in the future. This type of theology is epitomized by Karl Barth,[10] especially in his *Church Dogmatics*. The salvationists consider their liberationist counterparts to be advocates of the "social gospel" which, in Salvationist terms, is a deviation from the biblical message.

On the opposite extreme, other theologians insist that the Gospel challenges all its followers to become involved in the process of liberation, as "salt of the earth" and "light of the world" (Matthew 5:13–16). This challenge, they argue, involves direct involvement in social transformation. It is not possible for a person to separate spiritual conversion from actual witness in society. What one does in society ought to be consistent with one's inner convictions. Theologians who hold this view tend to consider their counterparts on the opposite extreme to be hypocritical in their proclamations, because of the "holier than thou" stance taken by the Salvationists. The liberationist theological perspective is exemplified by Soren Kierkegaard[11] and Ludwig Feuerbach.[12] According to the liberationist perspective, theology is at its best when it takes serious account of anthropological reality.

Between these two extremes there are many theological stances. Theological correctness is determined by the dominant tendency in the community of faith with which a theologian identifies. For example, if one identifies oneself with Pentecostalism, the tendency is toward salvationism, whereas liberationism is more likely to have supporters within mainline Protestantism and Roman Catholicism, especially in Africa, Asia, and southern America. The polarization indicated above presupposes that *liberation* and *salvation* are mutually exclusive, or mutually incompatible. However, it is quite clear that Jesus, in His public ministry, was actively and simultaneously involved in both personal and social reconstruction. He mobilized His followers to become involved in social change, having convinced them of the necessity and urgency to change their attitudes toward themselves and the world. The logical implication of this integral approach to evangelization is that liberation and salvation are theologically complementary.

> In the African context and in the Bible *salvation,* as a sociopolitical concept, cannot be complete without *liberation* as a sociopolitical concept. Thus Jesus, proclaiming his mission, quoted from the book of Isaiah to indicate the correctness and relevance of his concern (Isaiah 61:1–2).[13]

Theological discourse in Africa should come to terms with this integral approach to the Gospel. It is not necessary to opt for either the liberational or the salvational approaches. Rather, African theologians ought to discern an approach which integrates liberation with salvation, and *vice versa.*

Acculturation and Inculturation

Some Catholic theologians have tried to avoid the polarization between salvationist and liberationist categories by introducing another set of polarized concepts, one derived from the social sciences *(acculturation)* and the other from theology *(inculturation).* As a sociological concept, *acculturation* refers to the process through which the people of one culture absorb and internalize the norms of another culture during the period of encounter between the two cultures.

This process of internalization may be spontaneous or forced. The diffusion of cultural norms among African peoples in precolonial Africa has been spontaneous, whereas colonization forced African peoples to *either* adopt the norms of their masters or perish. Anti-colonial struggles throughout Africa have also necessitated spontaneous acculturation, creating bonds between peoples who previously lived in isolation. In the post-colonial era, African peoples have been compelled by ideological and market forces to become synchronized with the dominant culture in the world, through the mass media, advertising, and propaganda.

Cees Hamelink, in his book *Cultural Autonomy in Global Communications,* explains this process of synchronization and outlines some examples of national resistance to it. Then he concludes:

> If cultural expression is to contribute to the development of autonomy in a society, it must be an expression of internal equality as well as resistance to imperialist synchronizing forces. Furthermore, if it is to respect the cultural autonomy of other societies, it must also avoid the temptation that as a result of its success as an adequate cultural solution within its own national social system, it becomes an expansionist, imperialistic force.[14]

From the perspectives of economics and politics, Goran Hyden, in his book *No Shortcuts to Progress* has explained how the former colonial masters in Africa tried, during the 1960s and 1970s, to synchronize African nations and peoples with the international market economy, and the spontaneous resistance of the people in both rural and urban Africa. Instead of becoming incorporated into the market economy, Hyden suggests, African peoples have creatively evolved a different system, which he calls the "Economy of Affection."[15]

The so-called structural adjustment programs (SAPS), sponsored by the World Bank and the International Monetary Fund, are intended to synchronize African economies with the international market economy, but the resilience of African peoples remains largely intact in spite of the tough conditions imposed from without. Acculturation, when imposed, can have disastrous consequences for the cultural integrity of the vanquished people. Conversely, it gives the peddlers of the dominant culture a sense of success and pride which, in moral terms, is undeserved.

Inculturation is a term recently coined by Catholic theologians to explain the process by which the Catholic Church becomes rooted in every culture, without destroying Catholic ecclesiastical identity, tradition, and history. The semantic inspiration of inculturation is *incarnation*. In theological terms, incarnation is the manifestation of the divine in human corporeality. God becomes manifest in Jesus of Nazareth. Likewise, inculturation is the manifestation of the Church in the various cultures where it has been introduced and established.

Certainly, a semantic tension is generated by linking the theological concept of incarnation with the socio-ecclesiological concept of inculturation. The tension can only be resolved if one assumes that the Church (as a divine institution) is supernatural and "empties" itself into every culture just as God is "emptied" into Jesus of Nazareth (Philippians 2:1–11). The Church, however, evolves within history, and as a human institution is subject to the limitations of human achievement and weakness as it strives to emulate the ideals of its founder, Christ. It is clear, for instance, that the Catholic Church can hardly shed its Roman and Latin legacies without at the same time losing its centralized and hierarchical structure which it inherited from imperial Rome. In view of this fact, what does inculturation mean in practical terms?

The most well-known advocate of the theology of inculturation is Aylward Shorter. In his book, *Toward a Theology of Inculturation,* he has made a strong case for this label.[16] He traces the history of the term *inculturation* to Jesuit theologians in the early 1960s, and quotes a definition from the Jesuit priest, Pedro Arrup. Shorter himself defines inculturation as "the ongoing dialogue between faith and culture or cultures." For a longer definition, he refers to Arrup, whose definition of inculturation is:

... The incarnation of Christian life and of the Christian message in a particular cultural context, in such a way that this experience not only finds expression through elements proper to the culture in question (this alone would be no more than a superficial adaptation) but becomes a principle that animates, directs and unifies the culture, transforming it and remaking it so as to bring about a "new creation." [17]

It is interesting to note that, whereas in Latin America the theology of liberation was spearheaded by Catholic theologians, in Africa it has had Protestants as the strongest advocates, especially in South Africa. What is the implication of this observation? Could it be that Catholic theologians have been insensitive to the experience of oppression in Africa? Or was the rejection of the polarization between liberationist and salvationist perspectives based on discernment of a different set of theological axioms? Might it be that Catholic theological expression in Africa was too dominated by expatriate writers during the 1960s and 1970s? This third factor was certainly significant, considering that African Catholic thought began to appear in books and journals in significant quantity and quality only in the mid-1980s, although missionaries working in Africa have been writing on behalf of the Catholic Church in Africa for many decades.

Charles Nyamiti, one of the pioneers of African Catholic theology, categorizes African Christologies into two types—Christologies of *inculturation* and Christologies of *liberation*. This categorization is too sharp, because the African theologians who advocate for Inculturation–Incarnation are not necessarily against Liberation–Salvation, and conversely, those who promote the theology of liberation are not necessarily opposed to the theology of incarnation.[18] This point can be illustrated by the work of Jean Marc-Ela, the Camerounian Catholic theologian to whom Aylward Shorter refers when discussing the relationship between inculturation and liberation.

Marc-Ela rightly emphasizes that inculturation is not possible in Africa as long as Africans are not in control of their own lives and destinies, both outside and within the Church. This emphasis brings about a synthesis between inculturation and liberation. In response, Shorter concedes:

... It is true that the structures of ecclesial communion are culturally biased in favor of Europe, and it is true that authority in the Church is in no hurry to put the theology of inculturation into pastoral practice. It is also true that African cultural identity is by no means clear–cut, and that there are still far too many traces of colonial, cultural domination in Africa. These are even reinforced by neo–colonial structures of dependence. It is not only cultural liberation of which Africa stands in need, but a real political, social and economic liberation.[19]

Ela further insists that African theologians ought not to be satisfied with superficial window-dressing which might stir the curiosity of a tourist-minded North Atlantic visitor to the African Church. Rather, they should concern themselves with the fundamental tenets of the Christian faith as they relate to the challenges facing Africans today in all aspects of life. Such concern will necessarily lead to the questioning of the theological presuppositions upon which the Christian missionary enterprise has been based, and of the socio-scientific hypotheses which have justified the continuing plunder of Africa.

Reactive and Proactive Stances in Theology

During the 1960s and 1970s, Christian theological reflection in Africa tended to suffer from lack of definition and direction. In the 1960s, African Christian theologians were very few and far between, and they were under strong tutelage of their European and North American mentors. A younger generation of theologians emerged in the 1970s, and this generation was more self-confident. Its views, however, could not be taken seriously in the North Atlantic context owing to entrenched attitudes of superiority. The main reason was that African scholars at that time tended to write for the North Atlantic audience aspiring to answer questions in which their mentors were interested.

Theology, at best, must respond to the joys, sorrows, hopes, and fears of the community of faith which the theologian represents. The theologian's primary audience, therefore, must be the community of faith on whose behalf he or she engages in the theological quest. During the 1980s, several African Christian theologians of the younger generation began to write with African readership in mind. The 1990s opened with considerable theological literature produced in Africa by African scholars, primarily for African readership. Some of that literature has reached Europe and North America, stimulating interesting responses, which in turn have reached Africa. Such interaction is vital for the growth of Christian theology at the universal level.

The Ecumenical Association of Third World Theologians (EATWOT) which was launched at Dar es Salaam, Tanzania, in August 1976, had the aim of providing a discussion and consultative forum for ecumenically minded Christian theologians of Africa, Asia, and Latin America. This association has helped to emphasize that the non-Caucasian Christian community should be appreciated as an integral part of the theological Oikoumene. Since its inception, however, this association has tended to be *reactive* rather than *proactive*. The name it chose for itself indicated that the theologians involved were reacting to the marginalization they were suffering in ecumenical discourse. They chose to define themselves in terms of the three "worlds" which the Cold War had created. They were theologians of the "Third World" which also, emotively, seemed to imply that they were "Third Rate" theologians. This attitude has not subsided in North Atlantic theological circles. The label "Third World" continues to be used, many years after the Cold War has ended. This ideological lag is detrimental to Africa's intellectual development because of its reactive and residual stance.

Unfortunately, the ideological polarization between the capitalist North Atlantic and the socialist Eurasia tended to set the parameters for discourse in all disciplines, including theology. It is interesting to note that there was no corresponding "Association of First World Theologians." By launching EATWOT, the "Third World" theologians were defensively endorsing a classification of societies which was more ideological than geographical. Some of the African theologians who attended the launching conference pointed out the shortcomings of this reactive stance, but their caution did not carry the day. At that time, the Centre-Periphery paradigm was dominant, especially among the majority of Latin American theologians, who strongly felt that in accordance with the Marxian dialectics, the "Periphery" must assert itself and eventually promote itself into the "Centre." This dialectical approach to theology became very controversial, and accelerated the polarization between liberational-salvational stances on the one hand, and the acculturational-inculturational approaches, on the other. Now that the Cold War has ended, this threefold ideological classification of societies in the contemporary world is no longer relevant.

Many of the theological works produced by African theologians in the late 1980s and early 1990s have been more definitive, and are intended to meet the contextual needs of theological curricula in seminaries, pastoral colleges, and departments of religious studies in African universities. Unfortunately, most of those works remain largely unavailable to African students and researchers at home, owing to unaffordable prices and export-import constraints. With the dawn of a new century it is hopeful that we will see this problem overcome so that

African students in Africa will be able to interact in print with their own compatriot theologians.

The ecumenical movement can facilitate the achievement of this essential objective. It is clear that an integrated ecumenical approach to theological articulation will be more constructive than fragmented, sectarian approaches. It is necessary for trainee theologians to sharpen their original and critical insights with enrichment from the critiques of their mentors and peers, especially those who share the same cultural heritage. Such enrichment helped the development of theology in Europe and North America, and more recently, in Latin America. African theologians, therefore, should likewise be assisted to develop ecumenically interactive networks among themselves.

Reconstruction as a Theological Paradigm

The terms *construction* and *reconstruction* belong to engineering vocabulary. An engineer constructs a complex according to specifications in the available designs. Sometimes modifications are made to the designs, in order to ensure that the complex will perform the function for which it is intended. Reconstruction is done when an existing complex becomes dysfunctional, for whatever reason, and the user still requires to use it. New specifications may be made in the new designs, while some aspects of the old complex are retained in the new. Social reconstruction belongs to the social sciences, and involves reorganization of some aspects of a society in order to make it more responsive to changed circumstances.[20] Quality of leadership can be measured by the degree to which a leader is able to direct social reconstruction without destabilizing the society which he or she leads. Africa has been undergoing processes of social reconstruction during the past five hundred years. Some of the changes have been externally imposed, while others have arisen from internal pressures. The Bible is replete with illustrations of social reconstruction over a long span of time.

The history of the Arabian peninsula is a shop window through which we can observe several reconstructive efforts over four thousand years. The encounter between Israel and Egypt has been rehearsed several times, and each time there have been new dimensions in the relationship between the two peoples. In the Book of Exodus, Egypt is portrayed as an oppressor, from whom Israel must be liberated. The entry into Canaan, as recorded in the book of Joshua, is presented as a process of restoring old shrines which Patriarch Abraham had established many centuries previously. The relationship between Israel and her neighbors in the Arabian peninsula is a theme which recurs numerous times in the Bible.

The Book of Deuteronomy describes the restoration of the law under King Josiah, after Judah had deteriorated into idolatry and corruption. Jeremiah warned that the deterioration would inevitably lead to the destruction of Judah, and the exile of the majority of her people in Babylon. After the Babylonian exile, a new nation was reconstructed under the direction of Ezra and Nehemiah. The role of Nehemiah as the director of the reconstruction project is lucidly explained in the book bearing his name. Nehemiah becomes the central text of the new theological paradigm in African Christian theology, as a logical development from the Exodus motif. During the Inter-testamental period, the Maccabbee brothers led a resistance movement against the desecration of the temple by Hellenistic conquerors. They, too, were concerned to restore the sanctity of the Temple, after desecration by European invaders. Theirs was a reconstructive project.

Jesus of Nazareth enters history at a time when Judea is rife with the Messianic hope that some deliverer would come to liberate the people from the yoke of Roman imperialism. The critics of Jesus accused him of trying to destroy Judaism and its institutions. In response, Jesus replied that his mission was reconstructive rather than destructive. The Sermon on the Mount (Matthew 5–7) can be considered as the most basic of all reconstructive theological texts in the synoptic gospels. Although Jerusalem was destroyed in A.D. 70, the hope for the reconstruction of the nation remained alive in the Jewish community until the twentieth century. As the twenty-first century begins, new relationships are emerging through creative initiatives which are evidence of the ability of human individuals and groups to reconstruct their societies, under the guidance of imaginative leadership. The reconciliation between the Palestinians and the Israelis is a welcome relief, which will hopefully bring lasting peace to the enviable land between the River Jordan and the Mediterranean Sea.

Several paradigms have been proposed and utilized in the short history of African Christian theology. They include the liberation, deliverance, salvation, redemption, inculturation, and incarnation models. The *liberation* paradigm has been attractive to some theologians in Africa because of the historical experience of colonial and neo-colonial domination. However, the transposition of the liberation theme from the Old Testament to the African experience has led to some distortions of the theological message contained therein. This is because there are remarkable differences between the Israelite experience under the Pharaohs and the African colonial experience under North Atlantic powers four millennia later. These differences can be outlined as follows:

(i). Historical distance: The Israelites were in bondage in the second millennium before the Christian era. The African colonial experience has been in the second millennium within the Christian era. This historical distance also implies, considerable differences in historical circumstances.

(ii). Cultural distance: The Israelites had great affinity with the peoples of the Mediterranean region, and their cosmopolitan experience is much more evident than that of Africans in the twentieth century under European colonial domination.

(iii). Religious heritage: In the Old Testament, the charismatic leadership of heroes such as Moses derives inspiration from the religious heritage of the Israelites, whereas the association of messianic leadership in contemporary Africa is greatly influenced by biblical idioms.

(iv). Ideological distance: The ideological configuration of the Mediterranean region during the Exodus period is very different from that of Africa in the twentieth century.

(v). Religious plurality: Whereas in the Old Testament the Israelites claim to have the *only* true religion, in contemporary Africa several religions vie for recognition as heralds of divine and universal truth (Christianity; Islam; Judaism).

Given these differences, the parallels drawn between the Exodus and the process of decolonization have been rather contrived and far-fetched. Moreover, the analogy between the Exodus and the struggle against colonialism does not fit very well, considering that in the Old Testament the Israelites move physically over time and space, from Egypt across the Sinai to Canaan, whereas Africans remain in the same geographical space. Thus the Exodus, when transposed to the African situation, is over time, without any geographical movement. Could it be that the refugee situation is influenced by a desire to have movement in time and geographical space?

The theme of *reconstruction* is made attractive by the fact that it highlights the necessity of creating a new society within the same geographical space, but across different historical moments. This theme needs further development as a paradigm of Christian theological reflection in Africa.

Levels of Reconstruction

Personal reconstruction

In Christian theology it has traditionally been maintained that the starting point in social reconstruction is the individual. Jesus teaches that constructive change must start from within the motives and intentions of the individual. The confession of the Publican and the conceit of the Pharisee (Luke 18:9–14) are contrasts intended to show the appropriate stance in social change. Jesus said to the crowds (Matthew 23:1–13):

> The scribes and the Pharisees sit on Moses' seat so practice and observe whatever they tell you, but not what they do; for they preach, but do not practice. They bind heavy burdens, hard to bear, and lay them on men's shoulders; but they themselves will not move them with their finger. They do all their deeds to be seen by men; for they make their phylacteries broad and their fringes long, and they love the place of honor at feasts and the best seats in the synagogues, and salutations in the market places, and being called rabbi by men. But you are not to be called rabbi, for you have one teacher, and you are brethren (RSV).

This and other similar instructions, such as those in Luke 12–13, emphasize that the individual must continually reconstruct oneself in readiness for the tasks and challenges ahead. The same message is echoed by revivalist hymn writers:

> Amazing Grace, how sweet the sound,
> That saved a wreck like me,
> I once was lost but now I'm found,
> Was blind, but now I see.
> Teach me Thy way O Lord,
> Teach me Thy way!
> Thy gracious aid afford,

Teach me Thy way!
Help me to walk aright,
More by faith less by sight;
Lead me with heavenly light;
Teach me Thy way.

Take my Life and let it be
Consecrated Lord, to thee,
Take my moments and my days,
Let them flow in ceaseless praise.

Just as I am, without one plea
But that thy blood was shed for me,
And that thou bid'st me come to Thee
O Lamb of God I come.

Just as I am, though tossed about
With many a conflict, many a doubt,
Fightings and fears within, without,
O lamb of God I come.

These hymns are reminders that the key to social transformation is appropriate disposition of the individual members of the community concerned, especially its leaders.

Cultural reconstruction

Culture is the cumulative product of people's activities in all aspects of life, in their endeavor to cope with their social and natural environment. Its components include politics, economics, ethics, aesthetics, and religion.[21] In each of these components, reconstruction is necessary from time to time, to ensure that the social structures are finely tuned to the needs of the people. When some components of culture are not finely adjusted, there is uneasiness which can erupt into unrest.

Economics concentrates with reconstruction in matters of the management of resources. *Politics* deals with reconstruction in the management of social influence. *Ethics* is concerned with reconstruction of the system of values. When priorities change, the value system also has to be adjusted, either to remind the people of forgotten priorities, or to reorganize the hierarchy of values. *Aesthetics* is concerned with the sense of proportion and symmetry in all aspects of life. This component of culture also requires adjustment from time to time, depending on changing circumstances within a community.

Religion provides the world-view which synthesizes everything that is cherished by individuals as corporate members of the community. Cultural reconstruction should be consciously directed. If it is left to chance, the community risks losing its integrity and identity. Reconstruction of religion is perhaps the most vital project among a people undergoing rapid social change. In post-colonial Africa, the transformation of the religious order is indicative of the fundamental change of outlook among African peoples, especially south of the Sahara. It is worthwhile to examine this component of culture more closely, with Christianity as a case for illustration.

Ecclesial reconstruction

The Church is the organizational framework within which a peoples world-view is portrayed and celebrated. Its dimensions include mythological reformulation, doctrinal teaching, social rehabilitation, ethical direction, ritual celebration, and experiential (personal) response. Broadly, ecclesial reconstruction should include management structures, financial policies, pastoral care, human resources development, research, family education, service, and witness. Each of these projects is deeply involving, and they can best be explored with specialist attention. For the purpose of this book, it suffices to paint the mural of reconstruction in broad outline, hoping that others can supply the details with finer brushes and in more varied colors.

Theology is the means by which the Church rationalizes its process of ecclesial reconstruction. The theologian, at best, should be a catalyst —a facilitator—who makes it possible for the Church to adjust itself to the new social demands of the society to which its members belong. After the cold war, Africa needs theologians committed to the process of reconstruction as a multi-disciplinary endeavor. This book is intended to stimulate this process of reflection and action.

J.N.K. Mugambi, *From Liberation to Reconstruction: African Christian Theology After the cold War.* East African Educational Publishers Nairobi, 1995

NOTES

[1] For introduction to Theology of Liberation in Latin America, see *A Theology of Liberation,* by Gustavo Gutierrez, Maryknoll, New York: Orbis, 1973; *Frontiers of Theology in Latin America*, edited by Rosino Gibellini, Maryknoll, New York: Orbis, 1979.

[2] James H. Cone, *Black Theology and Black Power*, New York: Seabury, 1969.

[3] James H. Cone, *Martin and Malcolm and America*, Maryknoll, New York: Orbis, 1991.

[4] Gayraud S. Wilmore, *Black Religion and Black Radicalism*, New York: Doubleday, 1973.

[5] James H. Cone and Gayraud S. Wilmore, *Black Theology: A Documentary History*, Vol. 1 1966–1979, Maryknoll, New York: Orbis, 1979; *Vol II, 1979–1992*, Orbis, 1993.

[6] *Racism in Theology and Theology Against Racism*, Geneva: WCC, 1975.

[7] The papers at the launching conference were published as Sergio Torres and Virginia Fabelaa, eds., *The Emergent Gospel: Theology from the Underside of History*, Maryknoll, New York: Orbis. 1978.

[8] V. B. Thompson, *Africa and Unity*, London: Longman, 1969, pp. 57ff.

[9] My paper was published as "The Future of the Church and the Church of the Future", in *The Church of Africa: Towards a Theology of Reconstruction*, Nairobi: AACC, 1991.

[10] Karl Barth, *Church Dogmatics* (4 Vols.), London: Clark, 1957.

[11] Soren Kierkegaard, *Journals, 1834–1854*, London and Glasgow: Collins Fontana, 1958.

[12] Ludwig Feuerbach, *The Essence of Christianity*, New York: Harper, 1957.

[13] J. N. K. Mugambi, "Liberation and Theology", in WSCF Dossier No. 5 Geneva, June 1974, Later published in my book, *African Christian Theology: An Introduction*. Nairobi: Heinemann, 1989, pp. 12ff.

[14] Cees J. Hamelink, *Cultural Autonomy in Global Communication*, London: Longman, 1983, p. 33.

[15] Goran Hyden, *No Shortcuts to Progress*, London: Heinemann, 1983, pp. 8ff.

[16] A. Shorter, *Toward a Theology of Inculturation*, London: Geoffrey Chapman, 1988.

[17] *Ibid.*, p.11.

[18] C. Nyamiti, "African Christologies Today", in J. N. K. Mugambi and L. Magesa, eds, *Jesus in African Christianity: Experimentation and Diversity in African Christology*, Nairobi: Initiatives, 1989, pp. 17–39.

[19] Aylward Shorter, op. cit., p. 247.

[20] On this point see Peter L. Berger and Thomas Luckmann, *The Social Construction of Reality*, Harmondsworth: Penguin Books, 1967.

[21] I have dealt with this theme in my book, *The African Heritage and Contemporary Christianity*, Nairobi: Longman, 1989.

CHAPTER 11

"African Renaissance"
And the Challenge of Narrative Theology in Africa

Which story/whose renaissance?[1]

Emmanuel M. Katongole

Abstract

Т
he recent resurgence of hope in Africa—proclaimed by
political leaders as "reawakening" or "renaissance"—betrays
a commitment to a liberal capitalistic vision that sees in
economic liberalization the key to development and prosperity. The
meta-narrative underlying that proclamation hides the risks of new
forms of exclusion and exploitation and the perspective "from above."
African Christian theology should meet the challenge and force this
meta-narrative "to the ground" by itself being grounded within the daily
struggles and aspirations of ordinary Africans.

> African theology was born out of the struggle against colonial
> condescension and haughtiness; unless its future is now defined as a
> struggle against the fraudulent project of the post–colonial nationalist
> bourgeoisie, it might have no future or become pure entertainment.
>
> Itumeleng Mosala

> We must adopt methods of analysis that disturb the privileges people
> acquire under the protection of cadres who, in turn live in the shadow
> of power. A definitive analysis is the only way to get a clear picture
> of the reality, which is continuously masked by official reports,
> reinforced by myths disseminated in tourist leaflets directed at
> societies with itch for the exotic. Those who lead people to believe
> that Africans live in a world without conflicts fall back on ideology
> and ignore reality.
>
> Jean–Marc Ela

African Renaissance: just another meta-narrative, another story from above?

Winds of change are blowing over the African continent. Many countries find themselves faced with immense challenges of national identity as well as social, political, and economic reconstruction—*after* apartheid (in South Africa), *after* genocide (in Rwanda), *after* civil war (in Uganda and Eriteria), *after* dictatorship (in the former Zaire), and after so many other *afters*. Whereas these challenges are formidable, there seem to be significant signs of hope in the political, economic, and social infrastructures of many countries. No one has better expressed these signs of hope than Yoweri Museveni and Thabo Mbeki—two of the most respectable among the "new breed" of African leaders—when they announced an "African reawakening" (Museveni) and "African Renaissance" (Mbeki).[2]

To be sure, both Mbeki and Museveni see this "reawakening" primarily in terms of industrialization, regional trade, and the building of a strong African economic block. Says Museveni:

> Trade is the best tool of development, and African countries should develop their joint markets rather than aspire to become associate members of the European Union. Industrialization as a basis for the continent's renewal would succeed only if markets were integrated and enlarged through regional cooperation.[3]

For both Mbeki and Museveni this integrated and vibrant market will not only lead to economic prosperity, it will promote political stability on the continent. Africa's problems, they contend, are due largely to Africa's underdevelopment and poverty.[4] Thus industrialization and a strong market economics in Africa will not only solve a great many of Africa's problems, it will give rise to a radically new and positive African image and identity—away from the classical image of a continent characterized by interminable wars and tribal genocide, and inhabited by potbellied, naked, and starving children prowling about with begging bowls.

That Mbelti and Museveni see the African Renaissance in terms of economics and trade is perhaps not surprising. Both have accepted the International Monetary Fund's (IMF) and the World Bank's vision of development and policies of economic liberalisation. This is not to say they had much choice in so doing. For, with the collapse of the Marxist Soviet block, and with the conclusion of the Uruguay round of talks on General Agreement on Tariffs and Trade (GATT), and the subsequent formation of the World Trade Organization (WTO), economic globalization has become the dominant political/economic ideology. The hope which sustains this liberal capitalistic vision is that economic liberalization, investment, and free competition and trade are the keys to economic development everywhere and to a better and higher standard of living for everyone. In Africa, this economic gospel has been the object of IMF– and World Bank–sponsored programs of structural adjustments, and, as I have indicated elsewhere, the priority agenda of former President Clinton's visit to Africa.[5]

A Story from the Top

It is clear then that the story of African Renaissance or reawakening is a story which not only forms part of the wider story of economic liberalization; it is a story that is announced from the top by African leaders. For sure, it is a *big* story which comprises such big subplots as "common goals of modernization," industrialization, the creation of a unified African market, foreign investment and the construction of "an infrastructure between the sub-Saharan neighbours," that is, trans-African highways and railway lines. Its success will likewise depend on such *big* indicators as the growth of GDP, competitiveness, foreign investment, exchange rate mechanisms, the servicing of national debts, a narrow trade deficit, free flow of capital and stock markets, and other indexes. That is why, ultimately it is, in fact, not Museveni and Mbeki who tell the story of African Renaissance, but such high-placed institutions and bodies as the World Bank, the International Monetary Fund, and the World Trade Organization. From this perspective, it becomes clear that the story of African Renaissance is one whose plot as well as final resolution is designed, determined, and declared from the tenth floor of some air-conditioned offices in New York, London or Cape Town. No wonder it remains largely incomprehensible except to those with high degrees in economics—the same people who design or tell the story. It is a meta-narrative.

This is one reason that I find myself a little uneasy with the story of African Renaissance. What is "African" in the African Renaissance, apart from the fact that it is a story played out on the African continent? Is African Renaissance just another way of "naming" Africa, this time as the privileged parade-ground for the struggles of global forces and the new battleground for multi-nationals as well as urban minority elite interests? If so, what is the difference between this new ideology and the previous ideologies that have variously "named" Africa from outside as the "terra nullius," the "dark continent," the "Third World?" Where does my semiliterate, rural mother stand in this African Renaissance? She has been promised that with a liberal economy, free trade, industrialization, privatization, the encouragement of foreign investors —that is, with the African Renaissance—her life will become greatly improved. There will be clean drinking water, better health care, more and better food, and a future filled with hopes of prosperity and a longer life.

I am afraid she does not recognize herself in this story, since she does not yet see any of the above signs of "salvation." In fact, she has not yet experienced any "renaissance" in her own life, even as official reports have continued to celebrate the growth of the GDP and foreign investors appreciatively note the "economic miracle" taking place. To be sure, she hears the jumbo jets roaring over her head, she sees the hi–tech trains speed by, she encounters tourists with big cameras who ask to take her picture. She is bewildered by all the advertisements promoting Castle Lager, Protector Strong condoms, M-Net, and other satellite TV stations. She does not understand what all the fuss is about. On the contrary, she is seriously worried that she has less food to eat now than ten years ago. There is less medical care for her and her sick grandchild. Her son has been unemployed for the last year. She has been warned not to drink the water from the river, because it has been polluted by the chemical waste from the nearby oil factory, but she cannot afford the nicely bottled SPA mineral water. She is just one of the millions of other ordinary Africans who are similarly worried about the concentration of wealth in the hands of a minority, the corruption in the public offices, the pollution of the rivers, the unscrupulous destruction of the forests by the lumber companies, the massive number of young people rendered unemployed and homeless, the growing number of street children, and the scandalous gap between rich and poor.

These contradictions do not seem to feature in the official version of the African Renaissance story as it is told in New York, Cape Town, or Kampala. This is not surprising, for such is precisely the danger of meta-narratives. In their attempt to claim universal validity or be globally acceptable, they do not account for the particular and contingent, particularly the historically divergent variable. Instead, they tend to confirm and perpetuate themselves through a highly selective sociology of statistics, which not only successfully cover up any contrary indications, but as a result confirm the story as "inevitable."

But suppose my mother would have a chance to tell the story of the global market in Africa. Would she tell it as a renaissance or catastrophe? For she is just a rural, black, African woman (each of these adjectives places her in a peculiarly disadvantaged position of powerlessness). Who will tell her story? That she is a Christian is perhaps my mother's only hope for hearing the story truthfully. But what would it take for Christianity to tell the story in such a way that an ordinary African would be able to locate herself in it? These are disturbing questions. They present a challenge for Christianity not to engage in fanciful story-telling. It is a challenge as to what sort of theology we develop, and from which vantage point. It is a challenge to write theology in such a way that an ordinary African may be able to locate herself within it. It is an invitation for the theologian to be a story-teller—not in a naive sense, but to develop a narrative theology of the ordinary Christian's ordinary struggles and aspirations in the face of such overpowering and totalizing stories as the African Renaissance.

I take this to be the unique challenge of Christian theology in general and African Christian theology in particular; namely, to be able to write a theology not from the top, but from below, from the ordinary experience of the believer. Critically, the task of theology is to challenge the various meta-narratives that claim validity simply because they come from the top, but which fail to take people's life histories seriously. These are the stories that, because they are so committed to a theory, a program, or a system, fail and/or refuse to see the real, the concrete, that which resists reduction to, or is intentionally excluded by, the system (in biblical terms, the widow and orphan). In order to underscore this role of theology, it is useful to show why the construction of meta-narratives presents a real and constant temptation.

Meta-narratives and the Challenge of Theology:
Zaccheus, come down

Why meta-narratives?
There is something tempting about meta-narratives that makes their presence in our lives if not inevitable at least widespread. Historical existence does not come in an orderly fashion. The world not only seems aimless, it is chancy and huge;[6] it is full of tragic choices and possibilities. Within this world, as Martha Nussbaum has so rightly argued, life remains fragile, exposed to the vicissitudes of luck through one's dependency on others, by the chronic conflict inherent within the

plurality of one's engagements, and the ever-present fear of reversal and eventual loss (death).[7] Rather than facing or dealing with these painful and negative aspects of life, the individual may often seek to flee from them by engaging in big stories of a fantastic nature. The latter, which usually take the form of exaggerated claims for "my clan," "my race," "my tribe," "my country," "modernization," and so forth, tends to provide consolation for the self by hiding the painful and contradictory aspects within that story and within one's existence.[8] This is a moral reason why individuals readily take recourse to big stories or meta-narratives.

There is another reason which we have come to suspect, especially after Foucault, that is mostly political. Every society, as Foucault says, "writes its own history that legitimizes its own regime of truth, its 'general politics' of truth: that is, the type of discourse which it accepts and makes function as true" [9] This observation is connected with a central theme in Foucault (and Nietzsche); namely, the relation between knowledge and power. In fact, the overall effect of Foucault's analysis has been to show that the production of knowledge or history need not be seen as a faithful record of "what really happened," but as a certain "invention, behind which lies something completely different from itself: the play of instincts, impulses, desires, fears and the will to appropriate. Knowledge is produced on the stage where these elements struggle against each other."[10]

This means that what usually passes as knowledge or the voice of general well-being may well be the voice of a narrow range of economic and political interests. In this context, meta-narratives become a particularly useful and effective ideological guise: they keep large numbers of people from noticing the narrow base of real interest. However, once one has accepted this insight from Foucault, then one rightly begins to suspect the "politics" of exclusion, as well as the narrow base of interests which lies behind the production of such grand narratives as the "discovery" of Africa or America,[11] economic globalization, and African Renaissance.

The theological challenge: Zaccheus come down

Whatever the reason for their construction, meta-narratives, whether in personal or social history, tend to construct or view reality from a particular vantage point—the top. This way they not only tend to escape or flee from the rough and painful details of historical existence, they intentionally cover up the particular, the contingent, the historical, the real. That is perhaps why they represent a unique challenge to theology. For Christian theology, as I take it, has as one of its great challenges the reappreciation of the "small"—the local, the particular—which is always being covered up by grand narratives and totalizing structures. The challenge of theology is to fight what I call the Zaccheus Syndrome, narrated in Luke 19:1–10.[12]

Zaccheus, we are told, was a small man. However, everything around him is big or happens in a meta-narrative way. He lives in Jericho, a *big* city, second only to Jerusalem. He has a *big* top job. He is a *big* official. He is the *senior* tax collector—directly accountable to Rome, the imperial city, to which all roads lead. He is therefore a wealthy man. He has heard of Jesus, of the many *big* miracles and *powerful* speeches he (Jesus) has been giving in the countryside. Zaccheus does not only wish to see Jesus, he is (we are told) anxious to see him; that is, he has a *big* burning desire, a dream. Well, one day he has a chance, because Jesus happened to come to Jericho. But unfortunately, there is a *big* crowd. However, Zaccheus cannot be outsmarted. He runs ahead, climbs a *big* sycamore tree.

For Zaccheus, the climbing of the big sycamore tree is such a brilliant and smart idea. But it is as well a temptation, a temptation to dwell up there; of not getting involved with, and pushed around by, the crowd. He just wants to "see" Jesus clearly; to have a clear perspective of everything (false universalism) taking place. This is why Jesus calls to him to come down from the top of the tree to the ground; from the clouds to join the crowds: the smelly, disorderly crowd comprising both rich and poor, widows and orphans, well–fed judges and hungry children, muscular soldiers and feeble country women; a crowd, in other words, of the historical realities and contradictions.

Surprisingly, it is only when he had come down into this confused mess that he noticed the widow and orphan for the first time. Only then did he "see" his life and others clearly. His invitation to come down was at the same time an invitation to "see" small things, small events, small needs, small differences, to see realistically.

The greatest challenge for us today is to be able to "see" such small details, since we are accustomed to living with big stories. And, just like in Zaccheus' case, it is only when we have come down from the big sycamore trees—of big concepts like Globalization, The Market, The African Renaissance, as told on the tenth floor of air-conditioned offices in New York, London, or Cape Town (the sycamore trees of our day)—into the messy, uneven trivialities of everyday contradictions of the African villages, the shanty towns, the squatter camps, and the back streets (the home of starving street children), that we can begin to "see" the full effect of the African Renaissance. Only then can we begin to realistically and critically ask, "Who has done this to you, Africa?"

We have heard the story of Africa's renaissance from the top and I am sure we shall hear more variations. Can theology challenge whoever is telling that story—the World Bank, the IMF, the African leaders—to come down to the ground? What sort of skills would theology need to be able to do that? I am sure it will take more than pious words to be able to force Zaccheus down to the ground. One major requirement is that theology has to remain on the ground—within the realm of small stories, within the narrative context of the African's ordinary struggles and aspirations. But this is where the dominant form of African Christian theology has so far failed.

Questioning Africa's theological past

There is something of an ambiguity within the dominant theological forms of African Christianity, in as far as it has tended to identify itself with the quests for Africanization, indigenization, and/or inculturation. To be sure, this dominant form of African Christian theology was born (as noted in the epigram above) out of a struggle against colonial condescension. Its target was the missionary-dominated Church, and especially its theology, which was seen not only as tending toward the humiliation of the African peoples and their culture, but as (and therefore) offering a Christianity that remained essentially Western and only superficially grafted onto the African way of life. It was against this transcendental and superficial theology that African theologians —originally under the key influence of negritude and the existentialist quest for authenticity—began to emphasize the need for a theology of adaptation, inculturation, indigenization, or Africanization. However, even as it has become the dominant form of Christian theology in Africa, the theology of Africanization has greatly remained a theology from the top, caught up in the "sycamore" vantage point of the missionary Christianity it set out to overcome.

In the first place, theologies of Africanization remain grounded in a transcendentalist characterization of otherness and difference. This has not only contributed to the popular but highly misleading view of a monolithic African culture, it tends to conjure up the myth of a "pure" African past. It is this myth that has led (within African Christianity) to the preoccupation with and protracted search for these "exotic" cultural forms (usually identified with dance and drama), while neglecting the present historical concerns of African peoples. It is today's tragedies, struggles, anxieties, and conflicts which are the places where culture is being born. African culture is what we live today. However, by limiting culture to artistic forms, theologies of Africanization tend to make a parody of culture. Moreover, while there is a serious case to be made for authenticity, the temptation to "recapture" tradition or the past is a dangerous alibi, whose only effect is to provide a distraction away from the concrete historical struggles and actual contradictions of African societies.[13] In other words, by remaining confined to this "irreal sublime" of cultural forms and expressions, theologies of Africanization tend to offer a discourse about Africa that is not only theoretically thin, but politically impotent as well. Ironically, this is one reason these theologies have become popular and dominant—they have not seriously challenged or disturbed the status quo.

However, a major reason why African theology has remained captive to the sycamore vantage point has to do with Christianity's own failure to rise beyond the meta-narrative language of Universal Gospel, Church, and Truth. Such claims for universal validity could not but underwrite a Christianity of "mental beliefs," integration into a "system" and the subsequent bureaucratic management of believers. In any case, such a "zombie" Christianity, as Mudimbe calls it, does not take seriously people's concrete life history and their struggles, but only takes consolation in such official statistics and superficial figures as the number of baptisms, ordinations, or the richness and variety of cultural expressions. This is the sycamore Christianity which we need to move beyond if we are to allow the Christian story to work in a concrete and powerful way in the everyday struggles against such totalizing and yet marginalizing stories as "African Renaissance."

African Renaissance and the Power of the Christian Story.

African Christian theology as social critique—narratives from the ground

Every story not only engenders a certain social praxis, it fashions a distinct form of people. Every story is, therefore, ultimately judged by the richness of social practices it generates and the sort of people it produces. The critical challenge at any particular time is to know the sort of people we are becoming by accepting being controlled by a particular sort of story—in this case, the story of liberal economics and its proclaimed African Renaissance.

The first task of African Christian theology today, therefore, is to provide a sustained social critique by making available the concrete stories of people as well as of the actual contradictions within the societies formed by the story of liberal economics. Christian theology needs to tell the stories of increasing marginalization, exploitation, the scandalous prosperity of a tiny segment of the population (and the corresponding pauperization of the majority), of the deep chasm between the capital cities and the back country, the elite and the masses, the state and the people, of the stories of unemployment and homelessness of an increasing number of children and youth, and so forth. Such stories are either never told or intentionally covered up by the spurious promotion of liberal economics under the guises of modernization, industrialization, or African Renaissance. By making these stories available, African Christian theology would be challenging liberal economics to come down to the ground, to "see" and accept that they are not just accounts of isolated and minor irregularities on the way of being overcome by some structural adjustment program, but that such irregularities are part and parcel of the story of liberal economics, at least as experienced on the ground.

By playing this critical role, African Christian theology would find that she is beginning to take seriously the sociopolitical context in which Africans live. No doubt this would make African Christian theology deeply and dangerously "political." But this is inescapable if Christian theology is to tell and live the Gospel adequately. And, in fact, it is here that I locate the affinity between the sort of narrative theology that I am calling for with the main tradition of black theology. For a major insight from black theology has been the realization that Christian faith does not, and in fact cannot, transcend sociopolitical ideologies.[14] Even when she encourages a pietistic and ritualistic spirituality of salvation of souls, she ought to realize that this is deeply political, since it tends to justify a particular social, economic, and political status quo, while anesthetizing the individual against various forms of exploitation.[15]

There might be a tendency to play down the critical and subversive power of the Christian story which was so crucial to black theology. For, with the "liberation" of South Africa, and with an African Renaissance, we may feel that the exploitation, slavery, and apartheid against which black theology defined itself are a thing of the past. I think we might experience even worse forms of slavery and exploitation under the new economic arrangements, precisely because we fail to see them for what they are—false ideologies. We need therefore to make the social, materialistic analysis (within black theology) the dominant trend within Christian theology in Africa today; and to do this through a narrative display of the tensions, contradictions, and increasing marginalization of African societies under the story of liberal economics.

An embodied Christianity: an alternative story
African Christian theology can only play the above critical role if she herself is sustained by a genuine Christian praxis; that is, if she is grounded in communities which live by the Christian story. These are the communities of struggle and resistance that have learned to take the Christian story seriously as a social ideology which, like any social ideology, is capable of mobilizing specific goals and informing specific practices. Such communities will therefore not only offer a "witness" to the sort of characters and social praxes generated by the Christian story, they will provide an alternative to the individualism and agonistic competitiveness of the liberal economic story.[16] Such an alternative vision does not mean that the Church offers a new social/economic theory (that would be just another meta-narrative). The "alternative" is just another way of living, of embodying a different story as well as different practices and virtues, which may help to concretely show how some acclaimed values of liberal economics (individualism, competitiveness, acquisitiveness, consumerism, exclusion) clash with some of the most cherished Christian practices and virtues.

I found a recent experience in a Malaysian *kampong* very challenging in this regard. On a visit to Sarawak, friends invited me to celebrate the Eucharist in one village *(kampong)*. After the Eucharistic service, we were all invited to stay behind for "fellowship." What particularly impressed me was that the cans of Coca-Cola were not served directly; rather, they were opened, put into a jug, and served by one or two people from the same jug. It would certainly have been so much easier and faster to hand each one a Coke (or invite each to pick one) as there were enough cans to go around. What I saw was a culture trying to resist the individualism of the market (the cans are so packaged to conveniently serve "individual" consumption). I kept wondering what it would take for Christians to resist some of the values of the market. For I am sure that there are Christian practices (similar to those in this

AFRICAN THEOLOGY TODAY

kampong experience) which make it impossible for Christians to be good consumers in a liberal capitalistic economy. Take the "Our Father" and the Eucharistic communion, for instance. That people of various social, racial, and economic backgrounds can refer to the same God as "our Father" (not "my father"), and share the same cup and bread, is indeed a very powerful challenge. And, if one takes these practices seriously, then one begins to harbor valid doubts about, and to seek alternatives to, the liberal economic story that tries to convince us that we exist as individuals, driven by self-interest, who regard the other as a competitor for the same limited resources.

Conclusion

In this paper, I have sought to argue that the critical challenge of Christian theology in general, and African Christian theology in particular, is to force various meta-narratives to "come down" to the ground. The proclaimed African Renaissance seems to be one such meta-narrative which risks instituting new forms of exclusion and exploitation within the new realities of the world economic system. I have argued that African Christian theology can force this meta-narrative, and any other meta-narratives that may claim our allegiance, to "come down to the ground" by itself being grounded within the narrative setting of the daily struggles and aspirations of ordinary Africans. That is to say, African Christian theology needs to take her story seriously, as a sociopolitical ideology, capable of mobilizing creative social goals and possibilities, as well as of engendering a distinctive and alternative social praxis.

NOTES

[1] Prepared for the Doctoral Seminar, School of Theology–University of Natal, Pietermaritzburg (South Africa), 8th June 1998.
[2] At Cape Town, South Africa, May 27–28, 1997. See, "Africanews Homepage," on the Internet at http://www.html.africanews.com (August 1997).
[3] "Africanews Homepage."
[4] See Museveni K. Yoweri, *What Is Africa's Problem?* (Kampala: NRM Publications, 1992)
[5] Emmanuel Katongole, "Globalization and economic fundamentalism in Africa: on policies that intensify the cries of the poor," at ESEAT (Sagana, Kenya), March 1998.
[6] Iris Murdoch, *"Sovereignty," The sovereignty of the good* (London: Routledge, 1970) 96.
[7] Martha Nussbaum, *The fragility of goodness* (New York: Cambridge University Press, 1986)

[8] See, e.g., Stanley Hauerwas, "Self-deception and autobiography: reflections on Speer's 'Inside the Third Reich," Truthfulness and tragedy (Notre Dame: University of Notre Dame Press, 1977), 82–100.

[9] Michel Foucault, *Knowledge/power: selected interviews and other writings* (Brighton: Harvest Press, 1980), 72.

[10] Michel Foucault, "History of systems of thought," *Language, counter-memory, practice: selected essays and interviews by Michel Foucault*, ed. and tr. Donald F. Bouchard and Sherry Simon (Oxford: Blackwell, 1977), 202.

[11] On the politics of discovery and naming as they relate to Africa, see V.Y. Mudimbe, *The invention of Africa: gnosis, philosophy and the order of knowledge* (Indianapolis: Indiana University Press, 1988) and its sequel, *The idea of Africa* (Indianapolis: Indiana University Press, 1994). On the violence that is often masked by the story of the "discovery" of America, see Stanley Hauerwas, *After Christendom* (Nashville: Abingdon Press, 1991), 133–148. See also Michel De Certeau, *The writing of history* (New York: Columbia University Press, 1988).

[12] Biblical scholars will have to excuse me for such a gloss and careless reading of a biblical text.

[13] F. Eboussi Boulaga, *Christianity without fetiches: an African critique and recapture of Christianity* tr. Robert R. Barr (Maryknoll: Orbis Books, 1984).

[14] See e.g. Allan A. Boesak, *Farewell to innocence: a socio-ethical study on Black theology and Black power* (Maryknoll: Orbis Books, 1977) 99–122; Comel West, "Black theology of liberation as critique of Capitalist civilization," *Black theology: a documentary history*, Vol II: 1980–1992, ed. H. Cone & G. Wimore (Maryknoll: Orbis Books, 1993), 425.

[15] That is why I find Malukeke's question of whether African Christianity (to the extent it has encouraged a pietistic and ritualized theology) has been part of the African problem, a highly disturbing but a necessary first step toward a constructive introspection. See Tinyiko Maluleke, "Christianity in an unstable and poor Africa: towards a constructive introspection," Paper at ESEAT (Sagana, Kenya, March 26–29, 1998).

[16] I develop these issues more fully in *Beyond Universal Reason*, (University of Notre Dame Press, 2000).

CHAPTER 12

The Merging of Globalization with the Notion of an African Renaissance: A Practical Theological and Pastoral Assessment

D.J. Louw

Abstract

This article is an attempt to assess the notion of an African Renaissance from the perspective of a practical theological ecclesiology and a pastoral engagement. The link between an African Renaissance and the current processes of globalization and international communication is explored. In terms of the possible dangers of a romanticization of rural African spirituality and an imperialistic hijacking by global economic enterprises of an African revival, a globalization from below is proposed. In this regard a practical theological ecclesiology can play a pivotal role by making use of an "interpenetration model."

The so-called African Renaissance has become a political buzz word in South Africa. It is already setting the pace for social transformation and molding the framework for future thinking and development. To a certain extent its aim is to determine the social and cultural destiny of the African continent in the twenty-first century; its purpose is *Pax Africana* (African solutions for African problems) and *Pan-Africanism* (the social, political idea of interconnectedness despite the political divisions of the African continent).[1]

Closely connected to the notions of a *Pax Africana* and a *Pan-Africanism*, an African Renaissance is a new variant of protest policy and liberation theology. According to President T. Mbeki:[2] "The call for Africa's renewal, for an African Renaissance is a call to rebellion. We must rebel against the tyrants and the dictators, those who seek to corrupt our societies and steal the wealth that belongs to the people. We must rebel against the ordinary criminals who murder, rape and rob and conduct war against poverty, ignorance and the backwardness of the children of Africa." The "soul" of an African Renaissance is captured by Mbeki[3]: "Our vision of an African renaissance must have as one of its central aims the provision of a better life for these masses of the people whom we say must enjoy and exercise the right to determine their future"; it is a struggle for gaining dignity and humanity,[4] and to express Africa's need for a cultural identity.[5]

If meant as a philosophical verdict, the following question should be posed by Christian theology: What could the possible impact of such a cultural and even spiritual renaissance be on the enfleshment of the Gospel within the African continent; i.e., what is the implication of this new "ideological stance" on the formation of theory for a practical, theological ecclesiology? Should the church view an African Renaissance as a challenge to be met? If indeed, how will it influence the functioning of the church in Africa?

As an indication of a new frame of mind, one can assume that such a renaissance refers to a sort of enlightenment, or to the revival of the classic understanding of the freedom of the human spirit and its quest for meaning and search for dignity. Normally, the notion of a renaissance refers to the democratic ideal of Hellenism; the creative power of the human mind as well as a qualitative and quantitative transformation.[6] If one assumes that both meanings are incorporated, a renaissance provides an opportunity for creativity as well as new schemata of interpretation.

To home in on the concept "Africa," contextual issues which shape the daily lives of people immediately spring to mind. Issues such as poverty, unemployment, crime, violence, AIDS, and housing surface. How will an African Renaissance cope with these basic matters of daily survival?

These questions become even more complicated when one realizes that an African Renaissance cannot be isolated from that which is taking place in the bigger global world of current human thinking and technological development. It is inevitable that an African Renaissance cannot occur without taking into account one of the most influential factors in postmodern thinking: globalization. Hence the objective of this article: to reflect on the meaning of an "African Renaissance" and its possible link to universal trends as well as to those existential problems which mold Africans' life on a daily basis.

Gradually, it is dawning upon this continent: Africa is not necessarily the focal point of Western thinking. The main interest of the so-called global village is elsewhere. As a "Third World" country the real threat to Africans is being viewed merely as a marginalized coincidence on the agenda of those very powerful and global enterprises which set the pace for the twenty-first century.[7] For example, South Africa lost both bids for the Olympic Games (2004) as well as for the World Soccer (2006). One is forced to accept the fact: Africa is not necessarily the focal point of global thinking. If this assumption is true, how will globalization affect an African Renaissance?

The call for an African Renaissance could be interpreted as an urgent request for recognition, acknowledgment, and identity. It could even be seen as an attempt to mobilize Africa in terms of a revival of a new sense of inclusiveness and interconnectedness. However, for the church, the practical theological and pastoral question remains the following: Will an African Renaissance change Africans' basic experience of human dignity? How will it address their quest for meaning, and will it indeed improve life on this continent?

Pastoral Hermeneutics

In order to address the previous questions, the method of a pastoral hermeneutics will be applied. Such a "hermeneutics" means an attempt to understand conceptual schemata of thinking and their link to philosophical, cultural, and existential issues. A pastoral hermeneutics is engaged in an endeavor to understand conceptual models for interpretation, i.e., general patterns which govern our coming to cognitive terms with our world.[8] Furthermore, its task is to link these patterns of thinking to fundamental issues regarding our experience of significance and human dignity.

Within the parameters of a practical theological ecclesiology, a pastoral hermeneutics is basically driven by the ethos of the Christian faith, i.e., the ethos of sacrificial love. Its intention is to demonstrate empathy; to display solidarity; to change and transform structures which violate people's basic experiences of human rights; and to foster a vivid hope which inspires people to meet the challenges of life.

In order to apply this method of a pastoral hermeneutics to the investigation of the meaning of the notion of an "African Renaissance," this paper needs to probe deeper into the roots of contemporary philosophical thinking and its impact on life events. This article argues the hypothesis that international communication and globalization are the two most influential conceptual schemata which determine life on this planet. Both globalization and international communication are exponents of a market-driven economy which molds our being human into a new culture: the culture of achievement, entertainment, money-making, consumption, materialistic exploitation, technological development, and economic performance. Our daily existence is constantly being transformed from local experiences and national regionality into a new cultural identity: "transnationalism."

With these theses in mind, this article needs to ask: Is it possible to assess an African Renaissance without taking into consideration its inevitable link to the ethos of globalization and the demands of international communication? If not, what will the impact of an African Renaissance be on different cultural groups in Africa? What is the effect of globalization on the concept of differentiation?

In order to address these questions, one needs to reckon with a further assumption: essentially, an African Renaissance is about a cultural and sociopolitical renewal. Hence the fundamental hypothesis of this paper: *that unless an African Renaissance differentiates itself culturally from transnationalism and globalization, it will end up with a so-called African verdict of globalization, which is actually nothing but Americanization and economic colonization projected onto the idea of a better future, which is, in essence, constantly being determined by brute materialistic values. In the meantime, important spiritual issues and virtues which reflect local African culture and the core of a Christian ethos are being sacrificed without necessarily improving the quality of people's lives.*

This article is divided into three parts. Firstly, I will trace back the most important features of an African spirituality and link them to the basic philosophy of an African Renaissance. Secondly, I will make an assessment of a global economy and its possible influence on Africa. The last part will be devoted to a pastoral and practical theological reflection.

I. Spirituality Within the Framework of an African Renaissance

In Africa there is no division and/or differentiation between the animate and inanimate, between the spirit and matter, between living and non-living, dead and living, physical and metaphysical, secular and sacred, the body and spirit, etc. Most Africans generally believe that everything (human beings included) is in constant relationship with one another and with the invisible world, and that people are in a state of complete dependence upon those invisible powers and beings. Hence, Africans are convinced that in the activities of life, harmony, balance or tranquility must constantly be sought and maintained. Society is not segmented into, for example, medicine, sociology, law, politics and religion. Life is a liturgy of celebration for the victories and/or sacrifices of others.[9]

This quotation underlines the fact that, for the African, life is an integral whole of cosmic and social events. This implies that when one breaks society's moral codes, the cosmic ties between oneself and the community are broken. This factor then could be the main issue in a person's experience of suffering. Thus, recovery and cure obtain a new dimension: it is primarily not the person who must be cured, but broken ties and relationships.

Within the African social order and network of relationships, ancestors play a decisive role. As often stated erroneously, this does not mean that Africans *worship* their ancestors. The latter are not gods, but are merely part of the systemic network of relationships. Ancestors are the protectors of life and the community. "Africans do believe strongly in the presence and influence of ancestors in daily life, so much so that they do things, often unconsciously, to reflect such a belief, but they do not worship them as gods."[10]

African anthropology

For a practical and theological ecclesiology, it is of the utmost importance that the African be viewed as a holistic and social being. Systemic concepts, therefore, have important *anthropological impl-ications*. Thus, for example, personality is not a purely psychological concept. In Western psychology, personality usually refers to the self-structure of the human person. It is part of the I-nucleus with its conscious and unconscious processes. Personality thus becomes an individual category which reflects the constant factor of typical behavior and personal characteristics. Thus, the human being is autonomous and independent.

Within an African context, personality refers rather to a dynamic power and vital energy which allow a person to come into contact with ancestors, God, and society. Berinyuu,[11] for example, refers to an Akan tribe who have their own unique view of a person. "The *ntroro* spirit is the energy which links him/her to the ancestral lineage." They do not regard human spirit as an identifiable self, but as a personal con-sciousness of powers which they associate with the concept of "destiny." This destiny can be modified so that one can adapt within circumstances and within a social context.

The above-mentioned facts shed more light upon *Africans' non-analytical approach to life; they do not necessarily analyze life. Life,*

with its pain and problems, is lived despite there being no final solution.
This approach to life demands much patience and adaptability and it is
clear that, as such, it differs vastly from a Western model. Within the
latter (clock), time and the manipulation of life are important. This does
not mean that African rhythm does not also manipulate and often abuse
life and nature. The point to grasp is that, within an African model, time
is an *event* and life is a game of powers. Life and personality possess
dynamic energy within social relationships. Therefore, myth and
symbol, ritual and rhythm, determine everyday life, not analyses and
solutions. The human person, therefore, can never be a complete entity,
but is always embedded in social powers within which he/she has a role
to play. Your role in society determines who you are, and this is of
greater importance than your personal qualities and individual needs.
Role fulfillment becomes more important than personal self-
actualization.

A role does not indicate social position in the light of skills,
possessions, and professional status, but is a behavioral pattern
originating as a result of social expectations. Therefore, a role is not a
cloak to be donned or discarded. Your role is part of your social identity
and is part of the convictions of society and the tribal community.
Because the human person is a social being within the totality of
transcendental and religious powers, the *spiritual dimension* of the
African view of life plays a decisive role in people's experience of
meaning and significance.

This spiritual dimension must be understood corporatively: human
beings are part of a social order within which living energy is linked to
cosmic and religious powers which give meaning to everyday existence.
Hence, the importance of a holistic approach to the problem of suffering
within an African context. Therefore, one could say that the African
view of life, as a holistic social and spiritual enterprise, dovetails with
the systemic model's notion of interconnectedness and the human
person's place or position within this relational network.

African Spirituality
To determine what exactly is meant by the concepts African and
spirituality, is very difficult. Every generalization runs the risk of
forgetting that Africa consists of a multiple of peoples, beliefs, and
traditions. Therefore, an African spirituality refers to certain common
cultural traits and philosophical paradigms which reflect a general
mindset, belief system, or life approach.

According to Skhakhane,[12] the community is the core of African spirituality. "Community" means not only the living, but also the ancestors. "African Spirituality, as I understand it, consists in an intimate relationship of people with their ancestors which relationship initiates and governs their activity in life in such a way that they relate to all other beings in a manner that guarantees harmony and peace."[13] Community also includes the state of the whole family. Ackermann[14] refers to this state as the priority of a community: the extended family, within which role assignment and the quest for humanity are of the utmost importance. Hence the following statement made by Bellagamba:[15] "A spirituality which does not incorporate all people, their events, their richness, their hopes and concerns, cannot speak to Africans who are fundamentally communal and relational."

If we accept that "spirit" in an African spirituality means *spiritus*, a force concerned with day-to-day human activity, the following proposition expressed by Mtetwa[16] sums up our position very aptly. "One of the most remarkable and tangible dimensions of African Spirituality relates to the unique notion of communality and collective solidarity that the African society exhibits in all spheres of life. There is a profound sense of interdependence, from the extended family to the entire community. In a very real sense, everybody is interrelated; including relations between the living and those who have departed." The aim of an African spirituality[17] is harmony in interpersonal relationships: *umuntu ungumuntu ngabantu/motho ke motho ka batho* — roughly translated as: a person is a person through other people.[18]

Purpose of an African Renaissance

It is exactly at this point where an African spirituality merges with the *raison d'être* for an African Renaissance: "the need to empower African peoples to deliver themselves from the legacy of colonialism and neo-colonialism and to situate themselves on the global stage as equal and respected contributors to as well beneficiaries of all the achievements of human civilization."[19]

Both the need to be empowered as well as to be recognized by the global village are attempts to help Africans to rediscover their cultural roots. Both link with the notions of renaissance and spirituality and thus represent the idea of an inclusive communality, which assists Africans to understand their identity in terms of dynamic spiritual and communal forces which determine life. Daily life should, therefore, be experienced not in terms of individualization, fragmentation, and materialistic exploitation, but in terms of mutual respect for people and values which, in turn, reflects spiritual destination rather than secular survival. In both an African Renaissance and spirituality, the primary issue which needs to be addressed is: change and transformation; the shift from deprivation and suffering to recognition (identity) and significance (dignity).

However, it is exactly at this point where an African Renaissance becomes problematic. The real danger lurks that a globalist framing of this concept will hijack the notion of an African Renaissance and that moneyed elites in South Africa, whose understanding of the process of modernization is the generation of wealth, will embrace this notion enthusiastically. According to P. Vale and S. Maseko,[20] despite the three main pillars of economic development, global competitiveness, and regional cooperation and integration,[21] the features of the African Renaissance remain deliberately vague—high on sentiment, low on substance. Politicians use this concept for social sentiment and link it to economic development. Therefore, Vale and Maseko[22] are convinced that South Africa's renaissance implies economic globalization and a movement toward a notion that the country could anchor a chain of economies which, in time, might become the African equivalent of the Asian Tigers.

"Mbeki has favored this interpretation,"[23] implying that the African Renaissance posits Africa as an expanding and prosperous market alongside Asia, Europe, and North America in which South African capital is destined to play a special role through the development of trade and strategic partnerships.[24] But, and this should be the challenging question: What will then happen to the dream of a cultural reawakening and the revival of an African spirituality?

An African reading of the African Renaissance is often "post-structural," i.e., its aim is to move away from the romantic tourist view of dancing and smiling Africans to a reinterpretation of both African history and culture, away from its colonial construction towards a consolidation of true African values, culture, and folklore, and with an increasingly powerful appeal for a new future for Africa. In short, the epistemological shift proposed by an African Renaissance involves an understanding of human relations beyond the limiting sets represented by race and global polities. "It must simultaneously both recognize human worth and the diversity of cultural values it represents. To play this role a renaissance must represent both discipline and liberation;"[25] it should be forced back to issues at grassroots level.

The vital question which should be posed now is whether an African Renaissance can achieve recognition (identity) and significance (dignity) without a sort of alliance with the major forces of globalization and international communication within our universal, market–driven economy. If not, how will globalization and international communication affect the cultural and spiritual identity of Africa?

During a fact-finding mission to different countries in Southern Africa, delegates of the Faculty of Theology at Stellenbosch and the Western Cape[26] found that the quest for humanity and relationality, despite the process of modernization, is still of paramount importance. Among the most burning issues affecting life and African spirituality are poverty, unemployment, the AIDS threat, violence, and criminality. This finding corresponds with some of the negative features characterizing black urban townships in South Africa: crime, alienation, and protest/struggle.[27]

II. The Possible Impact of a Global Economy on an African Renaissance

It becomes clear that the agenda set for an African Renaissance, cannot be assessed separately from economic development within the global village. This truth had been clearly spelled out by T. Mbeki:[28] "And yet we must also recognize the fact that we cannot win the struggle for Africa's development outside the context and framework of the world economy." Hence attention must be paid to the interaction between globalization and Africanization.

The concept "political economy" is used to designate the fact that economics is basically a cultural, social, and political enterprise driven by needs and consumption. Owensby[29] defines economics as the study of the principles by which society organizes itself to use scarce resources for the production and distribution of goods and services in order to achieve a better life.

According to Meeks,[30] at least four basic components comprise every political economy:

Power/rule. What kind of politics serves a humane economy and what kind of economy serves humane politics?

Work and employment. How does a society understand production? What is meaningful work?

Needs and consumption. Are there ways in which our understanding of needs affect the ways in which we distribute resources, goods, and income? What is a human need as opposed to a human want? Does human freedom mean the right to luxury when the needs of others are not being met?

Property. What is the function of ownership and what is the meaning of possession? Who has rights, resources, and capital and why? Who should control planning and investment policies as well as monetary and fiscal systems?[31]

The basic problem of a global economy, determined by the previous components and value-laden convictions, is that it is becoming more and more an *economy from above*, i.e., an economy determined by big companies and the web of telecommunication systems. Plou[32] aptly captures the problem of a global economy by saying:

> As the globalization of markets moves relentlessly ahead, the globalization of communication is enabling the market to export its models of consumption by seducing those at the receiving end into adopting the rules of its game. How many will be left outside is not an issue. The goal is to increase individualism and social fragmentation so that persons come to perceive themselves only as consumers.

Within the social sciences, the term *globalization* attained different nuances. It refers both to the compression of the world[33] and to the intensification of consciousness of the world as a whole.[34] To a certain extent, globalization becomes a cultural process that tends toward homogenization and a high level of structural interconnectedness, which change local, cultural, and spiritual values. While it relativizes traditions, it simultaneously opens up a plurality of new options and possibilities.

The process of globalization becomes more and more systemic as it is determined by anonymous and impersonal systems such as technology and economics. Against such systems, the individual self is experienced as powerless.[35]

The effect of globalization is the disembedding of institutions. Social institutions are lifted out of social relations with local contexts progressively becoming abstract systems. Institutions become locally decontextualized and create a space separate from their environment. This leads to the globalization of the local and the localization of the global.[36]

Literature on globalization points out that this phenomenon cannot be understood without communication technology.[37] Scholars refer to "international communication" as a complex and fast-growing subfield within the major field of communication and media studies, and regard it as an important partner of the process of globalization. "It encompasses the issues of culture and cultural commodification[38] (the turning of cultural products into commodities), the diffusion of information and news broadcasting by media empires around the world, and the challenges faced by the developing world in the light of these processes."[39]

Gradually, international communication creates a multicultural environment which is run by transnational companies. Mega-cultural firms are based on the commodification of Anglophone culture with the aid of the electronic information highway. Indeed, globalization projects multiculturality but, in effect, and this is the challenging point, creates chaos where culture and economic imperialism (power) intersects with issues of human dignity, personal identity, values, social identity, and the production of wishes and desires. Often, telecommunication projects the illusion of a better world with happy people, ignoring the basic suffering of people deprived of luxury and electronic entertainment.

It is becoming evident that international communication and globalization raises questions of power, censorship, and human rights. It stirs up issues such as the freedom of information, the means of transnational communication, the nature of news, and the control of television, and behind all the lurking power of economics and the question of the control of technology. Furthermore, there are problems such as the imposition of news values, agenda-setting, and the imbalance between "the haves and the have nots," the incredible gap between rich and poor in the developing world and the gap surfacing everywhere between rich nations and poor nations.

The race for globalization puts the following challenge to a practical, theological ecclesiology: whether human life, its significance and value, can be assessed only in terms of unqualified competitiveness, projected as the so-called key to success. If one can assume that the process of globalization is not value-free, the question should be posed whether the concern in an African Renaissance for identity and human dignity can be separated from ethos and morality. Will the church find a way to challenge the new forms of knowledge, information, and economics whose only concern appears to be profit? "Will virtual reality for a small group of nations in the North be at the expense of an increasing actual poverty for people in the South?"[40] In short: "The future of the world depends, in large measure on how modernity can be tamed to ensure a continuing production of wealth without disastrous consequences for the global natural, social and cultural environments."[41]

During a visit to Accra, Ghana, for the 6th Congress of the International Council on Pastoral Care and Counseling (August 1999), I became aware of the huge gap between the practice of informal business and the policy of big business. The whole of Accra and its economy is structured according to the needs of poor people at grassroots level. The absence of malls and big shopping centers was striking. Back in South Africa, I attended a meeting where economists discussed the possibility of exploring new markets in Accra, Ghana. My immediate reaction was: but this will destroy the market economy from below. A new mall will create needs, demands, and opportunities which are foreign to the country's basic economy and the principle of entrepreneurship. The prices of informal business, scattered all over the city, will struggle to compete with the better propositions offered by big companies. My immediate pastoral question was: Despite the advantages of a new system, what will the impact be on the living standard of the poor and the problem of unemployment? My fear was that only a few would benefit, while many people might lose their jobs. In the long run the consequence could be more poverty and more unemployment.

This case study confronts an African Renaissance with the most basic challenge, i.e., whether such a renaissance can address the suffering of people at grassroots level and improve their economic and spiritual disposition. This challenge warns an African Renaissance against a relentless bond with the aspirations of globalization and international communication.[42] It brings the following awareness: in order to empower the people of Africa, an African Renaissance should start from "below" rather than from "above."

If it is true that an African Renaissance cannot be separated from the process of globalization, the following question should be posed: But what are the advantages of globalization? The advantages of globalization: it opens up a world–wide plurality of opportunities and a web of technological links and relevant knowledge—it can empower people and take them further than their local and cultural limitations. On the other hand, globalization can endanger our sense of local, cultural interconnectedness by molding people into a global similarity that fosters estrangement rather than promotes cultural communality.

III. A Practical Theological and Pastoral Assessment

To a certain extent, the concept African Renaissance coincides with what is meant in theology by an "African hermeneutics." The latter is the endeavor for contextualization. It is predominantly concerned with ways to construct African theology independent from Western theological influences. It represents the effort to understand and interpret the religious significance of African culture and to determine the theological character of African traditional religions and spirituality. According to Du Toit,[43] an African hermeneutics "is a contextual hermeneutics aware of the legacy of colonialism, the history of African oppression and exploitation, but determined to recover African identity and formulate a theology which takes cognizance of African Traditional Religions." As in the case of an African hermeneutics,[44] an African Renaissance should, therefore, be assessed as a hermeneutics of protest against factors crippling its people. It is a reactionary hermeneutics, trying to come to grips with post-colonial Africa.

The slogan "An African Renaissance" entails different meanings at different levels of interpretation. Four possible meanings can be identified: cultural; social and political; economic; and spiritual.

(a) Renaissance as a cultural revival and rediscovery of the African heritage

As an indication of a new understanding of the value of traditional culture in Africa, an African Renaissance is something of an appeal to Africans to make a reassessment of their indigenous heritage. Despite diversity, the Renaissance is presented as an opportunity to claim acknowledgment and to help Africans to grow from feelings of inferiority to a more positive self-esteem. In this regard, a cultural revival should foster a sense of inclusiveness against the global trend of individualism and fragmentation.

As a cultural revival, the most important contribution of an African Renaissance to the universal process of globalization is *ubunthu*, i.e., the sense of belonging and interconnectedness. *Ubunthu*[45] represents the idea that one is a human being only through relationships of caring and belonging. This, indeed, is important in terms of the probable dehumanizing effects of technocratization.

The problem with such a cultural revival is the diversity of various cultures in Africa. For example, is it possible to merge the ancient Egyptian culture with the Coptic culture and the Islamic culture? How will these cultures fit into the aspirations of traditional African spirituality and their understanding of ancestral life forces? Nevertheless, what is important for the effectiveness of a cultural revival is that it must be more than a mere reframing of a romantic image of Africa which no longer exists. The challenge to a renaissance is to help Africa to deal effectively with tribal violence and crime which endangers the experience of interconnectedness. Interconnectedness needs to be transformed from the slogan "black is beautiful" with its undertones of racism, to "Africa is humane" with its undertones of *ubunthu*, communality, and human dignity.

(b) Renaissance, as an attempt to promote social empowerment and political recognition

Indeed, a renaissance without democratization and enhancement of human rights will remain but a vague slogan. An African Renaissance must help people to be socially transformed from "colonial enslavement" and deprivation to political liberation and inner, personal freedom. Both democratization and human rights entail more than freedom from. . . . It represents the endeavor to free people, through social and political liberation, to be free for justice, co-humanity, and human rights. In order to materialize these, an African Renaissance should devote itself to basic virtues such as prudence, self-control, and humility.

If it is true that globalization feeds on individualization and fragmentation, the challenge for an African Renaissance will be to merge democratization, technocratization and urbanization with the philosophy of communality and interconnectedness. In this regard, an African spirituality should play a decisive role.

(c) Renaissance, as the striving for economic prosperity and structural independence

The intention of an African Renaissance is to gain more economic independence and to address the problem of poverty and unemployment. It strives basically for the upliftment of disadvantaged people and communities.

As already indicated, it is clear that economic globalization and intercultural communication have created a new possible discrepancy and schism: the huge gap between North (developed countries) and South (developing countries). In the meantime, big companies and their directors prescribe economic policies, while the poor become poorer and the rich richer. The gap between the "haves" and the "have nots" becomes so huge that the main obstacle to the implementation of an African Renaissance becomes how to create middle axioms which can guide the distribution of wealth on a fair and just basis.

(d) Renaissance as a new mindset and spiritual impetus

It is this article's contention that if a renaissance is to bear cultural, social-political, and economic fruit, it will be forced to depend very heavily on the development of the human mind and *habitus*. Renaissance then implies the development of people in terms of a new understanding of norms and values. Without a new experience of human identity and dignity, as well as the establishment of sound values, a renaissance will remain an ideology without "flesh."

By "spirituality" is meant the merging of cultural and religious values regarding our being human, with a new attitude and aptitude (*habitus*). The latter can be described as an attitude which renders the value of the human person as more important than objects and possessions. And it is exactly at this point that a practical theological ecclesiology and the Christian ethos of unconditional love and sacrificial service come into play.

By a "practical, theological ecclesiology" is meant a more functional and contextual understanding of the well-being of the church. It refers to the following basic ecclesiological functions, reframed and understood as a vivid program of action.[46]

Diakonia: concrete service and outreach to people in need

It is the task of the church to identify, not only with the suffering of people, but also to display solidarity. Identification and solidarity need to be enfleshed in projects and structures that make the church public and visible within communities. An example of such a project is the training of laypeople in caring for people suffering from AIDS and providing local support to groups who reach out to poor families who care for dying relatives, due to a lack of hospital and medical facilities.

Koinonia: people's mutual care for one another and the provision of a support system

Within *koinonia* people can be empowered and be assisted to rediscover their human dignity. The environment of unconditional love provides a forum within which people can experience positive self-esteem. People need to be helped to shift from the position of a victim during a crisis to the more hopeful position of new options, planning, decision-making, and creativity. If it is true that the church should support a globalization from below and try to promote informal business and entrepreneurship, it becomes the task of a community-oriented church to set up new structures and to provide instruction on how to survive despite the dehumanizing side-effects of a globalization.

Leitourgia

Leitourgia is about the celebration of God's presence within life's events. For example, in the post-NRC-period (the period after the work of the Truth and Reconciliation Committee in South Africa) it should become more and more the task of the church to provide a forum where people, who shared their stories of suffering and their experiences of discrimination and violence before the Commission, can be reconciled. Reconciliation is not a momentary event; it is the ongoing process of getting to know one another and accepting one another until prejudice and suspicion (even enmity) make room for unconditional acceptance (the ethos of the Christian love). There are new stories to be told if an African Renaissance makes an impact on spiritual experiences. Stories of embracing must be created so that people can rediscover a soul friend, a brother or a sister under the mask of the possible enemy. This should be done within the liturgy of the church. Such a liturgy should be structured along the lines of celebration and embracement.

Marturia

The Gospel needs to be proclaimed. The spreading of the Gospel and the missionary task of the church are still vital elements within a vibrant church.

In the past, *marturia* has often been interpreted as evangelization. Within this evangelical model, the Gospel focused mainly on content: the *kerygma* of salvation. By a "kerygmatic model" is meant: the conversion of people (often heathens) and the proclamation of salvation and forgiveness. In traditional missionary fields, this model often implied a total break with culture. It was a conversion not only to Christ, but also to the values of a Christiandom often driven by imperialistic intentions, which reflect more Western ideology than sound biblical values.

When taking contemporary life issues into consideration, as well as the processes of inculturation (the embodiment of the Christian faith within the cultural values of local communities) and interculturation (the mutual dialogue between different cultures), the church needs to reframe *marturia* in terms of a contextual Christian spirituality which puts faith into action.

Then Christian spirituality means: enfleshment of God's presence and will within life events and daily experiences. *Marturia* then means to witness the truth of the Gospel in such a way that people discover human dignity within the *kerygma* of salvation. In order to do this, the church needs to display both empathy (love and solidarity) and interpathy (the sensitivity to understand the difference between cultural values and the content of the Christian faith, as well as to understand culture from the other person's point of view).

Conclusion

The apostolate of the church needs to undergo a paradigm shift. It needs to move from a unilateral kerygmatic approach to a more pastoral, contextual approach. With the latter a sensitivity and solidarity is displayed which take social, cultural, local, structural, and communal issues into consideration. It is then, when the church descends from a hierarchical and patriarchal structure to a pastoral and public structure of service and sacrifice, that the church will make a contribution to an African Renaissance. But then this Renaissance must be more than the revival of traditional cultural values.

Africa cannot afford a romantic reinterpretation of the past. Africa needs to understand that we are indeed part of the global village. We all share in the cybernetic space of international communication. A global economy and the internet are there to stay. Perhaps these will be more influential in the twenty-first century than the possible threat of secularization during the twentieth century.

It seems that an African Renaissance should be aware of two possible dangers: on the one hand, a romanticization of an African spirituality which no longer exists due to processes such as industrialization and urbanization. Urban Africa is becoming increasingly estranged from rural life and communal values. On the other hand, an African Renaissance runs the risk of using terminology which reflects only the mindset and framework of thinking which represent conceptual schemata inherent to a *globalization from above* (market-driven economy). It runs the risk of becoming more and more estranged from a *globalization from below* (a people-oriented economy). Keeping in mind both the Scylla of romanticization and the Charybdis of globalization, an African Renaissance should be supplemented by a practical theological ecclesiology, i.e., a *doing theology* (actions which transform people's suffering at grassroots level) and *networking theology* (mediating between the interests of big companies, global enterprises, economic management and the needs of the poor). If both an African Renaissance and a practical theological ecclesiology do not join hands in order to address very vigorously the problems of youth unemployment, illiteracy, poverty, crime, AIDS and the exploitation of women in Africa, it will remain a fleeting ideology of politicians: "Thabo Mbeki's search for presidential status."[47]

To the church, the threat of globalization will be *agnosticism*: people who totally ignore the presence of God within daily events of decision–making and morals. Morality, and therefore the restoration of people's human dignity, should become focal points on the agenda of a practical theological ecclesiology. But then the church should realize that such an ecclesiology does not operate within the two antipoles: Church *and* society (the anti-model). Nor does it imply assimilation: the one absorbed by the other. A "practical theological ecclesiology" means: the church *in* society (the *interpenetration model*). This means a church which embodies God's presence in such a way that people discover new meaning in life. A practical theological ecclesiology then displays the meaning of "sacrament"—the enfleshment of God, the identification of God with daily events through his indwelling spirit (actual pneumatology).

A practical theological ecclesiology needs Christian organizations which can set up alternative structures of communication and public control of the mass media, through mechanisms linked with civil society independent of the state, "Telcoms" and broadcasting corporations. This pastoral task involves networking: the responsibility to link companies and their policies to the basic needs and struggle of suffering people. Such an endeavor is based on the human right to receive and impart information (Article 19 of the Universal Declaration of Human Rights),[48] as well as the right to telecommunication and the promotion of sound human values. The church should, therefore, embark on a program of active participation in the process of telecommunication. The church should start to telecommunicate in order to create a different world, established by embracement and geared toward the *courage to be* (hope). "To embrace" means to be close, to share, to feel in solidarity, to identify with the needs of others. Embracing unites and creates community. "It is important to begin to open up new spaces for communication based on solidarity, communication that enables people to embrace."[49]

In Palestine, bread and wine were not commodities which represented the aspirations of an affluent society. "Bread" and "wine" refer to the daily needs of poor people who struggled to survive despite the threat of a despotic, even imperialistic, Roman culture, as well as the demands of a fanatic, bureaucratic, and very hierarchic pharisaism. The way the church ought to operate is "globalization from below," i.e., the embodiment of Christ in structures and the experience of a mutual support system and fellowship which empowers humans to move with dignity from victimization to creativity, hope, and vision.

DJ Louw
Department of Practical Theology and Missiology, University of Stellenbosch
171 Dorp Street, Stellenbosch 7600
Tel. (021) 808 3259 Fax (021) 808 3251 E–mail: djl@maties.sun.ac.za

NOTES

[1] C. Landsberg & F. Kornegay, The African Renaissance: A quest for Pax Africana and Pan-Africanism, in: *South Africa and Africa: Reflections on the African Renaissance*, eds. G. le Pere et al. FGD occasional Paper no. 17 (Braamfontein: The Foundation for Global Dialogue, 1998), 16.

[2] T. Mbeki, The African Renaissance. Statement of Deputy President Thabo Mbeki SABC: Gallagher Estate, August 13, 1998, in *South Africa and Africa: Reflections on the African Renaissance*, eds. G. Le Pere et al. FGD occasional Paper no. 17 (Braamfontein: The Foundation for Global Dialogue, 1998), 40.

[3] T. Mbeki, Prologue, in: *African Renaissance. The new struggle*, ed. M.W. Makgoba (Cape Town: Mafube/Tafelberg, 1999), xvi.

[4] Mbeki, *Prologue*, xx.

[5] M. Makgoba, Introduction, in: *African Renaissance: The new struggle*, ed. M.W. Makgoba (Cape Town: Mafube/Tafelberg, 1999), iv–v.

[6] V. Mavimbela, The African Renaissance: A workable dream, in: *South Africa and Africa: Reflections on the African Renaissance*, ed. G. le Pere et al. FGD occasional paper no.17 (Braamfontein: The Foundation for Global Dialogue, 1998), 30.

[7] "The bi-polar world of the cold war has been replaced by the tri–polar economic and social world comprised of North America, Europe and East Asia. The material base of this world is the new advance in microelectronic and biochemical technologies that have revolutionized production distribution and the communication of knowledge.
Again this tri-polar competition is threatening to marginalize the African peoples. With the African countries no longer considered of strategic importance to the interest of big powers as they had been during the cold war, this marginalization could be exacerbated even further" (Mavimbela, *The African Renaissance: A workable dream*, 29).

[8] D. Capps, *Pastoral care and hermeneutics*. Theology and pastoral care series (Philadelphia: Fortress Press, 1984), 53.

[9] A.A. Berinyuu, *Pastoral care to the sick in Africa: An approach to transcultural pastoral theology* (Frankfurt: Peter Lang, 1988), 5.

[10] Berinyuu, *Pastoral care to the sick in Africa: An approach to transcultural pastoral theology*, 8.

[11]Berinyuu, *Pastoral care to the sick in Africa: An approach to transcultural pastoral theology,* 10.

[12] J. Skhakhane, African Spirituality, in: *The church and African culture,* eds. M. Makobane et al. (Germiston: Lumko, 1995), 110.

[13] Skhakhane, *African Spirituality,* 112.

[14] E. Ackermann, *Cry beloved Africa! A continent needs help.* (Munich, Kinshasa: African University Studies, 1993), 43.

[15] A. Bellagamba, New attitudes towards spirituality, in: *Towards African Christian Maturity,* eds. A. Shorter *et al.* (Kampala: St Paul, 1987), 107.

[16]S. Mtetwa, African Spirituality in the context of modernity, *Bulletin for contextual theology in Southern Africa & Africa* 3/2 (June 1996), 24.

[17]About the possible link between African spirituality and a renaissance, see L. Teffo, Moral renewal and African experience(s), in: *African Renaissance: The new struggle,* ed. M.W. Makgoba (Cape Town: Mafube/Tafelberg, 1999), 165–169.

[18] Mtetwa, *African Spirituality in the context of modernity,* 24.

[19] A.Van Nieuwkerk, South Africa's emerging Africa policy, in: *South Africa and Africa: Reflections on the African Renaissance,* eds. G. le Pere et al. FGD occasional Paper no. 17 (Braamfontein: The Foundation for Global Dialogue, 1998), 43.

[20] P. Vale & S. Maseko, South Africa and the African Renaissance, in: *South Africa and Africa: reflections on the African Renaissance,* eds. G. le Pere et al. FGD occasional Paper no. 17 (Braamfontein: The Foundation for Global Dialogue, 1998), 7.

[21] Mavimbela, *The African Renaissance: a workable dream,* 33.

[22] Vale & Maseko, *South Africa and the African Renaissance,* 8.

[23] Vale & Maseko, *South Africa and the African Renaissance,* 8.

[24] "From a policy perspective, however, the important question seems to be whether Mbeki is an Africanist or a globalist" (Vale & Maseko, *South Africa and the African Renaissance,* 14).

[25] Vale & Maseko, *South Africa and the African Renaissance,* 11.

[26] *Verslag van die Afrika–navorsingstoer van die Universiteit van Stellenbosch: Fakulteit Teologie en die Universiteit van Wes–Kaapland: Fakulteit Godsdiens en Teologie.* 4 Junie–1 Julie 1997 (Stellenbosch: Fakulteit Teologie), 1–3.

[27]T. S. Maluleke, The church in South African black urban townships. *Journal of Black Theology in South Africa* 8/2 (1994), 92–96.

[28] Mbeki, *Prologue,* xvii.

[29] W.L. Owensby, *Economics for Prophets* (Grand Rapids: Eerdmans, 1988), xiii.

[30] M.D. Meeks, *God the Economist: The doctrine of God and political economy* (Minneapolis: Fortress Press, 1989), 7–8.

[31] These components are determined by the following value–laden convictions, which underlie the seemingly objective theories, calculations, and policies of the capitalist economic system: *freedom* —"The heart of classical economic theory is that the individual, and the individual alone, has the right and the responsibility to decide whether or not to work, whether to buy or sell, whether to save or spend" (Owensby, *Economics for prophets,* 1); *scarcity and efficiency; and competition.*

[32] D.S. Plou, *Global communication: Is there a place for human dignity?* Risk Book Series (Geneva: WCC Publications, 1996), 61.

[33] A. Mohammadi (ed.), *International communication and globalization* (London: Sage Publications, 1999²), 3.

[34] R. Robertson, *Globalization, social theory and global culture* (London: Sage, 1992), 8.

[35] F. Schweitzer, Global issues facing youth in the postmodern church, in: *Growing up post-modern: Imitating Christ in the age of whatever.* The 1998 Princeton lectures on youth, church, and culture (Institute of youth ministry: Princeton Theological Seminary, 1999), 74.

[36] M.K.K. Tehranian, Taming modernity: Towards a new paradigm, in: *International communication and globalization*, ed. A. Mohammadi (London: Sage Publications, 19992),119–167.

[37] R. Negrine, Communication technologies: An overview, in: *International communication and globalization: A critical introduction*, A. Mohammadi (London: Sage Publications, 1999), 50.

[38] Some authors refer to cultural imperialism. See A. Sreberny-Mohammadi, The many cultural faces of imperialism, in: *Beyond cultural imperialism, globalization, communication and the new international order*, eds. P. Golding & P. Harris (London: Sage Publications, 1997), 49–68.

[39] Mohammadi (ed.), *Introduction*, 1.

[40] Mohammadi, *International communication and globalization*, 6.

[41] Tehranian, *Taming modernity: Towards a new paradigm*, 164.

[42] An analysis of different speeches on the notion of an African Renaissance gives one the impression that the Renaissance tends to be more about economic globalization than Africanization. "And yet a reading of his (Mbeki's) speeches (not only those that deal with the African Renaissance) suggests a strong commitment to the central tenets of globalization" (Vale & Maseko, *South African and the African Renaissance*, 14).

[43] C. Du Toit, African hermeneutics, in: *Initiation into theology: The rich variety of theology and hermeneutics*, eds. S. Maimela & A. König (Pretoria: Van Schaik, 1998), 381.

[44] Du Toit, *African hermeneutics*, 382.

[45] M.S. Mogoba, The church's task in reconciliation and harmony, in: *Ubuntu: Cradles of peace and development*, ed. A. Burger (Pretoria: Kagiso, 1996), 91.

[46] "However, without an integrated program of action to build upon those minimum factors, the dream of the renaissance will forever be deferred or remain a romantic idealist concept" (Mavimbela, *The African Renaissance: A workable dream*, 32). Such a program of action should be guided by the following question for becoming an effective church in Africa: "How can the Church effectively respond to the concerns of ordinary people—family strife, social injustices, jobs, teenage and social problems, religious conflicts, stability in a period of rapid social change and so forth?" [E.A. Obeng, Ministerial formation for an effective church in Africa, in: D.W. Waruta & H.W. Kinoti (eds.), *Pastoral care in African Christianity* (Nairobi: Acton Publishers, 2000), 38.]

[47] Vale & Maseko, *South Africa and the African Renaissance*, 13.

[48] Plou, *Global communication: Is there a place for human dignity?* 63.

[49] Plou, *Global communication: Is there a place for human dignity?* 63.